COMPUTER
BOOK SERIES
FROM IDG

Netscape Commun
For Dummie

MW00846559

Handy Information If You Have a SLIP or PPP Provider

Provider's name: _____

Dial-in telephone number: _____

Customer support telephone number: _____

Your provider's Usenet news (NNTP) server name: _____

Your provider's mail (SMTP) server name: _____

Your provider's DNS server name: _____

Your provider's DNS server IP address: _____ . _____ . _____ . _____

Your e-mail address: _____

Common File Extensions on the Web

Extension	Meaning
txt	Text
htm	Hypertext (also seen as .html)
ps	PostScript format (also seen as .eps)
gif	Image in GIF format
jpg	Image in JPEG format (also seen as .jpeg)
pcx	Image in Windows Paintbrush format
tif	Image in TIFF format (also seen as .tiff)
mpg	Video in MPEG format (also seen as .mpeg)
avi	Video in Video for Windows format
mov	Video in QuickTime format
mid	MIDI format (also seen as .midi)
wav	Sound in Windows sound format
au	Sound in one standard audio format
snd	Sound in another standard audio format

Ten Good Starting Locations on the Web

Name	Location
WWW Virtual Library	www.w3.org/vl/
Yahoo	www.yahoo.com/
Lycos	lycos.cs.cmu.edu/
WebCrawler	webcrawler.com/
AskERIC	ericir.syr.edu/
GamesDomain	www.gamesdomain.com/
World Wide Web Consortium	www.w3.org/
CommerceNet	www.commerce.net/
Internet Mall	www.internet-mall.com/
Publisher's Catalogs	www.lights.com/publisher/

IDG
BOOKS
WORLDWIDE

Copyright © 1997 IDG Books Worldwide, Inc.
All rights reserved.

Cheat Sheet $2.95 value. Item 0053-8.

For more information about IDG Books,
call 1-800-762-2974.

...For Dummies: #1 Computer Book Series for Beginners

COMPUTER BOOK SERIES FROM IDG

Netscape Communicator™ 4 For Dummies®

Cheat Sheet

Netscape's Navigation Toolbar

Icon	Name	Action	Icon	Name	Action
Back	Back	Go to previously visited page.	Guide	Guide	Go to one of Netscape's guides to the Internet.
Forward	Forward	Go to the page you were at before you went back.	Print	Print	Print the current Web page.
Reload	Reload	Get this page again from the Web server.	Security	Security	View the security information for this page or change your security preferences.
Home	Home	Go to your home page.	Stop	Stop	Abort downloading this page.
Search	Search	Go to Netscape's search page.			

The Parts of Communicator

Program	Use
Navigator	Viewing the World Wide Web.
Messenger	Reading and sending e-mail.
Collabra Discussion Groups	Usenet news and other discussions.
Page Composer	Creating Web pages.
Conference	Talking with other Internet users live.
Calendar	Keeping track of your appointments.
IBM Host On-Demand	Communicating with old mainframes.

My Favorite Addresses

_____

_____

_____

_____

_____

_____

_____

...For Dummies: #1 Computer Book Series for Beginners

®

COMPUTER BOOK SERIES FROM IDG

References for the Rest of Us!®

Are you intimidated and confused by computers? Do you find that traditional manuals are overloaded with technical details you'll never use? Do your friends and family always call you to fix simple problems on their PCs? Then the *...For Dummies*® computer book series from IDG Books Worldwide is for you.

...For Dummies books are written for those frustrated computer users who know they aren't really dumb but find that PC hardware, software, and indeed the unique vocabulary of computing make them feel helpless. *...For Dummies* books use a lighthearted approach, a down-to-earth style, and even cartoons and humorous icons to diffuse computer novices' fears and build their confidence. Lighthearted but not lightweight, these books are a perfect survival guide for anyone forced to use a computer.

> *"I like my copy so much I told friends; now they bought copies."*
>
> **Irene C., Orwell, Ohio**

> *"Quick, concise, nontechnical, and humorous."*
>
> **Jay A., Elburn, Illinois**

> *"Thanks, I needed this book. Now I can sleep at night."*
>
> **Robin F., British Columbia, Canada**

Already, millions of satisfied readers agree. They have made *...For Dummies* books the #1 introductory level computer book series and have written asking for more. So, if you're looking for the most fun and easy way to learn about computers, look to *...For Dummies* books to give you a helping hand.

TM

IDG BOOKS
WORLDWIDE

5/97

NETSCAPE COMMUNICATOR™ 4 FOR DUMMIES®

NETSCAPE COMMUNICATOR™ 4 FOR DUMMIES®

by Paul Hoffman

IDG Books Worldwide, Inc.
An International Data Group Company

Foster City, CA ♦ Chicago, IL ♦ Indianapolis, IN ♦ Southlake, TX

Netscape Communicator™ 4 For Dummies®

Published by
IDG Books Worldwide, Inc.
An International Data Group Company
919 E. Hillsdale Blvd.
Suite 400
Foster City, CA 94404
www.idgbooks.com (IDG Books Worldwide Web site)
www.dummies.com (Dummies Press Web site)

Copyright © 1997 IDG Books Worldwide, Inc. All rights reserved. No part of this book, including interior design, cover design, and icons, may be reproduced or transmitted in any form, by any means (electronic, photocopying, recording, or otherwise) without the prior written permission of the publisher.

Library of Congress Catalog Card No.: 97-70371

ISBN: 0-7645-0053-8

Printed in the United States of America

10 9 8 7 6 5 4 3 2 1

1O/SV/QX/ZX/IN

Distributed in the United States by IDG Books Worldwide, Inc.

Distributed by Macmillan Canada for Canada; by Transworld Publishers Limited in the United Kingdom; by IDG Norge Books for Norway; by IDG Sweden Books for Sweden; by Woodslane Pty. Ltd. for Australia; by Woodslane Enterprises Ltd. for New Zealand; by Longman Singapore Publishers Ltd. for Singapore, Malaysia, Thailand, and Indonesia; by Simron Pty. Ltd. for South Africa; by Toppan Company Ltd. for Japan; by Distribuidora Cuspide for Argentina; by Livraria Cultura for Brazil; by Ediciencia S.A. for Ecuador; by Addison-Wesley Publishing Company for Korea; by Ediciones ZETA S.C.R. Ltda. for Peru; by WS Computer Publishing Corporation, Inc., for the Philippines; by Unalis Corporation for Taiwan; by Contemporanea de Ediciones for Venezuela; by Computer Book & Magazine Store for Puerto Rico; by Express Computer Distributors for the Caribbean and West Indies. Authorized Sales Agent: Anthony Rudkin Associates for the Middle East and North Africa.

For general information on IDG Books Worldwide's books in the U.S., please call our Consumer Customer Service department at 800-762-2974. For reseller information, including discounts and premium sales, please call our Reseller Customer Service department at 800-434-3422.

For information on where to purchase IDG Books Worldwide's books outside the U.S., please contact our International Sales department at 415-655-3200 or fax 415-655-3295.

For information on foreign language translations, please contact our Foreign & Subsidiary Rights department at 415-655-3021 or fax 415-655-3281.

For sales inquiries and special prices for bulk quantities, please contact our Sales department at 415-655-3200 or write to the address above.

For information on using IDG Books Worldwide's books in the classroom or for ordering examination copies, please contact our Educational Sales department at 800-434-2086 or fax 817-251-8174.

For press review copies, author interviews, or other publicity information, please contact our Public Relations department at 415-655-3000 or fax 415-655-3299.

For authorization to photocopy items for corporate, personal, or educational use, please contact Copyright Clearance Center, 222 Rosewood Drive, Danvers, MA 01923, or fax 508-750-4470.

LIMIT OF LIABILITY/DISCLAIMER OF WARRANTY: AUTHOR AND PUBLISHER HAVE USED THEIR BEST EFFORTS IN PREPARING THIS BOOK. IDG BOOKS WORLDWIDE, INC., AND AUTHOR MAKE NO REPRESENTATIONS OR WARRANTIES WITH RESPECT TO THE ACCURACY OR COMPLETENESS OF THE CONTENTS OF THIS BOOK AND SPECIFICALLY DISCLAIM ANY IMPLIED WARRANTIES OF MERCHANTABILITY OR FITNESS FOR A PARTICULAR PURPOSE. THERE ARE NO WARRANTIES WHICH EXTEND BEYOND THE DESCRIPTIONS CONTAINED IN THIS PARAGRAPH. NO WARRANTY MAY BE CREATED OR EXTENDED BY SALES REPRESENTATIVES OR WRITTEN SALES MATERIALS. THE ACCURACY AND COMPLETENESS OF THE INFORMATION PROVIDED HEREIN AND THE OPINIONS STATED HEREIN ARE NOT GUARANTEED OR WARRANTED TO PRODUCE ANY PARTICULAR RESULTS, AND THE ADVICE AND STRATEGIES CONTAINED HEREIN MAY NOT BE SUITABLE FOR EVERY INDIVIDUAL. NEITHER IDG BOOKS WORLDWIDE, INC., NOR AUTHOR SHALL BE LIABLE FOR ANY LOSS OF PROFIT OR ANY OTHER COMMERCIAL DAMAGES, INCLUDING BUT NOT LIMITED TO SPECIAL, INCIDENTAL, CONSEQUENTIAL, OR OTHER DAMAGES.

Trademarks: All brand names and product names used in this book are trade names, service marks, trademarks, or registered trademarks of their respective owners. IDG Books Worldwide is not associated with any product or vendor mentioned in this book.

is a trademark under exclusive license to IDG Books Worldwide, Inc., from International Data Group, Inc.

About the Author

Paul E. Hoffman has written more than a dozen computer books, many of them about the Internet (including IDG Books' *The Internet,* the official book of the Public Television presentation *The Internet Show*). In fact, he's been active on the Internet for more than 15 years. As a founder of the Internet Mail Consortium, he is responsible for the popular Web service there as well as the mail response system. He also organized the Internet Computer Index. Since 1987, he has been the News Editor at *MicroTimes,* the largest regional computer magazine in the United States.

ABOUT IDG BOOKS WORLDWIDE

Welcome to the world of IDG Books Worldwide.

IDG Books Worldwide, Inc., is a subsidiary of International Data Group, the world's largest publisher of computer-related information and the leading global provider of information services on information technology. IDG was founded more than 25 years ago and now employs more than 8,500 people worldwide. IDG publishes more than 275 computer publications in over 75 countries (see listing below). More than 60 million people read one or more IDG publications each month.

Launched in 1990, IDG Books Worldwide is today the #1 publisher of best-selling computer books in the United States. We are proud to have received eight awards from the Computer Press Association in recognition of editorial excellence and three from *Computer Currents'* First Annual Readers' Choice Awards. Our best-selling *...For Dummies*® series has more than 30 million copies in print with translations in 30 languages. IDG Books Worldwide, through a joint venture with IDG's Hi-Tech Beijing, became the first U.S. publisher to publish a computer book in the People's Republic of China. In record time, IDG Books Worldwide has become the first choice for millions of readers around the world who want to learn how to better manage their businesses.

Our mission is simple: Every one of our books is designed to bring extra value and skill-building instructions to the reader. Our books are written by experts who understand and care about our readers. The knowledge base of our editorial staff comes from years of experience in publishing, education, and journalism — experience we use to produce books for the '90s. In short, we care about books, so we attract the best people. We devote special attention to details such as audience, interior design, use of icons, and illustrations. And because we use an efficient process of authoring, editing, and desktop publishing our books electronically, we can spend more time ensuring superior content and spend less time on the technicalities of making books.

You can count on our commitment to deliver high-quality books at competitive prices on topics you want to read about. At IDG Books Worldwide, we continue in the IDG tradition of delivering quality for more than 25 years. You'll find no better book on a subject than one from IDG Books Worldwide.

IDG BOOKS WORLDWIDE

John Kilcullen
CEO
IDG Books Worldwide, Inc.

Steven Berkowitz
President and Publisher
IDG Books Worldwide, Inc.

**Eighth Annual
Computer Press
Awards ➤1992**

**Ninth Annual
Computer Press
Awards ➤1993**

**Tenth Annual
Computer Press
Awards ➤1994**

**Eleventh Annual
Computer Press
Awards ➤1995**

IDG Books Worldwide, Inc., is a subsidiary of International Data Group, the world's largest publisher of computer-related information and the leading global provider of information services on information technology. International Data Group publishes over 275 computer publications in over 75 countries. Sixty million people read one or more International Data Group publications each month. International Data Group's publications include: **ARGENTINA:** Buyer's Guide, Computerworld Argentina, PC World Argentina; **AUSTRALIA:** Australian Macworld, Australian PC World, Australian Reseller News, Computerworld, IT Casebook, Network World, Publish, Webmaster; **AUSTRIA:** Computerwelt Osterreich, Networks Austria, PC Tip Austria; **BANGLADESH:** PC World Bangladesh; **BELARUS:** PC World Belarus; **BELGIUM:** Data News; **BRAZIL:** Annuário de Informática, Computerworld, Connections, Macworld, PC Player, PC World, Publish, Reseller News, Supergamepower; **BULGARIA:** Computerworld Bulgaria, Network World Bulgaria, PC & MacWorld Bulgaria; **CANADA:** CIO Canada, Client/Server World, ComputerWorld Canada, InfoWorld Canada, NetworkWorld Canada, WebWorld; **CHILE:** Computerworld Chile, PC World Chile; **COLOMBIA:** Computerworld Colombia, PC World Colombia; **COSTA RICA:** PC World Centro America; **THE CZECH AND SLOVAK REPUBLICS:** Computerworld Czechoslovakia, Macworld Czech Republic, PC World Czechoslovakia; **DENMARK:** Communications World Danmark, Computerworld Danmark, Macworld Danmark, PC World Danmark, Techworld Denmark; **DOMINICAN REPUBLIC:** PC World Republica Dominicana; **ECUADOR:** PC World Ecuador; **EGYPT:** Computerworld Middle East, PC World Middle East; **EL SALVADOR:** PC World Centro America; **FINLAND:** MikroPC, Tietoverkko, Tietovikko; **FRANCE:** Distributique, Hebdo, Info PC, Le Monde Informatique, Macworld, Reseaux & Telecoms, WebMaster France; **GERMANY:** Computer Partner, Computerwoche, Computerwoche Extra, Computerwoche FOCUS, Global Online, Macwelt, PC Welt; **GREECE:** Amiga Computing, GamePro Greece, Multimedia World; **GUATEMALA:** PC World Centro America; **HONDURAS:** PC World Centro America; **HONG KONG:** Computerworld Hong Kong, PC World Hong Kong, Publish in Asia; **HUNGARY:** ABCD CD-ROM, Computerworld Szamitastechnika, Interneto online Magazine, PC World Hungary, PC-X Magazin Hungary; **ICELAND:** Tolvuheimur PC World Island; **INDIA:** Information Communications World, Information Systems Computerworld, PC World India, Publish in Asia; **INDONESIA:** InfoKomputer PC World, Komputek Computerworld, Publish in Asia; **IRELAND:** ComputerScope, PC Live!; **ISRAEL:** Macworld Israel, People & Computers/Computerworld; **ITALY:** Computerworld Italia, Macworld Italia, Networking Italia, PC World Italia; **JAPAN:** DTP World, Macworld Japan, Nikkei Personal Computing, OS/2 World Japan, SunWorld Japan, Windows NT World, Windows World Japan; **KENYA:** PC World East African; **KOREA:** Hi-Tech Information, Macworld Korea, PC World Korea; **MACEDONIA:** PC World Macedonia; **MALAYSIA:** Computerworld Malaysia, PC World Malaysia, Publish in Asia; **MALTA:** PC World Malta; **MEXICO:** Computerworld Mexico, PC World Mexico; **MYANMAR:** PC World Myanmar; **NETHERLANDS:** Computer! Totaal, LAN Internetworking Magazine, LAN World Buyers Guide, Macworld Netherlands, Net, WebWereld; **NEW ZEALAND:** Absolute Beginners Guide and Plain & Simple Series, Computer Buyer, Computer Industry Directory, Computerworld New Zealand, MTB, Network World, PC World New Zealand; **NICARAGUA:** PC World Centro America; **NORWAY:** Computerworld Norge, CW Rapport, Datamagasinet, Financial Rapport, Kursguide Norge, Macworld Norge, Multimediaworld Norge, PC World Ekspress Norge, PC World Nettverk, PC World Norge, PC World ProduktGuide Norge; **PAKISTAN:** Computerworld Pakistan; **PANAMA:** PC World Panama; **PEOPLE'S REPUBLIC OF CHINA:** China Computer Users, China Computerworld, China InfoWorld, China Telecom World Weekly, Computer & Communication, Electronic Design China, Electronics Today, Electronics Weekly, Game Software, PC World China, Popular Computer Week, Software Weekly, Software World, Telecom World; **PERU:** Computerworld Peru, PC World Profesional Peru, PC World SoHo Peru; **PHILIPPINES:** Click!, Computerworld Philippines, PC World Philippines, Publish in Asia; **POLAND:** Computerworld Poland, Computerworld Special Report Poland, Cyber, Macworld Poland, Networld Poland, PC World Komputer; **PORTUGAL:** Cerebro/PC World, Computerworld/Correio Informatico, Dealer World Portugal, Mac*In/PC*In Portugal, Multimedia World; **PUERTO RICO:** PC World Puerto Rico; **ROMANIA:** Computerworld Romania, PC World Romania, Telecom Romania; **RUSSIA:** Computerworld Russia, Mir PK, Publish, Seti; **SINGAPORE:** Computerworld Singapore, PC World Singapore, Publish in Asia; **SLOVENIA:** Monitor; **SOUTH AFRICA:** Computing SA, Network World SA, Software World SA; **SPAIN:** Communicaciones World España, Computerworld España, Dealer World España, Macworld España, PC World España; **SRI LANKA:** Infolink PC World; **SWEDEN:** CAP&Design, Computer Sweden, Corporate Computing Sweden, Internetworld Sweden, MaxiData Sweden, MikroDatorn, Natverk & Kommunikation, PC World Sweden, PCaktiv, Windows World Sweden; **SWITZERLAND:** Computerworld Schweiz, Macworld Schweiz, PCtip; **TAIWAN:** Computerworld Taiwan, Macworld Taiwan, NEW ViSiON/Publish, PC World Taiwan, Windows World Taiwan; **THAILAND:** Publish in Asia, Thai Computerworld; **TURKEY:** Computerworld Turkiye, Macworld Turkiye, Network World Turkiye, PC World Turkiye; **UKRAINE:** Computerworld Kiev, Multimedia World Ukraine, PC World Ukraine; **UNITED KINGDOM:** Acorn User UK, Amiga Action UK, Amiga Computing UK, Apple Talk UK, Computing, Macworld, Parents and Computers UK, PC Advisor, PC Home, PSX Pro, The WEB; **UNITED STATES:** Cable in the Classroom, CIO Magazine, Computerworld, DOS World, Federal Computer Week, GamePro Magazine, InfoWorld, I-Way, Macworld, Network World, PC Games, PC World, Publish, Video Event, THE WEB Magazine, and WebMaster; online webzines: JavaWorld, NetscapeWorld, and SunWorld Online; **URUGUAY:** InfoWorld Uruguay; **VENEZUELA:** Computerworld Venezuela, PC World Venezuela; and **VIETNAM:** PC World Vietnam.   3/24/97

Author's Acknowledgments

The Web's a big place, and tens of thousands of people have put hundreds of thousands of hours into making it enjoyable. The vast majority of them haven't made any money from their work yet, and many did it for the joy of starting something new. These people deserve the most thanks for this book because there'd be nothing for me to write about, and for you to read about, without them.

Writing for computer novices is always easier if you have a few of them around asking you questions. My close circle of novices and ex-novices keeps me on my toes and reminds me of what is not obvious, how frustrating it can be when the system is designed by know-it-all dweebs, and what parts are fun. I'd particularly like to thank Morgan and Zoriah Tharan for their help in this area. I'd also like to thank my grandfather, Oscar Hoffman, for instilling in me a healthy mistrust of computer jargon.

Of course, this book also wouldn't exist without the work of the people at IDG Books Worldwide, Inc. Take a glance at the credits page to see the people who worked specifically on getting this book into your hands. I thank them all.

Publisher's Acknowledgments

We're proud of this book; please send us your comments about it by using the IDG Books Worldwide Registration Card at the back of the book or by e-mailing us at feedback/dummies@idgbooks.com. Some of the people who helped bring this book to market include the following:

Acquisitions, Development, and Editorial

Project Editor: Tim Gallan

Acquisitions Editor: Michael Kelly

Product Development Director: Mary Bednarek

Associate Permissions Editor: Heather H. Dismore

Copy Editor: Tamara S. Castleman

Technical Editor: James Michael Stewart

Editorial Manager: Leah P. Cameron

Editorial Assistant: Chris Collins

Production

Project Coordinator: E. Shawn Aylsworth

Layout and Graphics: Cameron Booker, Linda M. Boyer, Elizabeth Cárdenas-Nelson, Angela F. Hunckler, Brent Savage

Proofreaders: Sarah Fraser, Robert Springer, Karen York

Indexer: Sharon Hilgenberg

General and Administrative

IDG Books Worldwide, Inc.: John Kilcullen, CEO; Steven Berkowitz, President and Publisher

IDG Books Technology Publishing: Brenda McLaughlin, Senior Vice President and Group Publisher

Dummies Technology Press and Dummies Editorial: Diane Graves Steele, Vice President and Associate Publisher; Judith A. Taylor, Product Marketing Manager; Kristin A. Cocks, Editorial Director

Dummies Trade Press: Kathleen A. Welton, Vice President and Publisher

IDG Books Production for Dummies Press: Beth Jenkins, Production Director; Cindy L. Phipps, Manager of Project Coordination, Production Proofreading, and Indexing; Kathie S. Schutte, Supervisor of Page Layout; Shelley Lea, Supervisor of Graphics and Design; Debbie J. Gates, Production Systems Specialist; Tony Augsburger, Supervisor of Reprints and Bluelines; Leslie Popplewell, Media Archive Coordinator

Dummies Packaging and Book Design: Patti Sandez, Packaging Specialist; Lance Kayser, Packaging Assistant; Kavish + Kavish, Cover Design

◆

The publisher would like to give special thanks to Patrick J. McGovern, without whom this book would not have been possible.

◆

Contents at a Glance

Cartoons at a Glance

By Rich Tennant

page 79

page 9

page 135

page 293

page 235

page 311

Fax: 508-546-7747 • E-mail: the5wave@tiac.net

Table of Contents

Introduction

*T*he World Wide Web is a big place. It had better be: The hype for it is already so great that people have high expectations about what they'll find after they get there. The Web (I'll drop the "World Wide" stuff for now) is a new kind of online place in which you can find all sorts of interesting people and information. The Web is part of the Internet, which is part of the overall online world. But you can find plenty to do without straying far from the Web.

About This Book

Netscape is one program that enables you to use the World Wide Web. Imagine that you see a book about 1-2-3 and spreadsheets. You know that 1-2-3 is a kind of spreadsheet program. Any book about 1-2-3 should discuss spreadsheets in general and how to use 1-2-3 in particular. Well, this book is similar. Most of the book is about the World Wide Web, and some of the book is about how to use what is currently the most popular program for the World Wide Web — namely, Netscape.

Who Are You?

You are not a dummy. And if you can read this sentence, you're certainly not stupid. (This book's title comes from the name of a very popular book that started the entire series: *DOS For Dummies*. The book and the series are quite popular. Regardless of how you or I feel about the word "dummy," these books have introduced millions of readers to new computer concepts.)

You are, however, probably a novice at using the Web. If you weren't a novice, you'd probably have grabbed a different book from the shelf in the bookstore. Advanced users of the Web may find much (although not all) of the information in this book uninteresting because they already know it.

You're probably not a Web expert; this book is perfect for novices and even intermediate Web users. It assumes that you already know a little bit about your computer and a bit about the Internet, but not much. It is definitely written with the beginner, particularly the frustrated beginner, in mind.

Here are the assumptions I've made about you, the reader:

- ✔ You want to connect to the Internet to use the Web and other Internet services.

- ✔ You want to know what's on the Web and why everyone seems so excited about it.

- ✔ You may or may not already have an Internet account; if you do, you're not yet a "net.weenie."

- ✔ You may or may not want to use Netscape as your connection to the Web, but it seems likely that you will eventually use Netscape.

- ✔ Besides getting information from the Web, you may also want to put your own information out for others to see.

Again, you are not a dummy; the fact that you've picked up this book shows that you're actually quite intelligent. You simply have yet to master the Web and Netscape. Read this book and you'll know everything you need to go cruising around the Web like a pro.

What's a Netscape?

Good question, and the answer is a bit harder than it should be. Netscape is all of the following:

- ✔ The first part of the name of a company: Netscape Communications.

- ✔ The first part of the name of the software that millions of people now use to access the Web: Netscape Navigator. In a move that many people find confusing, starting with version 4, Netscape Navigator is part of a larger package called Netscape Communicator.

- ✔ The first part of the name of other software made by the same company (but you don't need to worry about this additional software in this book).

Thus Netscape Communications created a program called Netscape Navigator, and that's part of what this book is about. Everyone calls the software "Netscape" (not "Navigator"), however, and so that's the name this book uses as well.

How to Get Netscape

As I stated earlier, you don't need to use Netscape to get lots out of this book. In fact, if for some reason you are dead set *against* becoming a Netscape user, you'll find only a few chapters out of the more than 20 here that are specific to Netscape.

Netscape is inexpensive; at the time this edition of the book was being written, it costs you somewhere between $0 and $70, depending on who you are and where or how you get it. Netscape is also really, really good. There are many other Web browsers, and some of them are free, but Netscape is still a great bargain. Netscape's only serious competition is Microsoft's Internet Explorer, which is free, but Netscape has a tendency to make better software than Microsoft.

Netscape is available for PCs running Windows (including Windows 95), for Macs, and for some UNIX systems running XWindows. This book covers only Netscape for Windows and Macintosh. (UNIX users can probably figure out the differences on their own.)

Try before you buy

Netscape Communications, the folks who make Netscape Communicator (the program that is called Netscape throughout this book, that is), knew that it would be hard to get millions of people to fork out $50 for a product they weren't sure about, particularly if it competes against other products that are, in fact, free. The company decided to let individuals try out Netscape for as long as they want; corporate users evaluating Netscape can do so for free for up to 90 days before buying the product.

If you already have an Internet connection and that connection enables you to access files by FTP (that's the most popular way to get files over the Internet), you can get the latest version of Netscape from the FTP site called ftp.netscape.com. You'll have to navigate around to find the software that's for your computer, but it is well worth the effort.

At the time this book was written, the license agreement for evaluating Netscape was quite liberal: Anyone can evaluate it for up to 90 days before paying for it. Even if you're really slow, 90 days is as long as you need.

Consider yourself warned, however: Netscape Communications may change this policy at any time. That it will actually do so, however, seems quite unlikely because so much of the ethos of Netscape is built up around this policy. Even so, make sure that you check the license agreement you get from Netscape for the exact conditions under which you can evaluate the software.

It may be free

If you're at an educational institution or a nonprofit corporation in the U.S., Netscape is free to you. You can download it from the FTP server described earlier and not even need to "evaluate" it — you can use it as if you had bought it. Netscape is one of the only companies with this kind of policy, and (needless to say) Netscape has been well received by the educational market because of it.

At the time of this writing, Netscape says you are entitled to use the software for free if "you are a student, faculty member or staff member of an educational institution (K-12, junior college, or college) or an employee of a charitable nonprofit organization." They go on to say, "Government agencies are not considered charitable nonprofit organizations for purposes of this license agreement." I must agree: I haven't found too many government agencies to be all that charitable.

Updating from earlier versions

If you already have a copy of Netscape, it may not be up to date. This book covers Netscape version 4, but many people are still using copies from version 3, 2, and even version 1. Netscape allows you to update your software for a low cost (or even free).

To get the updated version, you should use your current version and go to Netscape's Web site (this is all described in Chapter 5, if you're patient). There is usually a link right on the first page on their site about how to get the most recent version of the software. Follow that link, and away you go.

The one thing that isn't always so clear is how much you're supposed to pay for your update. Netscape, the company, keeps changing the rules about this, so read the updating information on their Web site carefully.

Where and how to buy

To date, Netscape hasn't been a big seller in normal retail stores. You may, however, find it for sale at a few retail outlets. A few mail-order catalogs also sell the software.

If you already have a copy of Netscape — an evaluation copy, for example — you can purchase Netscape online by opening the Directory menu and choosing the Netscape Home command and then finding the location of the online ordering system from there.

You can also call Netscape directly to order the software. The telephone number is 415-528-2555.

What You'll Find in This Book

Yes, yes, you see this in the introduction of almost every computer book: a description of what you'll find in the rest of the book. This particular convention may seem a tad silly, given that all the headings are listed in the lovely table of contents. Yet every book does it, and so must this one, given the incredible bad luck that may befall the author if the Universal Rule of Introductions is broken.

Part I: Wild, Wild Web

The first four chapters of this book give you an overview of what the Web is and what it isn't. You also find a discussion of how to get connected to the Internet if you aren't already — or how to get a "better" connection if you already have one. By the time you finish with these chapters, you should have a solid foundation in using the Web.

Part II: How You See What You Get

The next four chapters describe the "how" of the Web: how to use Netscape, how to search for things, and how to get around problems. You may notice that not that much "how" is to be found in the rest of the book. The Web has so much "what" (and the "how" is so easy) that you'll find everything you need for the mechanics in these chapters.

Part III: Who's Webbing Now?

Most of the glowing descriptions of the Web talk about how much is out there to experience. The six chapters in this part show you more than 101 great examples of what's on the Web today. Even though the Web is still in its infancy, these examples can give you a pretty good feel for what you may see there next year as well.

Part IV: Your Name in Lights

If you find the material in Part III interesting enough to entice you to create your own Web information, you need to read the four chapters in this part. Putting information on the Web isn't that difficult, but it isn't terribly easy either. You must learn a bit about how to make your information look good, and you also need to know how to avoid the many pitfalls of publishing. This part helps you do all that — and more.

Part V: The Web in the Future

Predicting the future is impossible, but that doesn't stop many computer industry analysts (who get paid big bucks) from making wild guesses. Predicting the future of some parts of the Web isn't as hard as it may sound, however, because the groundwork for the future is already being laid by the people who create the standards on which the Internet and the Web exist. These two chapters talk about multimedia and how things will undoubtedly look in the next few years.

Part VI: The Part of Tens

Yep, you've gotten to the end of the main part of the book. To bring things to a close, this part contains a few short chapters, each containing ten items of interest to all Web users. These are things that didn't really fit in the rest of the book and make a nice closing.

The Glossary

Finally, what's a computer book without a glossary? You can use this book's glossary to find quick definitions for all kinds of techie terms.

HotSpots

In many chapters of this book, you will find special figures called *HotSpots*, which are screen shots showing special Web sites of interest. Each HotSpot has something to do with the material in the chapter in which it appears, although it doesn't relate to any particular paragraph. (That's what your ordinary, everyday figures are for.) Below each HotSpot is its Web address and a description of what you can find there. These extra goodies should whet your appetite for the Web, giving you even more places to investigate.

Note: You may notice that some screen shots in this book, both regular figures and HotSpots, display a slightly different URL than what you see in the captions. The most common difference is that some of them insert an *:80* between the host name and the request. Some Web client software adds this bit of unneeded dweebism into some of the URLs for no good reason. You can safely ignore it.

Type Styles Used in This Book

As you know, computer books look different from other books. One of the methods used to make things in the text clearer is to use different type styles to mean different things.

If you've read other computer books, you know that figuring out which text in a sentence is text that you are seeing on the computer isn't always easy. In this book, such text is shown in a special typewriter-like type style `that looks like this`. This style is also used for addresses on the Web or the Internet because these addresses are most often what you type into Netscape and other programs and thus see on-screen.

The computer field is full of jargon and unfamiliar words. In this book, the first time a word or phrase is used, it appears in italic type, *like this*. (Remember, too, that at the end of the book is a very complete glossary in which most of these new words are fully defined. If you see an unfamiliar word or abbreviation that isn't in italic type and isn't explained — and you don't remember it from what you've read so far — check the glossary; you're likely to find it right there.)

You also find sprinkled throughout the book short sections in yet a different typeface with a gray-shaded background. These are *sidebars* that contain (I think) interesting information that isn't essential to the flow of the main text. You can stop and read them where they appear or go back and read them after you finish the section, chapter, or even the entire book. (You'll recognize these sidebars when you see them.)

Icons Used in This Book

If you flip through this book, you should notice that some paragraphs have little round pictures — called *icons* — next to them. These icons are used to make important information stand out, just in case you're one of those readers who skims just a bit too quickly.

The icons you find in this book — and what they represent — are as follows:

This icon flags handy information that is just a bit more useful than everything else around it. It's like a gold star for some of the best information in the book.

Hey, not everything on the Web is all fun and games. You may need to pay extra attention to a few things so that they don't come back and bite you later. Warnings tip you off to these potential pitfalls

Most beginners like a bit of technical jargon once in a while. These sections, which you can feel free to skip, go into more detail than really needs to appear in a book such as this. Still, they can give you that special "propeller-head" (a.k.a. techno-geek) understanding.

This icon provides a friendly reminder of information you don't want to forget (even if you already have).

This book is part of the ...*For Dummies* series of books on many computer-related topics. (In fact, the series now includes many non-computer books as well!) Of course, this one book can't cover everything in the entire computer universe, so you often spot plugs for other books in the series that go into greater depth on particular subjects not covered in detail here.

The Web Awaits You

My, you are quite the reader, aren't you? You even read the obligatory end-of-introduction exhortation to start Chapter 1. Well, get to it! Zip through the first few chapters, get on the Web, and start exploring. You'll find an amazing wealth of information, a fair amount of fun, and who knows what else out there. As a novice, you're in good company on the Web; this book can help make you a seasoned Web user in no time.

Part I
Wild, Wild Web

The 5th Wave
By Rich Tennant

"Awww jeez- I was afraid of this. Some poor kid, bored with the usual chat lines, starts looking for bigger kicks, pretty soon they're surfin' the seedy back alleys of cyberspace, and before you know it they're into a file they can't 'undo'. I guess that's why they call it the Web. Somebody open a window!"

In this part . . .

*W*elcome to the Web! In the four short chapters of this part, you can gain a solid understanding about what the Web is, its parts, and how to use it. You even get a glance or two at a smattering of interesting things you may find on the Web during your wanderings. Enjoy!

Chapter 1

Welcome to Too Many Ws

. . . .

. . . .

*U*nless you don't read the newspaper and never watch TV, you have probably heard about the so-called "Information Superhighway." Politicians and businesspeople are promising you a rosy future filled with entertainment, information, and communications right in your home. Soon you can buy high-tech gadgets that give you access to more than everything in your local library and the local video store combined.

Yeah, right. No problem.

This is a great time to take a few steps back and look more closely at what people are promising, what already exists today, and what you really want. The Information Superhighway (or whatever silly thing computer pundits are now calling whatever it is) won't be running through your living room for many years, and you want to get going with the best of what's available right now.

The Internet of Today

One important component of today's version of the Information Superhighway is known as the *World Wide Web.* Understanding the World Wide Web without knowing the context in which it lives is impossible. The Web is part of the *Internet,* which is an international network of computers linked by certain rules and guidelines. You may already be a user on the Internet, or you may be coming to the Web and the Internet at the same time; it really doesn't matter.

Note: Just as the Internet has lots of names, so do the parts of the Internet. The World Wide Web goes under many names, such as *the Web, WWW,* and even *World Wide Web.* They are all the same thing, and this book usually uses the term *the Web* as the preferred name. Feel free to pick any of them — or even make up one of your own.

Describing the Internet is a bit like describing a city in that doing so well in less than a paragraph is impossible. Think, for example, about the many ways by which you may describe a city to someone who hasn't been there:

- ✔ Its location on a map
- ✔ The terrain
- ✔ Its architecture
- ✔ The kinds of people who live there
- ✔ The kinds of people who don't live there but just work there
- ✔ Its politics
- ✔ The business climate
- ✔ Some major tourist attractions
- ✔ Its history

Similarly, you can't simply describe the Internet as a particular place, the kind of information available, the people you may find there, and so on. You're unlikely, however, to be happy with the nondescription of "Gosh, it's hard to describe." Instead, the following sections provide a too-short description that should help demystify that which everyone likes to babble on about.

When you found this book, it was probably on the shelf near lots of other books about the Internet. If you want to know about the Internet in general, not just the Web in particular (that's why you're reading *this* book!), you should take a look at *The Internet For Dummies* and *MORE Internet For Dummies,* both from IDG Books Worldwide, Inc.

The Internet as a network

The Internet is a collection of thousands of computers that communicate through certain methods that have been agreed on for many years. The Internet started about 25 years ago with a small handful of computers run by a few people as an experiment. The initial results were successful; the network was useful, so it grew.

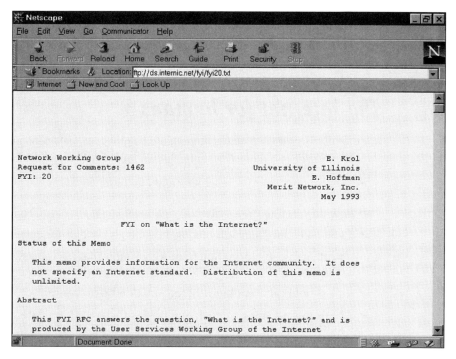

HotSpot 1-1: ftp://ds.internic.net/fyi/fyi20.txt
This document is a semiofficial introduction to the Internet for beginners. It gives a great overview of what you may find, and it contains pointers to other interesting documents on the same topic.

In fact, the Internet was partially intended to be an experiment for how to design a network that could grow easily, with very little central control. That concept is still considered radical today, and you find few networks as loose as the Internet.

If you use a computer on a network in your office, you are probably familiar with how you must ask some central administrator for help getting access to other computers or for permission if you want to add a computer to the network. One of the big experiments of the Internet (one that is still evolving) is how to make such growth as easy as possible.

Another experimental aspect of the Internet that was unique when it was created was the concept that messages passed between two computers may travel over a variety of paths. Think of the different routes you could use to drive from Los Angeles to New York, all of which take about the same amount of time.

On the Internet, a message between two computers may go on one path the first time you send it and on a different path the next time you send it. Even stranger, if the message is split into smaller parts, the parts may travel along different routes.

The Internet for humans

In the last ten years, some of the most interesting experimentation has revolved around the best ways for humans (that's you and me) to access information stored on computers that are on the Internet. Some of the questions arising from these experiments include:

- ✔ How do you find information if you don't know what you're looking for?
- ✔ If you find something interesting, how do you find other, related material?
- ✔ How do you get information from a computer that isn't always connected to the Internet?
- ✔ How should different kinds of information be presented?
- ✔ What's this all going to cost, and how is the cost to be determined?

To use the World Wide Web, you don't need to know many technical details of the Internet. In fact, only a tiny percentage of Internet users know more than a smattering of the *protocols* (a fancy term for rules and regulations), *standards groups* (the folks who define the rules), and so on. This is not to say that knowing technical details won't help you; however, in dealing with the World Wide Web, learning the little technical information that you do need will be fairly painless.

So a reasonably non-technical summary of the Internet may include the following facts:

- ✔ It is a network of hundreds of thousands of computers.
- ✔ These computers communicate with each other in a consistent fashion.
- ✔ Users on one computer can access services from other computers.
- ✔ You can access a wide variety of these services, most of which are free.
- ✔ Each service can give you many kinds of information.

The trickiest part of this summary is the word *services*. On the Internet, you can use many methods to communicate with a computer somewhere else on the Internet. These methods are called *services* because they service your requests. A few of the most popular Internet services that you may have heard of are the following:

> ✔ Mail
>
> ✔ The World Wide Web
>
> ✔ FTP (for getting files)
>
> ✔ Usenet news

If you haven't heard of these services, fear not: They and other services are described in Chapter 3.

The World Wide Web: Not a Thing, Not a Place

Given that somewhat vague definition of the Internet, you're probably wondering where this much-touted World Wide Web fits in. The Web is primarily a service — a method for obtaining information from a variety of computers on the Internet. If you think of the Internet as a supermarket, the Web is one section, such as the produce section. While you're in the market, you can go to other sections, and you don't need to go to the vegetable section at all if you don't want to.

The analogy can actually be extended a bit without stretching it too far. Have you noticed that, even in the produce section of most supermarkets, you can find lots of non-vegetables being sold? Depending on where you shop, you often find items such as salad dressing, charcoal, flowers, holiday cards — you name it. The Web is like that in the sense that you can locate other kinds of information — not only things that are made expressly for the Web — while using the Web. Convenient, yes?

This mixing of Webish and non-Webish information is due not to the structure of the Web itself but to the creativity on the part of those who write the software you use whenever you access the Web. Most Internet software programs enable you to access one (and only one) Internet service. With mail software, you use only mail; with Usenet software, you use only Usenet; and so on. Most Web software, on the other hand, enables you to access many services without switching to a different piece of software.

This mixing of services is a great help to users but tends to confuse even advanced users a bit. You often hear computer novices use phrases such as "I'm in Lotus 1-2-3" or "I'm in WordPerfect." If you use Web software to access Usenet news, for example, are you "in" the Web or "in" Usenet? The answer is that you are really never "in" any service; you are "in" your software. The more flexible your software is (and Web software is the most flexible on the Internet today), the more you can do with that software.

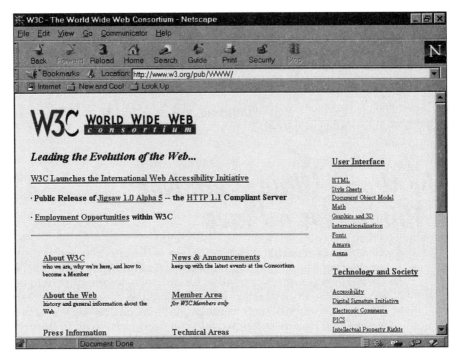

HotSpot 1-2: http://www.w3.org/
The industry group known as the World Wide Web Consortium (also called W3C) is a great place to start your exploration of the Web. The W3C coordinates the various companies that sponsor technical advancement, new standards, and other activities that help the Web grow.

As you can see, the vocabulary used for the Internet is often less than clear. Remember that just because you hear people use a phrase (such as "in Usenet") doesn't mean that the phrase is correct. In fact, many of the commonly misused phrases can be quite confusing. On the other hand, feel free to make up your own vocabulary if doing so enables you to keep things straight more easily; the term *Webish* a couple paragraphs ago is an example of something you may say to mean "things that pretty much pertain to the Web."

Chapters 2 and 3 describe in much more detail what is and isn't on the Web from different perspectives. Chapter 2 describes the Web in terms of its functional parts, and Chapter 3 describes the services that are part of the Web.

Hang On, It's About to Shift

This is probably not your first computer book, and if you're like most people, you've become used to the unfortunate fact that computer books sometimes become outdated. The bad news is that the book in your hands is probably one of those that will become outdated because the Web is changing even as you read this very sentence.

Fortunately, even the swift changes occurring on the Web are unlikely to make anything in this edition of this book totally wrong. More likely is that you'll discover that some new features on the Web aren't covered in the book at all. A year from now, for example, you can expect to find at least three times as many great places to visit and things to see on the Web as currently exist. In fact, after you've read this book, you, too, can publish your own (interesting, I hope) information on the Web.

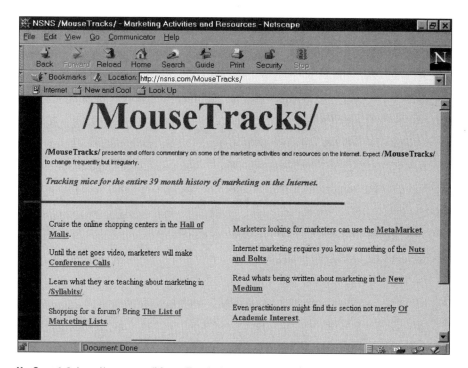

HotSpot 1-3: http://nsns.com/MouseTracks/
MouseTracks follows trends in marketing on the Internet, particularly the Web. Although no one can predict the future, this service is a good resource for ideas of what's coming next.

The Web is growing in other ways, too. The folks at Netscape Communications, for example, may add features to their Netscape Navigator software so that users can access a new Internet service they couldn't before. For example, Netscape added the capability to read and send electronic mail when it released version 2 of Netscape Navigator. (Such a change doesn't make any of the old services act differently, and it certainly doesn't make those old services any less interesting.) In version 3, they added many multimedia features, and in version 4, they added a slew of nifty geegaws like conferencing and desktop management. As the Web grows and becomes more diverse, you are sure to find more things that aren't covered in this book. But all the information here will still be valid and correct.

As you can see, the Web is quite a bit different than, say, a word processing package. If you buy a book for ZowieWord version 3, you may find that some of the commands in the book are no longer valid after ZowieWord version 4 comes out. That's not the case with the Web, however, because there are no "versions" of the Web. The Web changes slowly, and it almost always changes simply by adding new information providers and Internet services, leaving the older features essentially the same as they've always been.

You may, however, run across one possible *gotcha* as you read this book. Sometimes the locations of some Web spots discussed in this book change, similar to when companies move and change their mailing addresses. If the people or companies that maintain these interesting Web sites are nice, they leave a forwarding address at their old location so that you can then hop to their new one. Some people, however, aren't that conscientious of things and just up and split with no forwarding information. This problem is discussed in more detail in Chapter 8.

Another way the Web is about to change may be more important to you than either new places to visit or new services: *You*'ll be there. Your presence on the Web, even if you just poke around a bit, is going to be noticed by those who put their own information on the Web. The more people who are using the Web, the more likely is it that those service providers will put more effort into their sites.

In the past year or so, for example, the number and types of commercial services on the Web have expanded incredibly. This increase is mostly a result of companies realizing the potential for using the Web to reach the growing number of Web users. A publisher who didn't think that putting its magazine on the Web was worthwhile only a year ago may today be scrambling to publish it there, now that so many more users — such as you — are climbing the Web.

Some of the sites on the Web are community-based interactive sites, meaning that you can read something, respond to it, and have other people see your responses. As you may imagine, anything that is interactive and even barely interesting gets busier as more and more people start using the Web. Some of the fastest-growing services on the Internet are so popular, in fact, because people can say what they want to a small or large audience. As more of these services are encompassed by the Web, the Web itself will become that much more active.

Nothing in this section should worry you or make you think, "Ahhh, maybe I'll just wait until *next year* to start using the Web." Come on — face it: You'd rather be using something that is adding new and interesting parts than something that's stuck in one place, wouldn't you?

In this sense, the Web is somewhat like a good cable TV service: It's adding channels all the time. Some are really interesting and just what you've been waiting for, while others are worth about 10 seconds of viewing time before you decide to skip right over them. Either way, most people would rather be hooked up to a cable system that is always adding channels than one that isn't (especially one that's always raising its prices for the same old thing).

What You Need to Start Using the Web

Just like kids in the back seat of the family car on a long trip, you may be yelling: "Are we there yet? Are we there yet?" (On the other hand, you may *not* be yelling these words at the moment.) One important subject still needs to be covered before you jump onto the Web: What it takes to get going.

The starting point: a computer

First, you need a computer. That's obvious, you say? Not really. In fact, by the time the next edition of this book comes out, that sentence may not be in it. Today, most people need a computer; in only a few years, however, you may need only a good local cable provider or phone company, a *cable converter box* (also called a *set-top box*), and a television. The Web of the future is described in Chapter 19.

As I write this edition of the book, the first Web-to-television systems are being sold. The most widely known system, WebTV, got lots of initial interest but has made very few sales. The device is interesting, but I'm skeptical how well it will do over time. However, the folks at Microsoft have much more faith in WebTV than I do, because they just paid hundreds of millions of dollars for the company. Go figure.

Okay, for now, you still need a computer to get to the Web. To be specific, you need a computer that can communicate with the Internet. Today that kind of communication takes place through one of the following two vehicles:

- ✔ A modem
- ✔ A *local-area network* (LAN)

The vast majority of people use a modem to access the Internet because so few companies have yet installed Internet links to their LANs.

Someone to connect with

Next, you need an *Internet provider* that offers Web access. These providers are companies that offer access to the Internet, usually for a fee. That is, you need to connect to some computer that is already on the Internet, and that computer also must enable its users to access the Web.

Beware: Not all Internet providers give you Web access; in fact, an unfortunately high number do not. The only way to tell is to ask the provider's system administrator or its user consultants whether that system offers Web access.

If you are using a modem, you also need communications software so that your computer can use your modem. The software you can use depends on the type of Internet connection you get, as described in Chapter 4. (One unfortunate aspect of the Internet is that you cannot determine what hardware and software you need until you know what Internet service provider you will use.)

Modems: paying for speed

If you read the ads in computer magazines, you are probably under the impression that the faster the computer you own, the better off you are. That's true for many things, but not for Internet connections. Even a slow computer can always keep up just fine with a 9600-bps (bits per second, which used to be called baud) modem installed if you are communicating through character-based software. I use the term *bps* instead of *baud* because "baud" hasn't meant anything for almost ten years; if you read "baud" some other places, assume the writers mean "bits per second."

On the other hand, having a faster modem does make a big difference in how enjoyable and useful your Internet connection is. These days, you have basically three choices in modem speeds: 2400, 9600/14,400, and 28,800. A 2400-bps modem should cost you less than $50; many 9600/14,400-bps modems cost less than $110; and the prices on 28,800-bps modems are around $150 to $250 now but are still dropping.

And, now you can get faster than fast. In the past year, superfast modems called *ISDN* modems have started to become popular. ISDN modems run at about 4 times the speed of 28,8000-bps modems and only cost about twice as much. However, you need to get special phone lines to use them, and many local telephone companies are charging ridiculous prices for these lines. By mid-1997, ISDN should be cheaper and more useful, but if you can't wait that long, be prepared to spend lots of money for the faster speed.

Modems are a topic unto themselves, and not a pretty one at that. Even for computer experts, modems can be a terrible headache. Given how "standard" modems are supposed to be, you'd be amazed at how different they really are from one another. If you're happy with your modem and have no problems using it, great! If not, you probably want to check out IDG Books' *Modems For Dummies,* 3rd Edition.

Minimal Internet connection

Rest assured that all common computers made in the past 15 years or so can be used to access the Internet. Even a clunky old 286-based PC or a Mac Classic with a 2400-bps modem can be used to connect to the Web, although you may not be terribly impressed with the results. (In fact, some people still use even older computers with no problems at all.) If your Internet provider uses a character-based connection, almost any old thing will do. Figure 1-1 shows how a typical character-based Internet provider looks right after you log on.

Figure 1-1:
Using a character-based interface is a common but not terribly pretty way to connect to the Internet.

```
netcom8.netcom.com - CRT                          _ □ ✕
File  Edit  Preferences  Help

SunOS UNIX (netcom8)

login: phoffman
Password:
Last login: Mon May 12 12:18:19 from dharma.proper.co
            NETCOM On-line Communication Services, Inc.

05/28/97   There is a new phone number for the Houston, TX local dial-in.
           The new number is 713-881-1231.  The old number, 713-993-0989
           will still be available for the time being, but will eventually
           be disconnected.  Please begin using the new number.  As
           always, please check with your local telephone company to
           verify whether or not the number is a toll call. NETCOM will
           not be responsible for any telephone toll charges incurred.

You have new mail.
This disk usage summary is for the last 2 days.
Your average disk usage to date is    : 3.81 meg
At this rate, your disk charge will be: $0.00
Your account balance is temporarily unavailable.
bash$ █

Ready
```

For character-based Internet connections, you probably need to supply your own communications software. This software is usually called a *terminal emulation program,* a *terminal program,* or sometimes a *modem program.* For example, some popular terminal emulation programs you may have heard of include ProComm, SmartComm, and MicroPhone. These programs are usually very simple and don't do much other than dial your modem, display characters sent from the remote computer, and enable you to type to the remote computer.

If you are running under MS-DOS or on a Macintosh, you can use many freeware, shareware, and commercial communications systems. If you are running Windows 3.1 or Windows 3.11 on your PC, you already own such a program: Terminal. You may want to buy a shareware or commercial communications program that is better than Terminal, however, because Terminal has very few features of its own. On Windows 95, the HyperTerminal program has even more features that aid in a minimal Internet connection, but it is still far from complete.

Medium Internet connection

Each of the major online services has a different interface and a different level of Internet connectivity (the levels are described in detail in Chapter 4). All three of the services started offering Web access only in 1995, so they don't have a long track record. Figure 1-2 shows the Internet area of America Online.

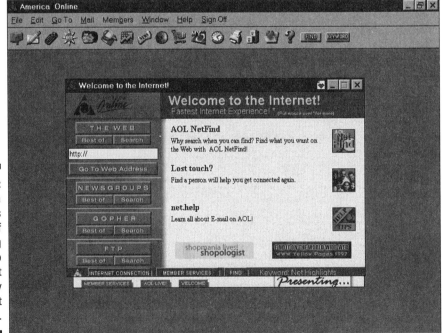

Figure 1-2: America Online was the first of the big networks to support many Internet options.

Modern Internet connection

Although you can get by with a minimal Internet connection, you may want to spend more money to get a better system. Such a system must run *TCP/IP software,* which is described in detail in Chapter 4.

In fact, to use the Netscape software described in Chapters 5 and 6, you must have a TCP/IP connection. As Chapter 4 describes, each kind of Web software that you, as a user, run requires a specific kind of connection. Netscape requires a TCP/IP connection because such a connection enables it to perform many neat tricks that the other kinds of connections don't.

Because TCP/IP software requires much more CPU power than do simple terminal programs, you need a more powerful computer to run it. On the PC side, you probably need at least a 486SX-based system, although some 386-based systems work if they have plenty of RAM. If you use a Macintosh, you can probably run the needed software on all Macintoshes made in the past five years — and probably on some older ones as well.

You absolutely need a modem that runs at 9600/14,400 bps or faster to use TCP/IP software. TCP/IP causes many messages to be sent back and forth over the modem, and a 2400-bps modem just can't keep up. In fact, most Internet providers that offer TCP/IP services specifically disallow you from using anything slower than 9600 bps.

The most difficult part of obtaining a modern Internet connection is that you also need to run TCP/IP networking software. A few years ago, doing so was incredibly tricky and not for the technically faint of heart. Recently, software manufacturers have made TCP/IP networking software easier to set up and use, but it is still confounding to many novice (and not-so-novice) users.

What's This about Netscape?

Okay, you've gotten through the Introduction and most of Chapter 1, and so far you've encountered almost no mention of Netscape, which is listed prominently on the cover of this book. You may be wondering where Netscape actually fits into the Web — and into this book.

Netscape Navigator (which is usually just called *Netscape* in this book) is a program that you run on your PC or Macintosh to give you access to the Web. Netscape is one of the best Web access programs available for any computer and is very inexpensive. (In fact, it's free while you are evaluating whether to buy it.) This book talks about many programs similar to Netscape but emphasizes Netscape because of its current popularity and the fact that its features go beyond those of the other programs.

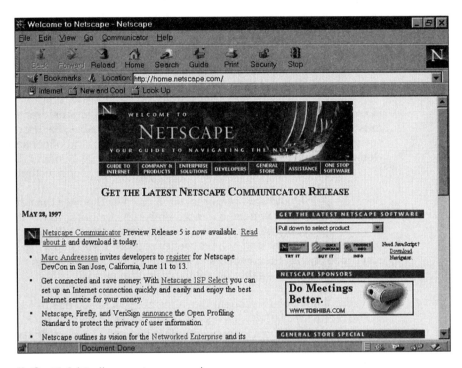

HotSpot 1-4: http://www.netscape.com/
Netscape's home page is a must-visit location for any Netscape user. This shot shows Netscape's picture interface, where you click the area of the picture that links to the kind of information you want.

Just to make things a bit more confusing, Netscape Communications changed the name of the package of programs when it released version 4. Now, the entire package is called *Netscape Communicator,* and *Netscape Navigator* is just one part of Communicator. Other parts include:

- ✔ Netscape Messenger, which used to be just the mail part of Navigator.
- ✔ Netscape Collabra, which does Usenet news and other groupware functions.
- ✔ Netscape Composer, which lets you create your own Web pages.
- ✔ Netscape Netcaster, which lets you receive "push" information from Internet broadcasters.
- ✔ Netscape Conference, which lets you talk and even see other users if your computer is properly equipped.
- ✔ Netscape Calendar, which acts like your personal appointment book.

 ✔ Netscape AutoAdmin, which lets system administrators help keep all the Netscape software at their site working well.

 ✔ Netscape IBM Host-on-Demand, which acts as a bridge between your computer and mainframe computers.

Chapter 2 in particular describes where Netscape and similar programs fit into the structure of the Web. Chapters 5 and 6 offer you good, detailed descriptions of how to use Netscape, and other chapters throughout the book discuss various Netscape features. Many of the computer screen pictures you see in the book show the Web through the eyes of the Netscape program. (For a bit of variety — and to keep you on your toes — a few of the figures use different programs.)

If you are not a Netscape user, however, don't despair: Almost everything in this book is still quite relevant to your own World Wide Web experience. In particular, if you are a Microsoft Internet Explorer user or want to become one, almost everything you read here (other than some of the specifics in Chapters 5 and 6) is just as relevant to Explorer as it is to Netscape.

Chapter 2

The Web:
A Concerto in Three Parts

* *

In This Chapter

▶ Breaking the Web down into its three components

▶ Defining Web content

▶ Glancing over the client programs

▶ Learning a bit about Web servers

* *

*A*s mentioned in the last chapter, describing the Internet is really, really difficult because it consists of so many parts that don't fit together neatly. Some parts of the Internet are simply computers; other parts are the networking software that access the Internet; some parts are what people publish on the Internet . . . and so on. Fortunately, describing the World Wide Web is a great deal easier than the Internet as a whole because everything about the Web falls neatly into three categories — *content, client software,* and *servers*.

Granted, three categories aren't as easy to describe as one unified structure. But if you understand the separate parts of the Web and don't try to mash them all together, you'll find what you want much more easily. Imagine trying to describe your local library as a single unified structure; it's probably impossible. However, if you could break it down into a few basic parts (the building, the books and magazines, the reference staff, the other staff), it makes much more sense.

For the moment, stop thinking about the Web as "the Web" and start thinking in terms of the main parts of the Web. By the time you finish this chapter, you should be able to put the three parts back together and talk about the Web as a sort of thing/place/idea combination again — and even help other novices as they start to get their footing on the Web.

The three fundamental parts of the Web — once again, in case you weren't paying attention — are content, client software, and Web servers. *Content* is the stuff you read, see, and hear on the Web. *Client software* is what you run on your computer to access the content you see on the Web. *Web servers* are the computers to which you connect (by using your client software); these computers are what store the Web's content.

As you read this chapter, keep repeating "content, client software, servers, content, client software, servers. . . ." The three are separate parts that, obviously, work together, but keeping them separate in your mind should make the rest of your Web experience much more understandable.

This book uses both the terms *Web client* and *Web browser* to mean the same thing. Web client is more technically correct because all the popular Web software do more than just browse. On the other hand, Web browser has crept into the vocabulary so much that both now mean essentially the same thing.

It Is Written: Content

Multimedia. Hypertext. Interactive entertainment. Buzzword-orama. Phooey! The stuff you get on the Web is the *content.* Ignore for a moment *how* you get it and where it comes from. The content is what you see as you move around in the Web. (By the way, in describing the Web, the words *content* and *information* are interchangeable. Unfortunately, *information* has lost its value as a word because many people now think that information is something you find on a superhighway.)

Even in our packaging-happy society, content is the most important part of what you do online. A book can be exquisitely bound, have really beautiful text, and smell just right, but if it's poorly written or covers some obscure, uninteresting topic, you won't find it worth reading. A TV show that offers nothing worth watching can't keep your thumb away from the remote control.

In many ways (such as the following), the Web is much like a well-stocked local library.

- ✔ A library houses materials on an incredibly wide variety of topics. Some of the materials are books about a single topic, and others are collections of information, such as multivolume encyclopedias.
- ✔ A library contains materials in many forms. Every library keeps books and magazines, and many libraries stock videos, CDs, tapes, pamphlets, computer databases, and other media.
- ✔ All the material in the library is freely available to anyone who can read it.

The content on the Web exhibits these three characteristics as well: a variety of topics, a variety of media, and (mostly) free access.

Topics on the Web

To say with any certainty exactly what topics comprise the Web's content at any given time is impossible because the list grows daily. A few years ago, the Web offered merely lots of topics; now it overflows with an incredible number, rivaling the breadth of a medium-sized college library; next year, almost every kind of content that you can find in print should also be available on the Web.

Throughout this book, you find examples of the type of content you can expect to see on the Web. (I hope that you also find something of interest in these examples.) Even if you don't see anything that grabs your attention right away (either in this book or your own browsing), rest assured that the Web probably contains something, somewhere that should interest you. (And if it doesn't, well, remember that you can go out and create your own content!)

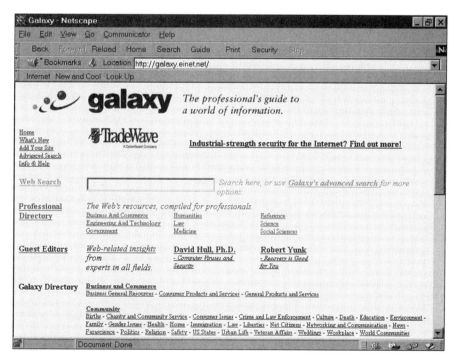

HotSpot 2-1: http://galaxy.einet.net/
The ElNet Galaxy is one attempt to index most of the interesting information on the Web. Of course, what's "interesting" is in the eye of the beholder, but ElNet Galaxy has done quite a good job of assembling the top picks for a wide variety of subjects.

You can find content that covers many topics but perhaps not in the depth you may want. The Web today is like a library with books and magazines on all the shelves in every category — but not as yet very many books in most categories. As time goes by, however, you can look for the Web's almost-empty shelves to fill up considerably — but don't expect the Web to replace your local library or bookstore any time soon.

The content on the Web is, in many ways, just like any content on paper. Nothing is especially magical about what you read on the Web that makes it more likely to be true than what you read anywhere else. Thirty years ago, some people believed that if they "saw it on TV, it must be true." (Some of those people are still around, of course, saying the same thing about what they see on the Web.) Just because the Web is a new medium, don't assume that the people putting content on it are any more progressive or honest than those putting content on TV, in magazines, or anywhere else.

The many media of the Web

The content you can find on the Web comes in many forms, and the number and variety of these forms also are increasing as more companies publish information on the Web. The most common form of Web content consists of just plain text — that is, text with no formatting or adornment of any kind. More and more, however, Web content is appearing with specific formatting, such as headings, character attributes such as **boldface**, and so on. But converting all the old, plain text takes a long time, so don't be surprised if you find a mix of plain text and formatted text at the same Web site for the next few years.

If the only form that Web content took was text, the wonder of the Web would never have caught on as well as it has. From the beginning, however, the Web was designed to handle almost any form of content, and people are experimenting more and more with those exotic forms that go way beyond plain, vanilla text. Today, in fact, you can find all types of multimedia content on the Web, including the following categories:

- Pictures and photographs
- CD-quality sound
- Video
- Interactive discussions (chat)
- Animation
- Games
- Programs that you can run on your computer

Tomorrow, you're sure to find even more exotic types of content on the Web.

As you can do to the content in a library, you can also divvy up the content on the Web into categories such as "books" and "periodicals." On the Web, you can find plenty of articles — and even many book-length tomes — that people have written on a one-shot basis. You can also find a fair number of Web-based magazines that circulate new issues weekly or monthly. Although other types of multimedia (such as audio and video clips) are still rare because these files are so large, even such offerings as these are definitely available on parts of the Web.

The Web already boasts a particularly impressive collection of reference materials that fall somewhere in that gray area between books and periodicals. Some states, for example, have already put all their laws on the Web. In printed form, these materials may fill up an entire bookcase and need to be revised in the form of inserts or reprinted in their entirety every year; on the Web, they are handily in reach (and out of sight) just a couple clicks away.

We interrupt this Web for a commercial announcement

One way in which the Web differs from the standard library is that a huge amount of plain old advertising also exists online. You are probably familiar with the process of looking through a magazine devoted to a particular topic, such as food, and finding yourself just looking at the ads. (A dirty little secret of the magazine world is that, for many topics, the readers care much more about the ads than they do about the articles. In fact, many readers rate magazines not on how good the articles are, but on how the ads make them feel.)

You can find ads upon ads upon ads in plenty of places on the Web. Many companies set up their own Web areas that contain little more than product literature. These kinds of Web sites are wonderful for Web users who want an interactive catalog that they can search through without some salesperson hanging over their shoulders. Depending on how creative the companies are, they can make the Web-based catalog more valuable to you than most print-based catalogs could possibly be.

The commercial Web content can be much more than just a catalog library, however. At some Web sites, you can purchase items immediately after shopping for them. In this way, some areas of the Web act like a shopping mall. Shopping in the stores on the Web may not be as much fun as browsing through a real mall (if you like that sort of thing), but you may find that the convenience of not having to leave your home or office makes up for the lack of ice cream parlors and the fun of searching for your car in the parking lot.

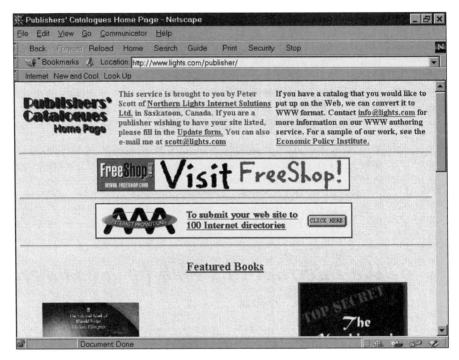

HotSpot 2-2: http://www.lights.com/publisher/
The Publishers' Catalogues Home Page lists many of the hundreds of book publishers' catalogs on the Web. The list is arranged by country, and you can get a feeling for how much commercial penetration has occurred in countries outside the United States.

Another growing area of commercial content is product support. If you've been frustrated calling the manufacturer of a piece of broken equipment, trying to secure help in getting it to work again, you can probably imagine the convenience of getting all the help you need over the phone — without being put on hold for 20 minutes (and listening to some awful CD or radio station).

So far, most of the companies offering Web-based support are computer hardware and software companies. Within a few years, however, you are likely to see many other types of manufacturers offering free Web-based support — if for no other reason than to keep you off the phone.

Filling in the blanks

One aspect of the Web that really separates it from other Internet services is that Web pages can include *forms* for you to fill out. A form can feature fill-in text fields, in which you type information, check boxes, radio buttons, and so on. Windows and Mac users are already familiar with these kinds of things in dialog boxes.

Forms are used for many things: Commercial spots on the Web use forms for taking your name, address, and the all-important credit card number. Other places use forms for surveys or just to ask questions about how you like the service. Still others use forms to help you search for a particular content based on specific words you want to find.

Web content is still mostly free

The comparisons between the Web and a local library are reasonably apt because in both places, reading the content doesn't cost the users anything. Of course, a library needs money to buy books, and people who publish on the Web incur a cost to put the information there as well. To the Web user, however, all that information is mostly just there for the taking.

"Mostly?" Um, yes, mostly. For the first few years, everything on the Web really was free. There was no way to charge for the information. In the past couple of years, however, some sites on the Web have started charging for their content, and a definite trend toward for-fee (as opposed to for-free) materials is growing on the Web.

Fortunately, because so much of the content on the Web is still free, any time someone is charging you for anything, you'll know it right up-front. It wouldn't be right for you to be shown something and then asked for money later; in fact, this practice is illegal in many states.

Your End of the Deal: Client Software

Now that you know that all this content is available out on the Web, the next logical question is "How do I get it?" For that, you need software that can access the Web itself and, therefore, access the Web's content as well. That software is called a *Web client* (or, sometimes, a *Web browser*).

If servers serve clients, what do clients do?

The word *client* comes from the technical term for the structure of the Web and many other Internet services. A *client-server* information system is one in which you run a program (the client) on your local computer and that program accesses information from a different computer running a different program (the server). The client and the server are programs; however, many people also refer to the computers themselves as clients and servers, which can be a tad confusing to people trying to think of the hardware and software separately. Client-server systems have been all the rage in the computer industry for the past ten years because they allow much faster and smoother changes in information systems.

Understanding a bit about the client-server mentality can help clarify how and why many things happen as they do on the Internet, especially on the World Wide Web. In the old days (up until the mid-1980s), to get information from a database, you needed access to a terminal that was connected to the computer on which the database resided. This style of monolithic computing is still in use in many places today.

The server program speaks in a *protocol* (which is similar to the structure of a human language) that can be spoken by client programs. Server programs speak only one language, while client programs can sometimes speak many languages. As the client starts to talk to the server, both programs verify that they can speak the same language and then start a conversation.

Using the client-server style for getting information from computers offers many advantages. The server program and the client program can run on different computers as long as they can communicate through some sort of network. Users, therefore, don't need a direct connection to the server before getting information from it.

Another wonderful feature of the client-server model for information retrieval is that people can write many different client programs that all speak the language of the server. This is precisely what has happened on the Internet. Instead of being forced to run a single client program to get information, Internet users can choose the program that is best for them from the dozens of different programs available.

In fact, a single client program can speak the language of many different server programs. This diversity, in fact, is what the Web is all about. Before the Web, almost all client programs spoke the language of only one server. Web client programs, however, speak the language of at least four, and often more, server programs, enabling you to get that much more information from the Internet.

To run a Web client, you need a computer or access to a computer. Most of the popular Web clients run on PCs or Macintoshes — that is, on the very computer that sits right on your desk. The most popular Web clients for these computers are Microsoft's Internet Explorer and Netscape. Figure 2-1 shows a typical screen from Internet Explorer; all the HotSpot screens you have seen so far are from Netscape. Other Web clients, such as Lynx, run on

UNIX systems that people dial into. Dozens of different Web clients are available, and almost every popular type of computer has at least one Web client available to it.

Chapter 4 goes into much more detail about choosing a Web client. The most important aspect of a Web client is how well it enables you to get around on the Web. All Web clients do certain basic things, as described in the following list (which contains a heap of technical jargon that isn't explained until Chapter 3 — or you can check out the glossary):

✔ Access files on HTTP (hypertext), Gopher, and FTP servers.

✔ Show HTML documents from HTTP servers with some formatting.

✔ Move between links in hypertext documents.

✔ Show pictures in Web pages.

✔ Save files you retrieve on your computer.

✔ Let you fill in forms.

Don't get the impression that Internet Explorer and Netscape are the only games in town for client software. Figure 2-2, for example, shows a typical screen from the Emissary software package, which includes a very capable Web client.

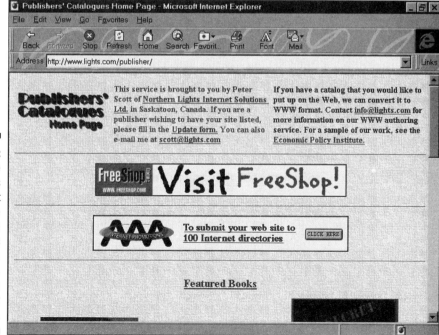

Figure 2-1:
Because the features in Internet Explorer are mostly the same as those in Netscape, the screens look fairly similar.

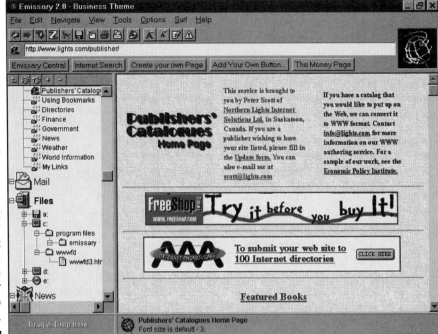

Figure 2-2:
The
Emissary
Web client
has a very
different
layout in
comparison
to other
Web
browsers.

Some Web clients also enable you to perform the following tasks, which you may find important:

- ✔ Access content from other Internet services, such as mail, WAIS, and Usenet news.

- ✔ Remember places on the Web where you went recently so that you can return to them quickly.

- ✔ Keep lists of interesting places you find on the Web so that you can easily find them again later.

- ✔ Print files.

- ✔ Mail documents to other Internet users.

- ✔ Look at the HTML source of hypertext documents.

- ✔ Change the look of formatted text, such as the fonts used or the background colors.

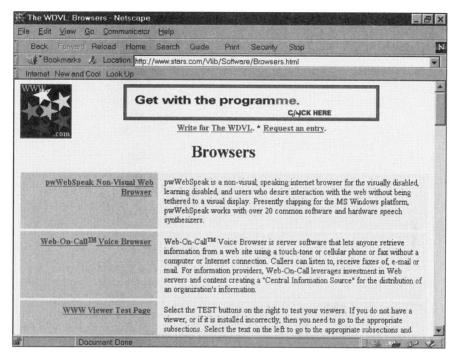

HotSpot 2-3: http://www.stars.com/Vlib/Software/Browsers.html
This page, part of the WWW Virtual Library section on Web development, contains the list of almost all the clients known to man. The WWW Virtual Library is discussed in much more detail in Chapter 9.

Some people would have you believe that the most important feature of a Web client is how good it looks. "Ooooh, this one has a *nice* toolbar." "Check out the *cool* background pattern on that one." Ignore the temptation to pick a client based on its visual appeal. The client's speed, its features, and how well it is supported are much more important than whether it exhibits a few extra gizmos on-screen that perform essentially the same functions as the menu commands.

If you are running your Web client on your PC or Macintosh, remember that you also need to run some sort of TCP/IP networking software in addition to the Web client. The networking software is not part of the Web client; it runs "underneath" the Web client to support it and make the connection to the Internet. (See the sections "Modern Internet Connection" in Chapter 1 and "TCP for You and Me" in Chapter 4.)

They Give It All to You: Servers

You have by now discovered the content and client software of the Web. The promise of accessing all that free content on your client software is tantalizing, but as you may know (or have guessed), that content doesn't simply appear out of nowhere, full blown and ready for you to access. Just as in the book world, someone must publish the content — and that's where the third part of the Web comes in. *Servers* are computers where you can go to get the content by using your Web browser.

In relation to the Web, a server is a computer that makes its content available through Internet services. To do that, it must run server software that can speak the same *protocol* (language) as your client software. Server computers are also sometimes called *host computers*. Each Internet service has its own protocol language. Having servers that act as both a computer and the kind of language the computer speaks to make a particular Internet service available to clients can be a tad confusing.

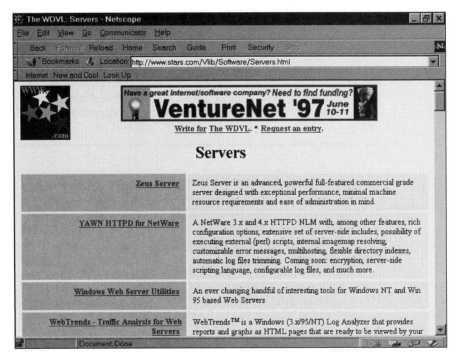

HotSpot 2-4: http://www.stars.com/Vlib/Software/Servers.html
As does the list of all the known Web clients, this list also contains software. This list, however, is of the software you may use to *serve* information on the Web, not receive it.

A few Internet services are considered the "core" of the Web. Any computer that serves either HTTP (hypertext), Gopher, or FTP, for example, is considered a Web server. Many computers, in fact, serve more than one protocol at a time.

On the Internet, most computers have a name, called the *domain name*. Domain names look like the following: `thomas.loc.gov`, `www.kantei.go.jp`, and `www.clark.net`. You use a domain name to identify the host computer on the Internet that has the content you want to access.

The case of the letters in the domain name is unimportant; you can enter them however you want. Thus `www.fv.com`, `WWW.FV.COM`, and `Www.Fv.Com` are all the same. In this book, domain names are usually shown in all lower-case characters. Be aware, however, that although the case of letters in the *domain names* is unimportant, the case of the letters in the *rest* of what you send to the server may be very important.

As described earlier, most Web servers do not charge money for access to their content. They need some other reason to offer the content, run the computer, and maintain the server software (which is often not all that easy). Each of the thousands of servers on the Web has a different reason for existing.

For the first few years, most of the Web servers were at educational institutions such as universities. In the long history of the Internet, universities have always been at the forefront of supporting free information. As long as people on the computer-support staff want to run a server, they are usually allowed to do so. Their motivation is often just to make the information free.

In the past two years, however, by far the fastest growth on the Web has been in servers at commercial sites. A few years ago, only a handful of brave companies experimented with having Web servers; now, tens of thousands of companies are expected to have their own servers. Some of these commercial servers are just there to promote the company's products, but others are there as bona fide experiments in online publishing.

A third group of people (other than those at universities and commercial companies) serves up content on the Web just because doing so is fun. They have accounts with Internet providers that give free or inexpensive Web service access. At these sites, any user can produce hypertext pages that become part of the site's content. People put all sorts of things at these sites — articles and novels they've written, political tracts, databases they've built, and so on.

Tying It All Together

Okay, you can stop repeating the "content, client software, servers" mantra now. On the other hand, you probably should keep it in mind as you continue your exploration of the Web while you read this book. If you come across an idea that doesn't make as much sense as you'd like, you may find at least a small measure of help by asking yourself in which of the three categories the critter best fits.

Be aware, however, that not everything fits neatly into just one category. Chapter 3, for example, covers the types of Internet services that are part of the Web. Each service relates to two parts of the Web triumvirate, client software and servers, because the client must be able to understand it and display it for you, and servers must be able to serve it to you. Keeping the differences among the three parts of the Web in mind, however, should help you more often than not get exactly what you want from the Web.

Chapter 3

HTTP or Not HTTP? What a Weird Question

Some folks are interested only in the content on the Web. They simply want to know where the good spots are located to find various types of information or entertainment. Why should anyone care much about what's behind the content on the Web? People turn to television for information and entertainment, but *TV Guide* doesn't spend much time talking about the electronics or even the politics of the television industry. The Web, however, is quite different from television (and we are all well off for that, some would say).

Within a country, all television is broadcast in a single manner, and all television sets offer approximately the same set of functions. (You can change the channel, adjust the volume, and so on.) To watch your TV, you don't need to know anything about how electromagnetic signals are broadcast or how your set electronically distinguishes between two channels. Furthermore, few viewers know who owns the various networks they watch, how much profit the networks make each year, and how many people are employed by the companies that create their favorite shows.

If the Web were so unified, you wouldn't need to know much either. In fact, you probably wouldn't need this book at all: You would use the Web the same way you just watch TV (or, at least, the way most people just watch TV).

But the Web isn't unified. As mentioned in the preceding chapter, a great deal of variety exists in all three areas of the Web. Of course, content comes in a variety of flavors in every medium, be it television, books, magazines, or radio. Considerable variety also can be found among the Web clients you can use and in the types of Internet services you can access by using those Web clients.

This chapter describes the different kinds of Internet services you find on the Web. As discussed in Chapter 2, not all Web clients give you access to the same set of Internet services. In essence, the clients that provide access to more services give you a bigger Web. In the next few years, the more-popular Web clients will probably add even more new Internet services to their universe; this chapter, therefore, also describes several Internet services that are not yet on the Web.

Overview of Internet Services

An Internet *service* is a vehicle through which two computers on the Internet communicate. More than 100 Internet services are currently available, although only a few dozen of these are common. Among the Internet services you may already have heard of are the following:

- ✔ Mail
- ✔ HTTP (hypertext)
- ✔ Usenet news
- ✔ FTP
- ✔ Gopher

(Don't worry, all these terms are explained later in this chapter.)

Most users on the Internet are connected to computers that use *TCP/IP* for networking. TCP/IP is one kind of networking, and it is the only one that is used between computers on the Internet. It's been around forever (well, okay, for 20 years anyway) and is one of the most-used systems of networking in the world. TCP/IP is a *protocol* — that is, a set of rules for how two computers communicate. Its popularity is not based on the fact that it is the best form of networking, because it isn't. Rather, TCP/IP is popular because most software operating systems work quite easily under TCP/IP. And adding a TCP/IP-based computer to an existing network is also easy.

Not everyone uses TCP/IP, however. Some people are connected to computers with only mail and Usenet connections. These computers do not require full-time TCP/IP connections. A few years ago, the majority of Internet users wasn't on the TCP/IP network; today the majority is.

I don't know anything about how the plumbing in my house works, and I don't want to know about TCP/IP either

If people say that the Internet uses TCP/IP for networking, they're actually being a bit loose with their language. Networking is a black art that can get incredibly technical in about two minutes of discussion. Part of the problem is rooted in history, back when people thought only computer dweebs would use networks. With so many different ways to network, the second — and more significant — problem is that you must use very precise language to describe just what it is you are doing.

TCP/IP stands for *Transmission Control Protocol/ Internet Protocol*. This mouthful (even the abbreviation is hard to say quickly) basically describes how the network works. Some people may have wanted to give it a more colorful name, such as "WonderNet" or "NetAmaze," but the network nerds in the 1970s didn't have that much marketing savvy.

Let me make it all a bit more confusing: TCP/IP isn't just one kind of networking; it's two. Notice that oddly-placed "/" in TCP/IP. The slash is dweebspeak for "over." In grade school, you may have learned that 8/4 can be read out loud as "eight over four." Well, TCP/IP can be read as "TCP over IP."

TCP and IP are *network protocols*, or sets of rules to which every computer on a network must adhere. Different layers of protocols exist in the networking world. The layers are very similar to the ever-popular American system of government. Federal laws take precedence over state laws, and state laws take precedence over city laws.

Everyone in the networking world has agreed to describe network protocols in terms of seven layers. TCP pretty much lives in layer 4, and IP pretty much lives in layer 3. Thus TCP over IP. (Because we're being precise, you may want to know that a bit of TCP slops up into layer 5, and a bit of IP slops down into layer 2 — but then again, who's quibbling?)

Why is this knowledge important to the Web user? If you hang around computer folk, you know that TCP/IP isn't the only network out there. You've probably heard of Novell NetWare, for example. A Novell network runs NetWare, not TCP/IP. Thus a computer running NetWare isn't, strictly speaking, part of the Internet. The person running the network can buy special software to make his Novell network act nice with the Internet and even be part of the Web, but the network isn't running TCP/IP.

In case you're wondering, yes, you can run something else over IP, but doing so is not nearly as common as TCP over IP. You can even run TCP over something else, but that's also rare.

Internet services are based on TCP, which are sometimes called *TCP services*. The term "TCP services," however, is also a bit of a misnomer because nothing in TCP relates to, say, giving you access to files or hypertext documents. TCP itself, however, is the part of TCP/IP that tells each host computer how to differentiate messages that are coming to it from over the Internet. This process prevents your e-mail message from getting tangled up in an HTTP request or a file that some other user is sending.

Each Internet service has its own rules for communicating. On the Web, you never need to worry about these rules because your Web client and the server do all the communicating for you automatically. You do need to know if you are using a particular type of service, however, so that you can predict the kind of content you'll get back.

If you send a piece of e-mail to another computer, for example, your computer and the other computer send a few start-up messages back and forth before your computer dumps the whole message out and over the Internet. After the complete message arrives at the other computer, that computer picks and separates out the nonmessage part of the communication that's at the beginning of the message and delivers the rest to the user.

Using HTTP to access hypertext documents is another example of Internet service communication. If your Web client receives a hypertext document from a Web server, it first contacts the host to make sure that the host wants to talk HTTP to you. The host sends back a message that pretty much says, "Yeah, sure." Your client then sends a request for the specific hypertext document you want, and the host sends the document and breaks the connection.

Ports of last resort

Every Internet service is addressed through TCP's *ports*. A port is a number that is significant to TCP but probably insignificant to you as a user. Each service has a standard port number that Web clients use in communicating with servers. The standard port number for HTTP, for example, is 80.

In the best of all possible worlds, users would never need to know about TCP ports. This, however, isn't that world. Sometimes, a particular host puts its Internet services on nonstandard ports. One host, for example, may put its HTTP service on port 8000 instead of on the standard port, which is 80.

The Center of the Web: HTTP

The Web started out with a single Internet service, *HTTP*, which sort of stands for *hypertext transfer protocol.* (The only time you see it written as "HyperText Transfer Protocol" is when computer book authors are trying to force the words to match the letters in the acronym; it really should have been called HTP, but that's another story for another time.) HTTP is the service that enables Web clients to receive hypertext content that can link to other hypertext content — and to nonhypertext content as well.

In and of itself, HTTP isn't anything special. It is just an Internet protocol like so many other protocols. If you look into its technical underpinnings, in fact, you find that HTTP has a few great features, a bunch of mediocre ones, and a couple dumb ones that can't be eliminated because of their history. (People on the Internet don't like changing things in a way that makes old things not work anymore.) In other words, HTTP is better than some other protocols because it is newer, but the protocol itself is nothing to get incredibly excited about.

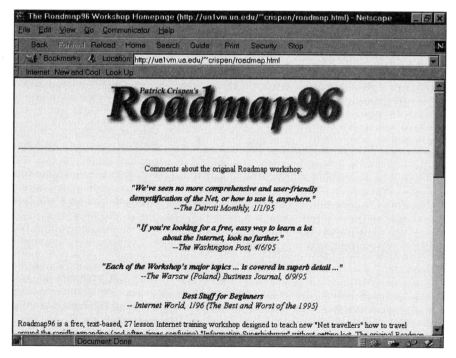

HotSpot 3-1: http://ua1vm.ua.edu/~crispen/roadmap.html
If you like structured lessons, the Roadmap is a great way to learn about the Internet, particularly about the Web. It is provided by the University of Alabama as a service to everyone on the Internet.

What *is* exciting about HTTP is the kind of content it serves up: namely, hypertext documents. These documents can actually be served by a number of different protocols, such as FTP and Gopher. Some servers perform fancy footwork behind the scenes to use other protocols to handle hypertext (such as FTP instead of HTTP). Because Web clients all know how to deal with HTTP-style hypertext documents, however, HTTP has become the de facto standard for serving hypertext.

A bit hyper about hypertext

Long before multimedia, there was *hypertext*. In fact, what people call multimedia today is what old-timers called hypertext back in the 1970s (the Dark Ages before the widespread use of personal computers). If you prefer current buzzwords, feel free to substitute the term *multimedia* everywhere you see *hypertext* in this book.

Hypertext is a type of content that can form links to other content. If you are using a hypertext reader (such as a Web client), you'll notice that some parts of the content are labeled as links to other content. (For example, Netscape normally shows links as underlined text.) The other content may be in the same document, or it may be somewhere else altogether. You can use the hypertext reader to jump instantly to those links, and then to others, or to go back to your original place. This is best described by example.

Imagine that, as you read this chapter, you encounter a sentence that reads: "See Chapter 14 for a list of government resources on the Web." To see that list, you must flip through the book to Chapter 14 and start reading there. After you finish reading Chapter 14 (or at least the parts you find interesting), you flip back to where you left off reading in this chapter and go on.

Now imagine a really nifty book that does things for you instead of forcing you to do them yourself. If you come to the sentence that reads, "See Chapter 14 for a list of government resources on the Web," you simply point to that sentence and the book flips directly to Chapter 14. When you want to go back to your original location, you point to a button labeled "Back," and the book flips back to the page you started from.

Keep your imagination turned on for a while longer. Suppose that Chapter 14 is actually interesting (imagine that!), and you see a sentence that reads: "Congress has made a list available to you of all the bills it is considering." Point at that sentence, and the book instantly produces a copy of that list for you to read. You get the list even though it *doesn't actually exist in the book itself.*

As you browse the list, you spy a piece of legislation that concerns you. A sentence in the list reads, "Representative Hornblower is the author of this bill." Point at that sentence and click, and suddenly you are creating an electronic mail message to Representative Hornblower (although you can still see the list in the background). You finish the message, indicate that you want to send it, and — voila! — it's sent. Next, you decide you'd rather be reading your book about the World Wide Web (or, at least, this author certainly hopes so). You point to the button labeled "Back" and click it a few times to return to the list of bills, to Chapter 14, and then back to the original chapter you were reading.

Pretty nifty, huh?

The *hyper* in hypertext means that you're not just reading text; you're reading content that knows how to refer to other documents. As long as your hypertext reader — your Web client — knows how to find what the content is linked to, you can wander off and go roaming from link to link to link. (Unfortunately, not every Web client knows how to find every kind of content that you may find in links.) Most people find their first few experiences with hypertext quite engrossing and possibly even addictive. Throughout this book, you're reminded that the nicer Web clients such as Netscape give you extra features to make your wandering even more productive. For example, Netscape can show you which links in a hypertext document you've followed in the past month so that you don't go back to things you've already seen unless you want to.

Why hypertext is popular

Many people like to wander around bookstores even if they don't intend to buy anything. Hypertext on the Web is like a giant bookstore that you can roam around in, jumping from book to book. Many people also like to conduct research by exploration instead of in a linear fashion. This kind of research is easy when using hypertext documents because you can go from the inside of one document to the inside of another with a single click of the mouse and then wend your way back when you feel like you've gone too far.

As mentioned earlier, hypertext is somewhat of a misnomer because the content can encompass much more than just text. Hypertext documents can include pictures, sounds, and movies — and in the future will probably incorporate still other types of content that haven't even been thought of yet. Each type of content can contain links to other hypertext. The most common use for these links is a picture in a hypertext document that offers links based on parts of the picture. Imagine a picture of a baseball team, for example, where you can click each player's image and view his current statistics as well as his history with the team.

Remember that hypertext documents can also be linked to nonhypertext documents. Hypertext documents are commonly used as tables of contents for text documents or pictures. Thus you can create a hypertext document as an organizer for other documents containing information that you may want to keep track of. Creating hypertext documents is covered in Chapters 15 through 18.

A hypertext document can also have links to parts of itself. This feature is most commonly used as a table of contents for a document. Although not as exciting as links to other documents, such links enable you to skim a document much faster.

What hypertext looks like

Enough text about hypertext. Figure 3-1 shows a hypertext document as seen through the Netscape Web client. For now, ignore all the menus and buttons; those are covered in Chapters 5 and 6, which describe how Netscape works (as compared to how hypertext works, which is what's important here). The most relevant part of Figure 3-1 is that the hypertext links to other documents are shown as underlined text.

As you can see in Figure 3-1, links to many different documents exist. Notice, however, what is not in Figure 3-1: the names of those documents. The underlined text, the *link,* tells you about what you'll see if you follow the link, but it doesn't tell you where that document is or what kind of document it is.

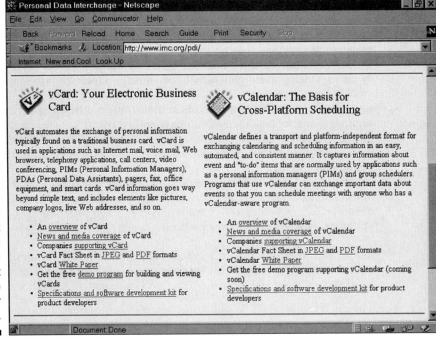

Figure 3-1:
The underlined text sections are hypertext links to other documents.

This fact is one of the most confusing parts of using hypertext. You must look at a different part of the screen (in this case, the bottom) to see where you go if you select the link. Even worse, you don't know what kind of document you're selecting until you select it, although you can learn to look for certain hints on the Web that tell you about the type of content in a link. You learn these hints as you get more experienced with the Web. For example, if you see ".txt" at the end of a filename, you have a good clue that it is a text file, not a hypertext document.

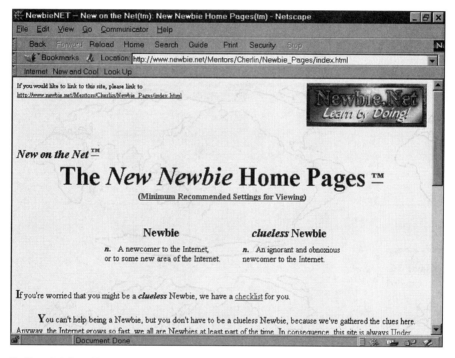

HotSpot 3-2: http://www.newbie.net/Mentors/Cherlin/Newbie_Pages/index.html
We were all new users once. Newbie.net is a friendly site that emphasizes access to information hints for new users. Even not-so-newbies can find some good ideas here.

How to hypertext: HTML

Hypertext documents don't magically appear; they must be created by someone. On the Web, these documents are written in a language called *HTML*, which stands for *HyperText Markup Language*. (Yes, there's that silly capital *T* in the middle of *HyperText* again.) HTML has two major features: it enables you to add formatting to plain text, and it enables you to specify hypertext links.

A *markup language* is a set of special characters you put in a text document to indicate something other than regular text, such as "make the next characters boldface" or "make a hypertext link from the following characters to a different document." You don't need a special word processor to create HTML documents — any old text editor is sufficient. (By the way, using HTML is discussed in detail starting in Chapter 15.)

In case you're curious, Figure 3-2 shows a sample of some HTML. In fact, that text is the HTML that created the hypertext you saw in Figure 3-1. Even if you don't want to create your own hypertext documents, knowing a bit about HTML is useful because it's the structure that holds the Web together. For now, you don't need to mess with any of that glue; you need only to know that it's there.

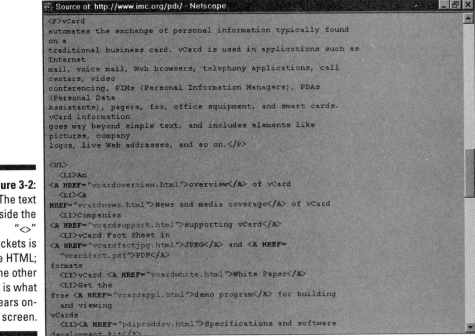

Figure 3-2:
The text inside the "<>" brackets is the HTML; the other text is what appears on-screen.

A Little Farther Out: Other Services on the Web

Although hypertext documents are the starting point for the Web, they are by no means the only part. One of the great beauties of the Web is that it encompasses so many other Internet services as well.

The Web is generally considered to consist primarily of the following three services:

- ✔ Hypertext (HTTP)
- ✔ FTP
- ✔ Usenet news

As you move around the Web, you frequently run across FTP servers, often on the same server with HTTP. Because many people don't have access to Web clients, those who run some servers give other Internet users access to the same information via these different forms.

FTP

FTP is HTTP's inferior sibling. FTP is little more than a glorified file-retrieval system. Its basic commands are the same as UNIX's directory commands, and all you see are directory names and filenames.

On the other hand, FTP has shown incredible resilience over the years. All the major file repositories and many file-duplication utilities are based on FTP. Still, in the face of HTTP, FTP looks more than a tad arcane. Figure 3-3, for example, shows how an FTP directory looks in Netscape.

Because FTP servers merely show a view of a regular file structure, a server site may easily have both an FTP server and a Web server viewing the same files. Some Web server software, for example, enables a Web administrator to show directories that don't have any real HTML content. The administrator can instruct the Web server software to add some formatting that makes the directories a bit more informative.

The vast majority of FTP sites, however, do not yet use this kind of software, and you're left with the basic view of the files and directories. (Be thankful, therefore, that you are using the Web and not a character-based FTP client software and its myriad of arcane UNIX-like commands.)

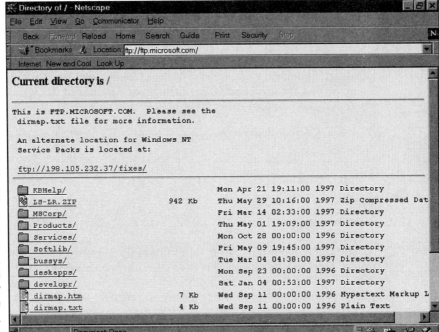

Figure 3-3:
In Netscape, FTP directories are pictured as file folders, and files display discernible icons.

Usenet news

Usenet news is often incredibly more interesting than FTP, and this fact should make it a core part of the Web. Unfortunately, most Web clients have meager (if not lame) methods for showing Usenet news. These Web clients may change in the future because Netscape includes quite a nice Usenet viewing mode.

As Internet services go, Usenet news is by far the most interactive, personal, and fun. It's like a huge party with thousands of topical conversations going on at the same time. You can just sit and listen to a conversation or pipe in at any time. Each conversation has a title that somewhat describes the parameters of the topic, but as in regular conversation, the topic often shifts away from what you're supposed to talk about into what you *want* to talk about.

The content in Usenet news is created by anyone who wants to talk. This fact can be both its blessing and curse. Usenet enables people who would otherwise not communicate in public to finally break out of their shells and say something, even if they're just speaking on a technical subject. On the other hand, it also empowers pushy and overbearing people to be even pushier and more overbearing than usual. To really enjoy Usenet, you must accept a wider range of people than you may normally choose to associate with in your daily life.

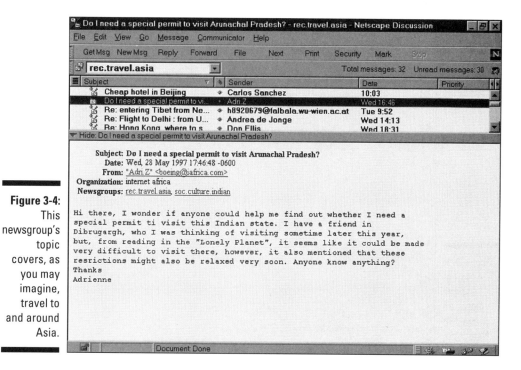

Figure 3-4:
This
newsgroup's
topic
covers, as
you may
imagine,
travel to
and around
Asia.

Usenet is just starting to be considered a significant part of the Web. Figure 3-4 shows Netscape's view of one Usenet newsgroup. More than a dozen popular Usenet browsers exist, most of which are difficult to use and burdened by too many commands for most novice Internet users. Netscape, on the other hand, has pared down the range of commands to a manageable number.

Gopher

Before the Web, there was Gopher. Gopher is an all-text hierarchical interface that was designed to be easy to set up and maintain. Everything in Gopher is a simple, line-oriented menu. For a while, it looked like Gopher would be as popular as HTTP, but now, finding Gopher sites on the Internet is almost difficult. Figure 3-5 shows a Gopher site, as seen through the Netscape client.

In my mind, it's really too bad that Gopher has all but disappeared. For novice users, Gopher is much easier to understand than hypertext. Of course, it doesn't look nearly as nice, being only text, but you could figure out where you were easily when you were using Gopher. And I'm not just pining for the good old days: I really think that helping new users wherever you can is important. Gopher did a good job of doing just that, but it got lost in the "has to look pretty" shuffle.

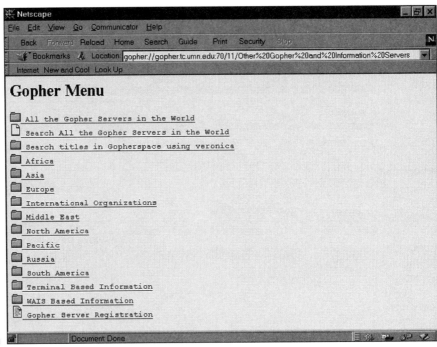

Figure 3-5:
A typical
Gopher
menu, as
viewed in
Netscape.

WAIS

A few years ago, people noticed that no standard existed for accessing databases on the Internet. That problem was resolved by establishing a standard for access requests that bore the not-so-colorful name Z39.50. This standard is better known, however, as *WAIS* (*W*ide *A*rea *I*nformation *S*erver).

Many people widely expected that WAIS databases and WAIS servers would sprout up everywhere. They thought people would access them as much as they do other Internet services, such as FTP. Well, that didn't happen. In fact, WAIS is barely mentioned anymore. Very few Web clients support WAIS directly, and the few WAIS clients available are not terribly interesting.

Telnet

Probably the least used (and least useful) part of the Internet is the telnet service. *Telnet* was one of the very first Internet services, and it shows. If you telnet to another computer, the effect is the same as using a modem to dial up the other computer. The interface you get on the other computer is always character based.

Today, telnet is generally used only for university library catalogs and computer bulletin board systems (BBSs). The biggest problem with telnet is that, after you reach the remote computer, you have no way of knowing how to interact with it. University libraries, for example, use dozens of different programs to access their catalogs. If you telnet to one of these systems, you must first figure out what commands to issue to access its content.

Consequently, few Web clients offer built-in support for telnet. Instead, they start a different program on your computer to run the telnet session. Of course, you must have such a program for this procedure to work, and many people don't because they have little need for telnet.

The Internet Outside the Web

As mentioned before, the Web is not the Internet. Many Internet services are not yet available to Web clients. That "yet" is there because no real reason exists for these services not to be available on the Web, other than an insufficient demand for them from users.

Another possibility for this lack is insufficient creativity from the folks who write the Web clients, but that's a whole other story.

A great example of this is the fact that Netscape now has integrated electronic mail, a feature that's missing in other Web browsers and was, in fact, missing from version 1 of Netscape Navigator.

Where's the mail?

The biggest unrepresented piece of the Internet on the Web is electronic mail. Because your mail is private, the folks who constructed the Web didn't include it in the early design. No one other than you can read your mail, so it made little sense to include it as an Internet resource on the Web.

Now let me clarify that the Web doesn't ignore mail altogether. One method, supported by most Web clients, is available to enable the client to send mail to someone (but not receive it). These links are commonly used by people who create Web pages and want you to be able to send them mail. This method, however, is a one-way device; the recipients can't send any mail to you without you first sending them mail or without you filling out an online form of some kind that you have linked to from somewhere else.

A mail hypertext link contains only the recipient's address — not a message. After you select a mail link, the Web client enables you to fill in the message. Figure 3-6, for example, shows the mail window that Netscape opens after you select a mail link. (Other Web clients, by the way, offer fewer options in their mail section than Netscape.)

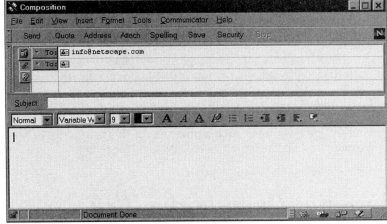

Figure 3-6:
After you
select a
mail link,
Netscape
fills in the
recipient's
mail
address.

The big push

The latest fad for Web-like content has the not-so-attractive name *push*. Push technologies, such as Netscape's Netcaster, allow companies to send you data that you have specified that you want to "tune in." This data appears as separate "channels" similar to (but not nearly as fun as) television.

Netscape's Netcaster also lets you download parts of the Web for reading when you're not connected to the Web (called *offline viewing*). For instance, you can take the first few levels of a Web site and store them on your hard disk, and then disconnect from the Internet so that you aren't running up modem charges.

The supposed advantages of push are that you can get up-to-the-minute news and stock market reports sent to you without any effort. But how much effort is involved in clicking one place and going to your favorite news site?

Frankly, I'm skeptical of push. The offline viewing part is fine, and I use it sometimes when I travel, but the rest of the push market seems really intrusive. Instead of letting me choose where I want to go on the Web, I'm supposed to trust someone to tell me. That seems to get pretty far away from what I think is the advantage of the Web. Web content still isn't nearly as compelling as television (and even that can seem like a cultural wasteland at times), and I think that the excitement about push technologies forgets that people using the Web can think for themselves.

Other non-Web Internet services

A few other Internet services are not yet represented on the Web. In fact, dozens of other standard Internet services exist that aren't on the Web, but most of them don't make any sense for 99 percent of Internet users. You may, however, have heard of a few of the following services that are still not on the Web:

- ✔ Finger
- ✔ Talk
- ✔ whois
- ✔ X.500 directories

Because these services aren't on the Web, they aren't described in this book. You may want to check out *The Internet For Dummies* and *MORE Internet For Dummies* (IDG Books Wordwide, Inc.) to find out more about these services. Nothing currently prevents these services from being added to the Web eventually — maybe even by the time you read this. The Finger service, for example, which is used to describe users on a remote system, is already starting to appear on the Web and in the standards committees that loosely coordinate the Web.

Gateways: on and not on the Web at the same time

Before you start to think that you have it all down when it comes to the Web, a certain gray area exists in the "on or not on" question. Some Internet services that are not on the Web can still be accessed through Web clients by using a Web site called a *gateway*. A gateway is a program that translates between two protocols, somewhat like an automated dictionary for two human languages.

Gateways are very useful for giving users access to a service for which they don't have a client. The University of Michigan, for example, has an experimental X.500-to-Gopher gateway program. If you have a Gopher client (or, of course, a Web client that can speak Gopher), you can send X.500 requests through this gateway. The gateway translates your request into X.500, contacts the X.500 server, gets the response in X.500 format, and translates that back into something Gopher can understand.

Many kinds of gateways are available on the Internet. One of the more interesting (but so far underused) is the mail-to-HTTP gateway. Such a gateway enables Internet users who have mail-only access to receive hypertext documents in their mailbox. As the Web gets bigger and more popular, this gateway will probably become more popular as well.

You Need URL in That Engine

By now, you should be wondering: "What do the hypertext links to these wonderful Internet services look like?" Well, that subject has been put off until now because, um, well, they aren't very pretty. In fact, they're downright ugly. Suffice it to say that they were designed by people who didn't put ease of reading or typing first. Seems that if you leave these kinds of designs to dweebs, they often choose, well, fairly *dweeby* designs.

The correct name for these links is *URLs* (*U*niform *R*esource *L*ocators). A URL tells the Web client the following three things:

- ✔ The type of Internet service that your client uses to get the item.
- ✔ The name of the computer on which the service resides.
- ✔ The request for the item you want (this part may be blank).

The biggest redeeming value of URLs is that you don't often need to type them. Because they mostly exist as links in other hypertext documents, you can simply select them in your Web client if you want to see the documents to which they refer. This section tells you enough about URLs to enable you to recognize them whenever you see them; Chapter 16 gives more detail about how to create your own URLs — if, of course, you create your own Web content.

Note: Throughout this book, URLs are usually shown in all lowercase letters. If you need to type a URL, you can type the service name and the computer name in lowercase letters, uppercase letters, or a combination of both. However, you usually must match the case in the request part exactly as it is shown in this book (or wherever you see the URL). In a perfect world, the case of the request part wouldn't matter, but it all too often does.

Service names in URLs

Each Internet service on the Web has its own name for URLs. As you can see in Table 3-1, the URL names match the service names fairly well. The hardest one to remember for beginners is usually *http* for *hypertext*. Also notice that each service name has a colon after it to keep it separate from the host name or request that follows it.

Table 3-1	URL Service Names
Service	**Name in URL**
Hypertext	`http:`
FTP	`ftp:`
Usenet news	`news:` and `nntp:`
Gopher	`gopher:`
WAIS	`wais:`
Telnet	`telnet:`
Outgoing mail	`mailto:`
Prospero directories	`prospero:`
Local files	`file:`

Note: The committee that creates the names for services may add new official names in the future. At the time this book was written, the `wais:` name may have been given two additional, similar names: `z39.50r` and `z39.50s`.

The last two items in Table 3-1 are probably new to you. Prospero is a networked directory system that has not been widely implemented, so the URL name is rarely seen. The `file:` name is used if a URL refers to a file on your local computer or on your local network, not on the Internet. PC users may be all too familiar with the file that has a URL of `file://C:/AUTOEXEC.BAT`. (PC users are also probably familiar with the use of all uppercase letters for filenames on their PCs.)

Host names

As you saw in Chapter 2, almost every computer that serves as an Internet service host has a domain name. The domain name is the best way to identify the location of the desired computer in a URL. Thus, in a URL such as `http://vvv.com/HealthNews`, the `vvv.com` is the domain name of the host computer, and `HealthNews` is the request.

You occasionally find URLs that have IP address numbers instead of host names. An example of such a URL with an IP address is `telnet://152.4.101.50`. IP addresses are now rarely used in URLs because domain names are much more flexible for administrators and less prone to typing errors by users.

Some URLs add an additional bit to the host name part: namely, a TCP port number (described earlier in this chapter). If the URL specifies a TCP port number, the number falls after the host name with a colon between them. In the address `http://cancer.med.upenn.edu:3000`, for example, the TCP port number (3000) is placed at the end of the address.

What's in a domain name?

Domain names are one of the Internet's greatest features. They enable you to have a nice, usually easy-to-read name for each computer. You don't really need to know much about domain names to use the Web, but you may enjoy some of their fancy tricks.

Every computer on the Internet has an address, called an *IP address*. The address is made up of four numbers; the numbers are always between 0 and 255. The numbers are always shown with periods between each individual number (for example, 152.4.101.50 — in which 152 is one number, 4 is another number, and so on).

If you specify a domain name on the Internet, software converts that name to an IP address by looking up the name in a table of addresses. The method for converting the name to an address is a tad complicated, but it basically boils down to: "If I want to know the address for the name *xxx.yyy.zzz*, I'll ask the computer at *yyy.zzz* because it will know the address of everything that ends with *yyy.zzz*. If I don't know the address of *yyy.zzz*, I'll ask the computer at *zzz* because it knows the address of everything that ends with *zzz*."

On the Internet, the names in *zzz* are predefined by committee, as is the location for finding the computer that knows about the names at *yyy.zzz*. Some of the most common names you see in place of *zzz* are *com*, *edu*, and *net*, although more than a hundred other names are defined. These names, which are always at the right side of a domain name, are called *root domains*.

The great part of this scheme is that, if you control the computer at mycompany.com, you can make up your own domain names such as www.mycompany.com and snorky.mycompany.com without having to ask anyone's permission. If you make up a domain name, you tell the tables what IP address the name is affiliated with (as long as you also control the IP addresses). You can change the table of names and addresses that start with mycompany.com at any time.

Allow me now to make what I consider an interesting point. Don't assume that the computer identified by a particular domain name is always the same. The server whose address is identified by www.mycompany.com today, for example, may be a computer in North Carolina, but that server may change addresses to a computer in New York tomorrow while keeping the same name. The physical location of the computer identified by the name is not important to you — you need to care only whether it is serving the information you want.

Another fun oddment of the Internet: One domain name can point to more than one IP address. If so, the two or more computers with different addresses are, for all intents and purposes, the same computer to someone on the Internet. This feature should see more use in the future as parts of the Internet become so busy that server administrators must create duplicates of their servers to speed up access for Internet users.

```
Netscape                                                              _ 5 X
File  Edit  View  Go  Communicator  Help
  Back  Forward  Reload  Home  Search  Guide  Print  Security  Stop        N
   Bookmarks    Location: http://www.nw.com/zone/WWW/dist-bynum.html      ▼
  Internet  New and Cool  Look Up
```

Host Distribution by Top-Level Domain Name

Domain	Hosts	Domains Queried	Domains Missed	Percent Domains Missed	
TOTAL	16146360	824791	293442	26%	
com	3965417	507513	225989	31%	Commercial
edu	2654129	12694	1588	11%	Educational
net	1548575	24296	15281	39%	Networks
jp	734406	18864	1621	8%	Japan
de	721847	28071	1008	3%	Germany
mil	655128	1128	224	17%	US Military
ca	603325	13995	2450	15%	Canada
uk	591624	27314	5993	18%	United Kingdom
us	587175	15086	5289	26%	United States
au	514760	16811	1065	6%	Australia
gov	387280	1714	481	22%	Government
org	313204	24737	9602	28%	Organizations
fi	283526	3456	525	13%	Finland
nl	270521	10360	332	3%	Netherlands
fr	245501	6422	415	6%	France
se	232955	11180	1189	10%	Sweden

```
  Document Done
```

HotSpot 3-3: http://www.nw.com/zone/WWW/dist-bynum.html
This list is a breakdown of the recent distribution of domain names on the Internet, sorted by root domains. The company that keeps this list, Network Wizards, performs other statistical calculations on domain names every few months and publishes the results for free.

URL requests

The last part of the URL is the request itself. The request tells the host which of the many pieces of information on the host you want.

Often, the request part of a URL looks like a UNIX filename. Truthfully, it often *is* a UNIX filename. Because of how most servers such as HTTP and FTP work, the URL is really just the name of a file that holds the content you want.

In many URLs, the request part is left off altogether. This absence tells the server that you want the *default* content, which is usually a welcome page or home page of some sort. This page is commonly called a *home page* because it is the starting point for your exploration around a server. One URL minus a request, for example, is http://www.info.apple.com, which is the welcome page of the Apple Computer Web server. If you select a link from that page, you discover that it leads to another page with the full URL `http://www.info.apple.com/documents/whatsnew.html`, which is a specific page on that same Web server.

Some novices call every page on the Web a "home page," which is really not correct. The term *home* should mean something along the lines of *beginning* or *introduction*. Pages other than a home page should probably be referred to simply as *pages*. (You don't often hear anyone describing content on nonhypertext servers as home pages.)

The request part of a URL may be case sensitive, meaning that uppercase and lowercase characters in the request are different, even if they are otherwise the same letter.

Note: Some requests end with a slash (/) while others don't. Whether the request should or shouldn't have a trailing slash depends on the server software at the host and the type of information you are requesting. In general, if you request a file by name, the request never has a trailing slash. Also in general, if no actual request is listed (just a service name and a host name), the request doesn't include the trailing slash — but it may. If the request names a directory (such as a request for a directory listing to an FTP server), the request often can have a trailing slash. Not all server software works well with trailing slashes, however, and other server software doesn't work well unless a trailing slash is present. If in doubt, use exactly what you see in the place from which you are copying the URL.

Chapter 4

Before Getting on the Web

. . . .

. . . .

*Y*ou should by now be ready to start looking around on your own (which is, admittedly, much more fun than reading this book). But before you can wander the Web, you need to choose the program you are going to use to access the Web. As soon as you do, you're ready to wander off on your own.

As noted in the Introduction, this book covers two separate but related topics: Netscape and the World Wide Web. Not everyone reading this book is a Netscape user. Even Netscape users will want to read the entire chapter because it is good to know the numerous ways other people use to access the Web. This information is particularly important to people who plan on publishing their own material on the Web, as described in Chapters 15 through 18.

The choice of which Web client software to use may be very, very easy: You may have only one choice, depending on the Internet provider you select. If you chose Prodigy as your Internet provider, for example, you can use only the Prodigy Web client. If you chose a TCP provider (described later in this chapter), you have available to you a much better selection, including Netscape.

Choosing your Web browser is a bit like choosing a college: You can possibly change later, but doing so may be much harder than you'd like. The choice you make of Internet providers can either limit you severely or give you a wide range of options. Choose carefully.

This book uses both the terms *Web client* and *Web browser* to mean the same thing. So if you see references to a Web browser, you can mentally change this to "Web client" — or vice versa, as you prefer.

You May Already Be a Webber

Before you start to get too involved in making your decision about how to get on the Web, remember that you may already have access. You may not have the kind of access you want in the long run, but if access is available to you now, you can use it for your initial exploration.

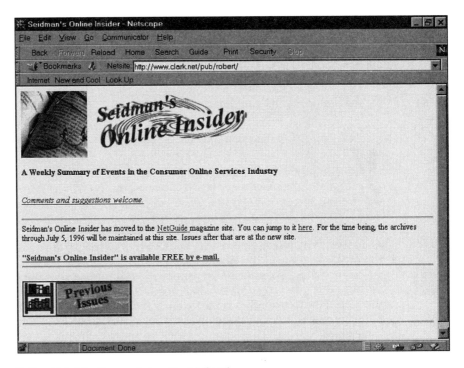

HotSpot 4-1: http://www.clark.net/pub/robert/
Seidman's Online Insider is a free weekly newsletter that covers the online services environment, including the providers such as CompuServe and America Online. Unlike many other Internet newsletters, this newsletter covers the non-Internet side of the online world in more depth than it covers the Internet.

One good reason you may not have known that you already have Web access is that all three of the popular network services — Prodigy, CompuServe, and America Online — tend to de-emphasize their Web connections whenever they get too busy. Figure 4-1 shows the Web browser that comes with America Online.

You may even have access to the Web through a local network at your office — but the network administrator doesn't want to publicize it. Network administrators often do this out of the mistaken belief that people will "misuse" the Web connection, which is sort of silly given how much people "misuse" their computers or even the photocopy machine anyway.

If you want to access the Internet through TCP/IP, such as you can with Netscape, none of the big network services can help you; only the rarest company offers the kind of TCP/IP connections needed to run TCP-based Web clients. Most of the TCP/IP world today consists of individual users who pay for their own accounts or people who work for universities and colleges and receive their accounts for free. (Universities, in fact, are about the only sector of the workforce that actually makes getting TCP/IP Internet accounts easy.)

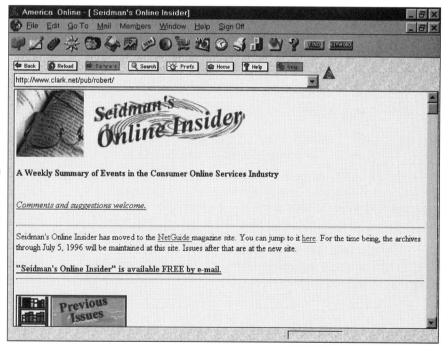

Figure 4-1:
America
Online's
Web
browser
has many
(but not
all) of
Netscape's
features.

Will the Web Hurt My Wallet?

The Internet is one of those funny things because people can pay wildly different prices to access it. Many people get on the Internet for free, and others can pay more than $100 per month for their access. After you obtain Internet access, accessing the Web usually doesn't cost anything above your normal connection fee.

If you access the Web through Prodigy, CompuServe, or America Online, your Web access costs the same as your normal Internet access. Each of these services gives you a certain amount of free time per month and then charges extra for each hour you go over your free time. (Notice that this "free" time isn't really free because you pay a monthly charge, but you get the idea.) By the time you read this, one or more of the major services will have likely changed their pricing structures. In fact, if you read this chapter again in two months, the pricing structures will probably have changed again. Thus, you're better off not to make any long-term assumptions about how much your Web access will cost.

Many Internet providers offer a common fee schedule: a certain number of hours free each month and a surcharge for each hour beyond that. TCP/IP connection services usually work the same way. The trick is to find a local provider that gives you the most free hours for the lowest cost.

Shopping around for an Internet provider is certainly worth your effort. The following fee variations, for example, are typical for TCP/IP service in some areas:

- ✔ $20 per month, 30 hours free, and $1 per hour past the free hours.
- ✔ $20 per month, unlimited use.
- ✔ $30 per month, 100 hours free, and $1 per hour past the free hours.
- ✔ $3 per month, 3 hours free, and $2 per hour past the free hours.

Picking the best provider often requires estimating how many hours per month you expect to use the Internet. That may be particularly difficult at this point because you may not even have started to explore the wonders of the Web, much less other Internet services. You also must factor in the quality of service you'll receive, how reliable the company is, the number of modems it has, and so on.

TCP for You and Me

The Web was designed with TCP in mind. Oddly enough, the first Web software didn't have snazzy graphics and point-and-click interfaces; it was character based all the way. Later, after Mosaic was introduced, everyone started thinking that the Web was designed with graphics in mind.

All the computers that can access the Internet have one thing in common: TCP/IP. This fact may not be readily apparent, but every computer directly connected to the Internet is connected through TCP/IP. Not all Internet computers are alike, however, and that's where you find the difference in Web browsers.

Why do some computers have so many choices of Web interfaces, yet others are limited to only one? The network software you run on the computer in front of you is what determines your number — or lack — of choices. And the software you run on your computer is dependent on what your Internet provider gives you or tells you that you can choose.

Running TCP/IP right there

With some Internet providers, you run TCP/IP on your computer and communicate with your provider through TCP/IP. Whenever you dial in or hook up with your Internet provider, you are using TCP/IP to talk to that provider. Running TCP/IP on your own computer is good because TCP/IP gives you the most choices in Web browsers — and enables you to run Netscape, as described later in this book.

These kinds of Internet providers have many names. Most of them call themselves or their service *SLIP, PPP,* or *SLIP/PPP* services. Not too clear, huh? SLIP and PPP are different protocols that enable two TCP/IP computers to communicate if they're connected by *serial lines.* Most often, a serial line is the combination of two modems and the telephone system. This jargon is rooted in computer antiquity and should probably be quietly forgotten.

SLIP and PPP enable your computer to act like a full-fledged Internet host computer. To people out on the Net, your computer looks like any other computer. The only difference is that the last link between them and you is a tad slower than most of the other links on the Internet.

A few years ago, having a SLIP or PPP connection to the Internet was considered to be a luxury affordable to only a few lucky souls. Nowadays, you can find SLIP or PPP providers in hundreds of cities across the country. Turns out that it doesn't cost the Internet provider any more to run a SLIP or PPP service than it costs to run the old-style *shell accounts*. (A shell account is a character-based account, usually with an ugly UNIX interface. Shell accounts were all the rage until a few years ago. Now they're often shunned because they are much harder to use than TCP/IP accounts.)

If your provider gives you a choice between SLIP and PPP and you can choose either kind of software for your local computer, choose PPP. SLIP is more popular only because it has been around longer — not because it is better (doesn't that sound familiar?). PPP is technically more sound, and most providers that give you the choice generally tell you that people who run PPP have fewer problems than do those who run SLIP.

If you choose to connect to the Internet using TCP/IP, you do need to run TCP/IP software on your computer. Some operating systems come with TCP/IP built in. Windows 95, OS/2, and Mac OS are examples of this. Others, notably MS-DOS and Windows 3.1, require you to get shareware or commercial software to run TCP/IP.

Choosing and configuring TCP/IP software for your computer isn't easy and is well beyond the scope of this book. (You're trying to get on the Web, remember?) Your SLIP or PPP Internet provider, however, can probably help you get going with TCP/IP. To reduce the number of questions you may ask, the provider probably even gives, or sells at low cost, a favorite set of programs to help get you started.

If you are a PC user, you may want to consider upgrading to Windows 95, which has everything you need to run TCP/IP built in. Although setting up TCP/IP connections in Windows 95 isn't all that easy, the software is more reliable than in Windows 3.1.

Restricted TCP/IP

Some Internet providers connect to you through TCP/IP but don't let you choose the software you use. Interchange is a good example of this type of service. You must run its own software for TCP/IP, so you can't also run Mosaic or Netscape to access the Web. Some of these providers use their own Web clients, others don't. (But the latter probably will promise you that they'll have them "real soon now" — yeah, right, and the check's in the mail.)

Restricted TCP/IP isn't very flexible and is really no better than offering only non-TCP/IP service.

'Taint TCP/IP at all

As you probably guessed, many Internet providers do not connect you through TCP/IP. Instead, you dial into their systems by using their own non-TCP/IP software, or you use a character-based terminal program. In either case, you usually have only one option for Web browsers — if the provider gives you a Web browser at all.

You are now at the point where many novice Internet users (and veterans, for that matter) get a bit confused. Your logic may go something like this:

> ✔ All computers that can access the Web run TCP/IP.
>
> ✔ Therefore, my Internet provider must run TCP/IP.
>
> ✔ So I should be able to connect to my provider and, therefore, to the Internet via TCP/IP.

Good logic, but the Internet doesn't work that way, and you probably won't like the reason: history. The biggies such as CompuServe and America Online do have TCP/IP connections to the Internet so that you can access the Web. But just because *they* use TCP/IP to connect doesn't mean that they let you connect that way.

Instead, the big services often make you use their own WWW browsers, which often are not nearly as good as the more popular browsers such as Netscape. And if you use one of these browsers, you can upgrade only after your service provider makes its own upgrade, which can take, well, forever. (Ask any Prodigy user how slowly things change there!)

The little guys, the BBSs of the world, have the same problem even if they offer you Web access themselves. You must dial in to the BBS by using one method (such as a BBS-specific protocol or a character-based interface), and the BBS connects to the Web by using another (TCP/IP).

The procedure doesn't need to be so complicated, but it is unlikely to change any time soon for the small BBSs or the big services. You wouldn't believe, for example, how much hardware and software CompuServe uses to serve its current customers with normal service. For CompuServe to try to shift everything over so that its common customer had TCP/IP access to their network would cost a fortune (and not a small one), although it looks like CompuServe is going to try. The other major services are in the same boat.

If you choose one of these kinds of Internet providers, you are stuck with whatever Web access the provider gives you. Some of these companies, such as Prodigy, provide you with reasonable graphical clients. Others give you not-too-thrilling character-based clients (although many such clients are actually underrated and do an adequate job of getting you around the Web).

Web Clients for TCP

Three of the most popular choices for browsers in the Web market are
Netscape, Internet Explorer, and Mosaic. This may, however, be the first time
you've heard them listed in that order; people used to talk about Mosaic as
if it were the standard for all Web browsers. Netscape leapfrogged over
Mosaic quite quickly, however, and history on the Web is, well, history.

For a while, it looked like Mosaic would be the only browser. Then Netscape
took over. More recently, Microsoft's Internet Explorer is getting more and
more converts. Internet Explorer is free (remember, Netscape still costs
money for most people), it has the massive backing of Microsoft, and it
works quite like Netscape. This year, Netscape is still much more popular,
but Microsoft has been known to come from way behind and take over
markets.

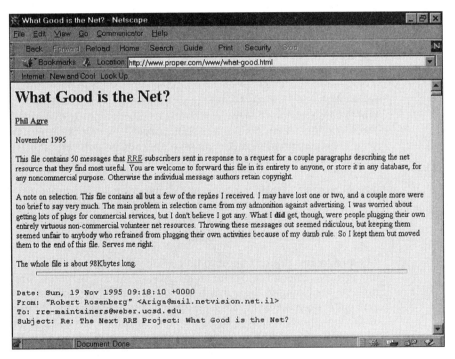

HotSpot 4-2: http://www.proper.com/www/what-good.html
Ever wonder what real people do with the Internet? This question was posed on a popular
mailing list, and the result was 50 people talking about what they do with the Web and other
parts of the Internet. These responses should give you a few ideas of what there is on the
Web that is of real value.

What makes Netscape and Internet Explorer so great? Many things, but the most obvious one is graphics. People who create Web pages can include pictures to appear anywhere in their documents. Instead of just text, which is what you get from almost every other Internet service, you get a mixture of text and graphics.

As people first started seeing and using Mosaic, however, its fancy graphics weren't all that got its users excited. They were really jazzed about Mosaic's point-and-click interface for accessing the Web's hypertext links. In character-based browsers, you have no point and no click; you use the boring old cursor control keys to move a selection bar to a link. In Mosaic, and in all subsequent TCP/IP-based browsers, the Macintosh and Windows concepts of pointing and clicking finally came to the Internet via the Web.

This section discusses several different Web browsers, many of which you can't use because of the type of Internet service you choose. This information may help you, however, if you decide to change Internet providers (something many people do over the course of a few years) or just want to keep up on how other people access the Web.

You may, for example, have free access to a character-based service running a Web browser such as Lynx. (Lynx is a character-based Web client described later in this chapter.) Knowing about programs such as Mosaic, Netscape, or the browser in Prodigy is still worthwhile in case you ever decide to take a step up to a browser with a better interface (in exchange for paying for the better service, of course!). Or your free account may disappear at some point in the future if, for example, you are getting your service through your job or university and change employment or graduate.

As you read these descriptions, remember that the technology underlying the Web is moving forward quickly, and so are its browsers. By the time you read this, some of the programs may have added additional features.

The first big thrill: Mosaic

When some folks talk about the Web, they used to call it *Mosaic* because that's all they had heard of. If you've been following along with the early chapters of this book, however, you know that calling the Web Mosaic shows a deep misunderstanding about what's going on. It's like calling roads "carriageways" because for years all the vehicles on them were horse-drawn carriages.

On the other hand, until Mosaic came on the scene, the Web was merely a rarely explored experimental backwater of the Internet. Sure, other Web clients were available, but very few people used them because they just didn't look all that great on-screen. In our packaging-happy society, as you may know, looks often are everything — and Mosaic sure has the looks.

The Web was born separately from Mosaic. In its first incarnation, the Web was used by physicists to share information by using hypertext. At first, they used character-based Web clients — and not terribly good ones at that. Mosaic was developed by the National Center for Supercomputer Applications (NCSA) at the University of Illinois at Urbana-Champaign, a center that supports physicists and others who use supercomputers. Mosaic and the Web have nothing to do with supercomputers or physicists other than the fact that supercomputer users were the first Web users; the Web could just as easily have been developed for doctors or accountants.

Of course, the fact that Mosaic was free also helped grab people's attention. The biggest group of early Web users were scientists, most of whom had UNIX computers on (or under) their desks. These computers, usually called *workstations,* run a display system called *XWindows*. The first popular version of Mosaic was, in fact, designed for XWindows and was followed by versions for the Macintosh and for Windows on the PC.

Today, Mosaic is barely even a blip on the radar of the Web. NCSA has stopped development of Mosaic and has moved on to other things. Figure 4-2 shows a typical screen from the last version of Mosaic.

Figure 4-2: Mosaic has been the standard against which other Web browsers are measured.

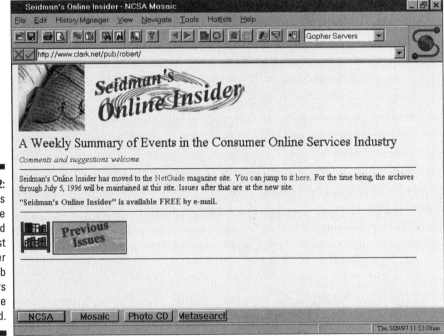

January 1997 was the end of an era for the Web. On their Web page, the NCSA folk say:

> The Software Development Group at NCSA has worked on NCSA Mosaic for nearly four years and we've learned a lot in the process. We are honored that we were able to help bring this technology to the masses and appreciated all the support and feedback we have received in return. The time has come for us to concentrate on other areas of interest and active development on all three platforms is complete.

The great leap forward: Netscape Navigator

For more than a year, Mosaic was the only game in town for graphical, TCP-based Web browsers. In early 1994, however, all that changed. The primary authors of Mosaic at NCSA left to start a new company, which they called Netscape Communications. Within a few months, they started releasing beta-test versions of their new Web client, which they called, naturally enough, *Netscape Navigator* — or just plain *Netscape* for short. The world took notice.

At the time, Netscape was much more stable than the versions of NCSA's Mosaic, which certainly garnered good publicity for Netscape. Netscape also seemed much faster than Mosaic, thanks to certain technical tweaks the Netscape programmers had built into their client. (In fact, it wasn't really faster, but it appeared that way because Netscape shows you content, as it is downloading it, sooner than Mosaic does.) Several indications that the folks at Netscape had a silly side to them (such as the reptilian mascot cartoons on their server's pages) added to the good feelings Netscape gave most Internet folk, especially after seeing how corporate NCSA was becoming. Because of Netscape's liberal policy with respect to evaluating Netscape, it almost seemed like Netscape was being given away for free.

People wondered how Netscape Communications could put out and maintain a good Web browser that they could evaluate for free and buy for less than $50. The management at Netscape Communications is very different from the management at universities where most Web clients are designed. Netscape Communications intends to make its money selling Web server software and other server utilities. (Universities rarely try to make money on the software their staff writes and puts out on the Internet.) The best way to do that is to have everybody on the Internet know the name of the company and associate it with the Web.

If you think about it, what better way exists to get name recognition than to almost give away a good, technically sound Web browser? Of course, the Netscape Navigator is not really "free" unless you're using it at an educational institution or a nonprofit corporation. The folks at Netscape Communications, however, want as many people to use Netscape Navigator as is possible without losing their legal rights to the software, and they want to make at least a little money on selling copies to regular users. Thus they devised an extremely liberal, but legally sound, way to let people use Netscape for "kinda free."

Their solution was fairly novel: You can continue to use the program as long as you are evaluating it for purchase. You have no time limit on your evaluation. So as long as you think you may buy the software at some point, you can still use it for free. Neat legal trick, huh? Of course, you should actually buy the software when you are sure that you are finished evaluating the product.

You can get the latest version of Netscape Navigator (for your evaluation, of course) from the Netscape FTP server at `ftp.netscape.com` (see also the Introduction to this book for information). As with Mosaic, Netscape versions for Windows, Macintosh, and XWindows are available.

Browsing other browsers

For a while, it seemed like Mosaic would be the only game in town. Then Netscape arrived and rapidly took over the market. More recently, however, the balance has shifted again, and all sorts of Web browsers are getting toeholds in the market. Many people expect that in the next few years, there will be many times as many people on the Web, leaving lots of opportunities for different browsers.

For example, Microsoft's Internet Explorer, shown in Figure 4-3, is gaining popularity and has completely eclipsed Mosaic in the market. Microsoft is aggressively pushing Internet Explorer, and has made versions available for Windows 95, Windows 3.1, and the Macintosh. Many Internet Service Providers are giving away Internet Explorer instead of Netscape because Microsoft makes doing so much easier for them. A year ago, it looked like Netscape was the only game in town; now Internet Explorer is looking like it could take away some of Netscape's market.

Many other freeware and commercial Web browsers have features that not even Netscape has. Of course, that's today: If the folks at Netscape see something in another browser that they think is interesting, they'll probably put it in their own in a future version. The same is true for Netscape's competitors: They're constantly trying to keep up with Netscape's features.

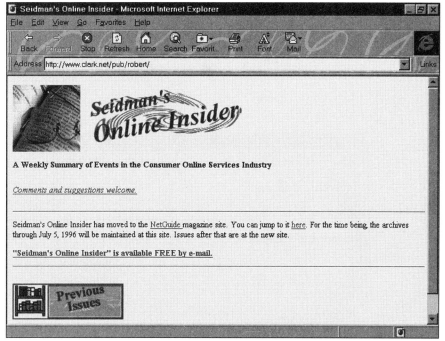

Figure 4-3:
Internet
Explorer
doesn't
have as
many
features as
Netscape
but does
have
excellent
integration
with
Windows 95.

The Best of the Rest

The world of Web browsers consists of many more offerings than those clients discussed so far, although these interfaces are by far the most popular. Dozens of other Web clients are available today; given the popularity of the Web, many more are likely to pop up in the coming years.

Terminally Lynx

Despite the current hype about the Web, nothing is inherently graphical about it. In fact, 99 percent of the interesting content on the Web is text, not pictures. So you don't really need a Web browser that displays graphics. In fact, millions of Web users have no access to graphical Web browsers. (At the time that this book was written, more people on the Web were using character-based Web clients than were using NCSA Mosaic.)

What they do have is *Lynx,* by far the most popular character-based Web browser around. If you have a shell account on a UNIX system, and that system gives you access to the Web, you can bet that it is through Lynx. A version of Lynx also is available for MS-DOS because some DOS users have TCP access but cannot run Windows (and, therefore, cannot use a much better-looking browser such as Netscape).

Lynx was developed at the University of Kansas. It runs on most character-based UNIX systems and on DEC's VMS operating system. It requires you to have a computer terminal or, if you are dialed into a host computer, to be running a terminal emulation program. Fortunately, almost every PC and Macintosh communications program has such emulation, usually for the DEC VT-100, with which Lynx works just fine. Figure 4-4 shows what Lynx looks like in a typical telnet program.

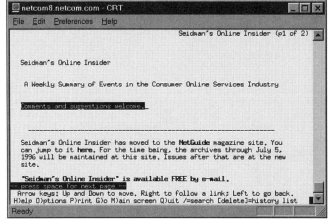

Figure 4-4:
Lynx shows links to other parts of the Web as highlighted text.

If you are familiar with other UNIX-based programs, you'll find Lynx fairly easy to use. You interact by using the arrow keys on your keyboard or by pressing single letters to give commands. Lynx offers most of the basic features of Netscape and Mosaic and has some other UNIX-specific features as well. (If you're not familiar with UNIX-based systems but are on one anyway, I can only wish you the best of luck.)

Be aware, however, that many UNIX systems do *not* run Lynx. In the past, Lynx was plagued with bugs, and that kept many system administrators away from it (although it is clearly more stable now than it has been). Support for Lynx has also been spotty, and many administrators have (probably wisely) decided not to offer possibly flaky software to beginning users.

Lynx, as does other UNIX software, comes as source code written in the C programming language. Getting source code for the program is completely different than is the case with PCs, where software is almost always distributed as ready-to-run programs. Thus, a system administrator (or some other UNIX weenie) must compile Lynx's programming code on the host system. Unfortunately, compiling Lynx is not easy on some systems, and administrators again often choose to wait for a great deal of user demand before they go through the bother of compiling the software and later supporting it.

These potential problems, however, should not discourage you from using Lynx if you have it available. Millions of people use Lynx, and it is particularly popular at universities, which generally allow only character-based access to the campus computers. Some snooty Web sites insist on making their information available only to those with graphical browsers, but those sites are in the minority and usually are not the most valuable ones out there.

If you are at a UNIX site that is not running Lynx, you can get the C source code from the FTP server at `ftp2.cc.ukans.edu` in the directory `/pub/lynx`.

And even more browsers

Many Web browsers come as part of complete Internet packages, usually designed for TCP access. Many of these packages are already available, and many use Enhanced Mosaic as their Web browser, although a few companies have chosen to write their own browsers for their packages.

Most of these browsers offer fewer features and are less interesting than Netscape or Internet Explorer. A few feature interesting interfaces — but none are so compelling as to entice you to buy the entire package just for its Web browser. Figure 4-5, for example, shows the Web browser in the NetCruiser package from Netcom, which encompasses some of the basic features of Netscape but in a different interface.

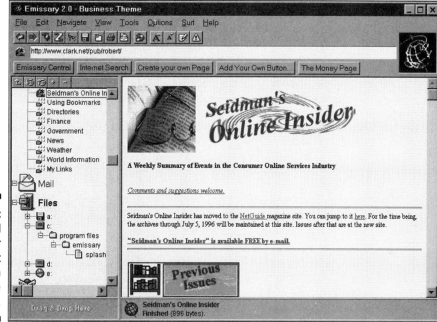

Figure 4-5: A typical browser that is part of an all-in-one package.

Again, if you're already a Netscape user, you're not likely to find features significant enough in other Web clients to make you want to switch. The following two chapters describe how to use Netscape and show some of its best features. If you're not a Netscape user, you'll get a feeling from these chapters for what the touted Netscape has to offer.

Part II
How You See
What You Get

The 5th Wave   By Rich Tennant

IT WAS ACTUALLY ON THE WEB ONE NIGHT THAT CAPT. AHAB CAUGHT UP WITH HIS OBSESSION.

©RICHTENNANT

WHALE CHAT

White? Really? Where can we meet?

In this part . . .

Here's where you get to the meat of Netscape — its many features and how to use them. You also receive an introduction to searching for information on the Web, regardless of which Web client you use. You even find in this part an overview of what happens if you encounter any of those nasty error messages during your explorations of the Web.

Chapter 5
Navigating Basics for Netscape

• •

In This Chapter

▶ Moving around the Web with one finger

▶ Getting where you want when you want

▶ Saving what you see to disk

▶ Opening files on your computer in Netscape

▶ Deciding whether or not to view pictures

• •

*A*s you can tell from the cover of this book, it deals with *Netscape Communicator*. Most of this book is, in fact, about getting around the World Wide Web and the things you find as you do that. Netscape is just the Web client of choice for this book.

Writing a book with *Netscape* in the title that didn't tell you how to use Netscape, however, would be silly. Sure, the Netscape information may not be of interest to people who use another Web browser, but it won't be totally useless to them either.

Because Netscape is still the premier Web browser, most other Web browsers try to incorporate features similar to Netscape. Many of the features you find on Netscape that aren't in other Web browsers may appear in them within a year or two. These features probably won't be implemented just the same, and some are likely to appear in different commands and menus, but many of Netscape's best features are almost certain to make an appearance.

If you don't care at all about Netscape and are comfortable with your current Web browser, feel free to skip this chapter and Chapter 6. Before you do so, however, you may want to read the headings in these two chapters so that you get at least a flavor for what Netscape (and possibly your Web browser) can do.

Where Does It All Begin?

The Introduction to this book described the many ways available to get your own copy of Netscape Communicator. The most common methods, of course, include the following:

- ✔ Buying it directly from Netscape Communications.

- ✔ Downloading copies for evaluation from Netscape's file server.

- ✔ Getting it as part of a software package that comes with other Internet programs.

- ✔ Downloading copies for free use if you are at an educational institution or nonprofit organization.

- ✔ Buying copies in some software stores and bookstores.

A system administrator at your company or university may even have installed a copy on your computer already.

All these options mean that you may install Netscape on your PC or Macintosh in many different ways, which makes writing a book that covers every way of installing the program on your computer pretty much impossible. To make matters worse, Netscape from time to time changes its installation procedures.

The preceding statements lead to what you may have guessed by now — this book doesn't cover Netscape installation. But don't worry. So far, Netscape has been one of the easiest Web browsers to install. Still, to put the exact directions in this book would be a bit pointless because they are bound to change by the time you read this.

For most people, setting up Netscape consists of answering a few questions about what name you want to use, where you get your mail, and so on. The answers to these questions usually come from your Internet Service Provider (ISP), and because Netscape is so popular, most ISPs can tell you what to fill in each of the setup dialog boxes.

One hint I will give you, however, is that you should not have two different versions of Netscape on your computer at the same time. It appears that Netscape has tried hard to make this possible so that you could be running both version 3 and version 4, but a few people have had problems with this. Because every version of Netscape is really much better than the previous one, I always just overwrite the old ones and go with the new.

The fact that you install Netscape differently at different times, or that someone else may have installed Netscape for you, means that what you see as you first run Netscape may be different than what you see in this book.

This fact makes writing a book for beginners a bit difficult. A solution exists, however, that should have everyone starting at the same place.

Remember that this book covers version 4 of Netscape. If you're running an earlier version, many of the commands will be different from what you see here, and the screen will probably be different also.

After you first start Netscape, click the Home button. You should see a screen similar to that shown in Figure 5-1. This screen is the home page for Netscape Communications, and it may be what your copy of Netscape is already set to show after you start it up. (It's okay to click the button anyway.)

The Web weavers at Netscape change the contents of this page quite often, so it will certainly not actually look like this on your screen. It changes because Netscape puts all the latest company news on this page to get you excited about its products. Of course, this variability makes it a tad difficult to show you something in this book that will look like what you see on-screen. Although things won't be arranged the same way each time, you shouldn't have any trouble adjusting to the changes. Just don't let them confuse you.

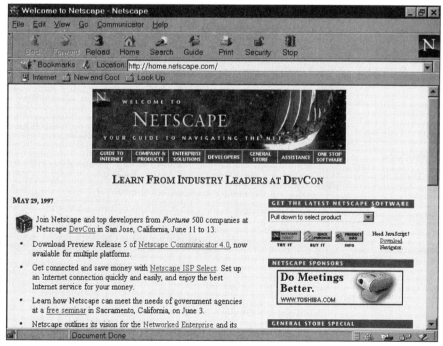

Figure 5-1:
The
Netscape
Welcome
page.

Figure 5-2 lists the names of the parts of the Netscape window. The navigation toolbar (the top toolbar in the picture with all the icons), the location toolbar (the second toolbar from the top, with the text area), and the personal toolbar (the third toolbar from the top, just above the content area of the window) may not appear on your screen, depending on the settings in the View menu.

The component bar is that little area in the lower-right corner of the screen. When you first start up Netscape, it is a big window that is always on top of the main Netscape window. I have no idea why Netscape made it that way, because it is annoying and always in the way. Fortunately, you can easily make the component bar small and push it into the lower-right corner by using the Communicator⇨Dock Component Bar command.

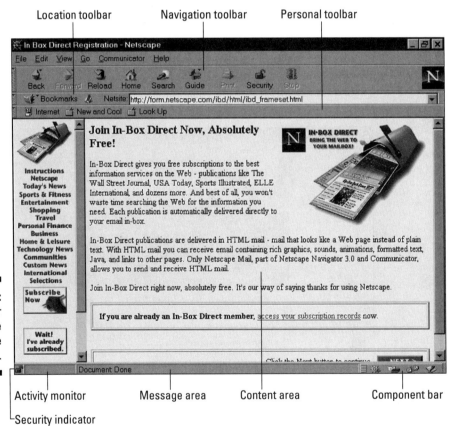

Figure 5-2:
A bit farther down the Welcome page.

Windows 3.1? Windows 95? Macintosh? Who Cares!

You've probably noticed that all of this book's screen pictures come from a PC running Windows 95. If you're using Netscape Navigator on a PC running Microsoft Windows 3.1, or on a Macintosh, you may be thinking, "Oh, great, the instructions in these chapters won't work for me." Fret not, dear reader! Fortunately, the good folks at Netscape Communications made the software for Windows 95 work almost exactly like the software for Windows 3.1 and for the Macintosh. A couple of small differences exist, but they are pretty much unimportant to most Netscape users. (I cover them anyway, just to keep the people who don't run Windows 95 happy.) A few folks use Netscape Navigator on UNIX systems running under XWindows. They, too, can follow along with the directions in these chapters, although they'll probably find a bit more divergence than will the Windows 3.1 and Macintosh users.

Click-O-Rama: Following Links

As described in Chapter 2, hypertext is based on *links*. A hypertext document can have links (sometimes called *pointers*) to many other documents or to certain spots within the same document. To jump to the link's destination, select the link, which indicates to the browser that that's where you want to go.

In Netscape, links are shown by default as underlines. For example, look at the text on your screen. Some of the text is underlined, and each set of underlined text is a link. Jumping to linked text is easy as can be: Just click any of the text in the link. (If you're using a PC, always click with the left mouse button; on the Mac, you don't have any choice because you have only one mouse button to click.)

For example, click on any link from the Netscape main page. After a moment, this takes you to a different document on the Web — for example, the one shown in Figure 5-3. Congratulations, you've just started your Web journey!

You can tell where you are by looking in the *location toolbar* near the top of the Netscape window (it's the middle toolbar). This area tells you the URL (the address) of the Web page you are viewing, which is often useful to know in case you just jumped someplace without first looking where you were going.

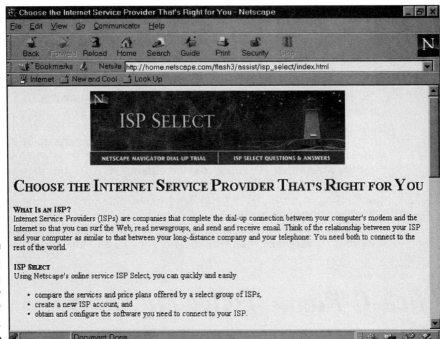

Figure 5-3:
Discovering
what's new
on the ISP
Select page.

You may notice that many of the screen pictures in other parts of this book don't display the navigation or personal toolbars. Hiding the toolbar and directory buttons enables you to view more text in the content area, which is usually what you want. In general, you don't want to hide the location toolbar, however, because knowing where you are at any given time is valuable. You can hide and unhide the navigation and personal toolbars and directory buttons by using the commands in the View menu.

Look before you link. Just because a link looks interesting doesn't mean that you actually want to follow it. It may, for example, be a link to a system that you recognize is very slow or often unavailable. Or it may be a link to a Web site that contains content you would find offensive and prefer not to link to.

Looking at a link in the main part of the Netscape window tells you what the person who wrote that content thinks is a good description of the link. It doesn't tell you where the link takes you. Fortunately, Netscape gives you an easy way to figure out where you go if you click a link.

Just look at the bottom of the Netscape window: See the large blank area that takes up most of the bottom of the window? Move your cursor over a link on-screen but don't click it. Notice that the blank area (the *message area*) now contains a URL. That URL is the URL for the link underneath the cursor.

Backward and forward

Okay, say that you followed a link and now you want to get back to where you were. After you jump to a different Web page, that page doesn't know or remember where you came from. Netscape does remember, however, and you can return to your starting location in any of the following ways:

- Click the Back icon in the navigation toolbar.

- Choose Go⇨Back.

- Press Alt+← (PC users) or ⌘-[(Mac users).

All three of these options do the same thing, so you want to use only one.

Netscape usually remembers at least a dozen backup steps. So if you start at Web site A, select a link to go to Web site B, and then travel to Web site C, you can go back twice from C to get to A. Going backward in Netscape is a bit like undoing changes in a word processor.

Going forward is easy with Netscape as well. The three possible actions that take you forward are just what you would guess if you remember the Back command:

- Click the Forward icon in the navigation toolbar.

- Choose Go⇨Forward.

- Press Alt+→ (PC users) or ⌘-] (Mac users).

By using these methods, you can go back and forth in a chain of links to check where you've been and where you're going.

Knowing where you've been

If you choose to use the Go menu's Back and Forward commands, you may notice something after you choose your first link: the Go menu changes. Each time you go somewhere new, that location is added to the list near the bottom of the Go menu. The name in the menu is the title of the page you went to. (This may be a tad confusing, but the new places are added to the top of the list that's at the bottom of the menu.)

Instead of using the Back command, you can choose the location you want by selecting its name from the Go menu. This method is much faster than repeatedly using the Back command to navigate. Figure 5-4 shows a typical Go menu after you've been meandering around the Web for a while.

Figure 5-4:
A history of
where
you've been
appears in
the Go
menu.

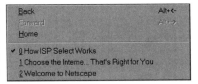

Who says you can't go home again?

Sometimes you can get lost in all your wanderings around the Web. You may want to get back to the place from which you started. Getting to home, the page you see when you start Netscape, is quite easy. (Actually, Netscape had to make this process easy because people often use it to bail out of a fruitless search. Even advanced Web users regularly go home.)

To go home, you can either click the Home icon on the navigation toolbar or choose Go⇨Home command. If you haven't roamed too far, your home page is the last item on the Go menu; you can also just pick it up from there.

Stop right there

As you link from one Web page to another, you never know how big a new page may be. If you're accessing a file by FTP, the page could be hundreds of kilobytes long. Depending on how fast your modem is and how fast the Internet seems to be running at the moment, you may realize that getting all the text or images on a page is going to take much longer than you anticipated.

No problem! Simply click the Stop icon on the toolbar, open the View menu and choose the Stop Page Loading command (sounds a bit weird, I know), or press the Escape key (PC users) or ⌘-Period (Mac users). Netscape immediately stops downloading whatever it was getting and lets you go on with your life. If you were downloading an HTML document or image, you can still see what you received before you stopped.

In fact, you don't really need to stop downloading to move on while Netscape is downloading more HTML or images. If you see a link on-screen that you want to explore, simply click that link, even if Netscape is still downloading. Netscape stops what it's doing and takes you to that link, similar to the way that you can skip the rest of a song on a CD by pressing the fast-forward button.

Stopping the downloading process is more common than you may at first think. Because some Web sites are incredibly busy, many links that aren't broken are horribly slow to access. You click a link and then wait, wait, wait. If you get tired of waiting, or are just plain bored, stop the process and go somewhere else.

Get it again

The opposite of "stop right there" is "give it to me again" — something you want to do occasionally when you're using Netscape. For example, some Web pages are frequently updated (such as current weather reports and stock market quotations).

You can make sure that you are looking at the most recent version of a Web page by *reloading* (getting it again). To reload the current page, click the Reload icon in the toolbar or open the View menu and choose Reload.

Entering Links Instead of Clicking Them

The Web isn't all click-click-click. You find URLs in other places that you want to investigate. I hope, in fact, that you will find some interesting URLs in the later chapters in this book. To get to those places, you need to tell Netscape where to go. (You are, of course, already learning how to tell Netscape what to do.)

The easiest way to do so is to choose File➪Open Page command. The Open Page dialog box that appears asks for the URL or file you want. Type the new URL in the text box, click the Open button, and away you go. You can also achieve the same results by selecting the text in the location toolbar, erasing that URL, typing in your new URL, and pressing Enter.

 You may notice that URLs are often long and complicated. Typing them can be tedious, and mistyping them is all too easy. If the URL appears on a document you already have in another program on your computer (such as in a word processor or a mail program), Netscape gives you a great, no-typing-needed option. Just follow these easy steps:

1. **Copy the URL listed in that program to the Clipboard.**

2. **Switch to Netscape by using the Alt+Tab key (Windows users) or whatever other method you use to switch between programs.**

3. **Choose File➪Open Page command.**

4. Paste the URL in the text box in the Open Page dialog box by pressing Crtl+V. (And yes, Mac folks use ⌘-V.)

Save That File

The Web is for more than just looking. You can save the text you're reading (or the pictures you're viewing) to disk on your computer. By doing so, you can read them again later without having to go back out on the Web.

Saving HTML documents and text files takes a single command: the File menu's Save As command. The Save As dialog box in Netscape looks the same as it does in most programs, but with a single addition. In Windows, the option located directly below the file list is labeled Save File as Type; on the Mac, it's a simple Format. For Windows, the choices are "HTML Files" and "Plain Text"; for the Macintosh, the choices are "Source" and "Text."

If you are saving an HTML file (on the Mac, this is a "Source" file), name the file with an HTM extension. (Mac users can use HTML or html if they want.) For example, if you are looking at a Web site that is having a contest and you want to save the list of prizes, you might call the file PRIZES.HTM. If you are saving a text file, choose Text and name the file whatever you want.

If you save an HTML file by using the Plain Text option, you'll lose all the formatting. In fact, HTML files converted to text usually come out looking pretty awful — lots of extraneous spaces, odd line breaks, and so on. Generally, you should always save HTML files by using the Source option to retain the HTML codes.

The Save As command also works for images. If the Web page is a single image, such as a GIF or a JPEG file, choose the File⇨Save As command, and Netscape will tell you the file type.

You don't need to save the file as Source if you just want to look at the HTML in the file. Instead, choose View⇨Page Source command. Doing so opens the source document as a text file that you can scroll through and, if you want, save to disk. This document appears as a new text window in Netscape.

Use What You Have: Opening Local Files

Netscape can do more than open links off the Web. It can open files off your computer's disk as well (such as the files you saved by using the File⇨Save As command). The same Open Page command can open an HTML file, a text file, or a graphics file.

In fact, Netscape can read these files no matter what program created them. For example, if someone mails you an HTML file, you can save it by using your mail program and give it the extension HTM. Netscape opens this file just fine. The same is true for the JPEG and GIF files you may have on your system.

Imagining a Web without Images

To some people, the pictures are the things that make the Web exciting. To others, pictures are what make the Web slow. If you don't want to download all the pictures on each Web page you come to while you're cruising around the Web, you don't need to. Simply give the Edit⇔Preferences command, choose Advanced from the list at the left, and then deselect the "Automatically load images" checkbox. You can choose the command again to cause Netscape to start downloading pictures once more.

You immediately notice that you get your Web pages much faster. (Web pages commonly have 5K worth of text and 100K worth of images.) And the pages you see are still quite readable. Figure 5-5 shows a typical Web page that was downloaded without its images.

If you turn off automatic downloading, you can still download all the images easily. Choose the View⇔Show Images menu command or click the Images icon in the toolbar to load all the images for the current page. To download just one of the images, click it, and Netscape brings only that one in.

If you have a 14.4-Kbps modem, you probably want to spend most of your time cruising around without automatically downloading images. Every time you come to a page and think, "Hmmm, I wonder what kind of images they've got here?" you can load them for just that page. The improvement in speed should make your Web travels more enjoyable.

Many Windows to the Web

So far, everything you've done in Netscape has been in a single window. If you click a link, the old page disappears and the new page replaces it. What do you do if you want to view more than one Web page at a time?

Easy! (Or at least it's easy in Netscape; some other Web programs don't offer this feature.) Choose Communicator⇔Navigator. A second window appears. You can use it to roam around the Web while the first window stays the same.

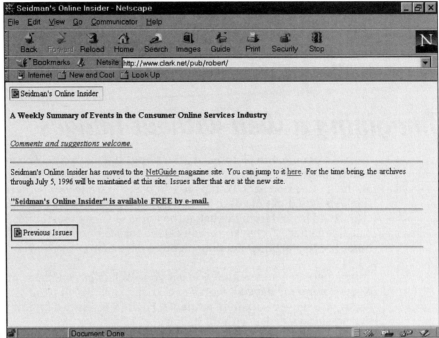

Figure 5-5:
A Web page
downloaded
without its
images.

In fact, Netscape keeps separate history lists for each window you open. This feature means that you can easily keep track of your wanderings in different windows. You can also change the windows' appearance separately. For example, you can have the toolbar showing in one window but not in the other.

So Go Out and Have Fun

You now know 80 percent of what you need to use Netscape well and 100 percent of what you need to really start exploring. Follow links. Click here and then click there. Get lost. Get found. Get lost again. Go home and start over. Enjoy.

Chapter 6, by the way, fills you in on the various Netscape commands and options not covered here. You really should read it at some point, but you don't need to read it now. Go ahead and play. Hey, you can even feel free to experiment with the commands that aren't covered for you. Come back if you want to find out about the other 20 percent.

Chapter 6
Getting Farther with Netscape

· ·

In This Chapter

▶ Filling in Web forms

▶ Reading news and sending mail

▶ Storing bookmarks for your favorite Web sites

▶ Changing how Netscape looks and acts

· ·

Chapter 5 describes everything you need to traverse the Web. You can do more with Netscape, however, than just wander around the Web. This chapter discusses how to handle Web sites that have fill-in forms that look pretty much like dialog boxes. You also find information on how to use Netscape to read and post to Usenet newsgroups, and how to use Netscape to read and send electronic mail.

This chapter also describes the other features of Netscape that are most likely to increase your long-term enjoyment of using the Web. Bookmarks, for example, are a way to remember the best spots on the Web you visit. You can treat them like your own page of the best links on the Web. The end of this chapter describes the choices accessed through the Options menu. You use this menu to change important settings in Netscape and control how the Netscape window looks.

Filling In Forms

One of the great features of the Web — one that differentiates it from other popular Internet services such as Gopher and FTP — is forms. A form is pretty much like a standard dialog box. Web forms are basically Web pages that contain dialog boxes.

Web forms can have most of the features you've gotten used to in Windows and Mac dialog boxes. Figure 6-1 shows a typical form. If you know how to use dialog boxes, you don't need to learn much to use Web forms.

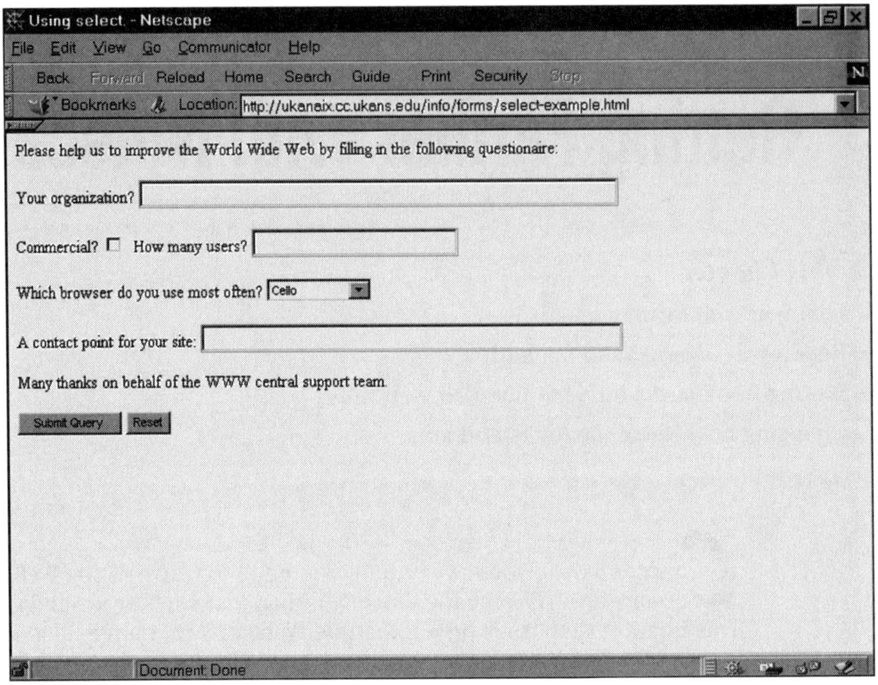

Using select. - Netscape

File Edit View Go Communicator Help

Back Forward Reload Home Search Guide Print Security Stop

Bookmarks Location: http://ukanaix.cc.ukans.edu/info/forms/select-example.html

Please help us to improve the World Wide Web by filling in the following questionaire:

Your organization?

Commercial? ☐ How many users?

Which browser do you use most often? Cello

A contact point for your site:

Many thanks on behalf of the WWW central support team.

Submit Query   Reset

Document: Done

Figure 6-1:
A sample
Web form.

Every Web form has at least one button, usually labeled Submit or OK, that sends the data you fill in to the host computer for processing. Many forms also often have a button labeled Cancel that causes all the information you've entered in the form to be removed.

After you submit a form, it goes to a program, usually located at the same site from which you got the form, which takes the information you fill in and processes it. The program can do just about anything with the information. If the form is an order form, for example, the program can record all your information and start processing your order. If it is a survey form, the program may just write your responses into a file to be tabulated later.

After you submit a form on the Web, the information you have entered is usually sent over the Internet as plain text; encryption of forms (making their contents secret) is still quite new to the Web. Any information you put in the form, therefore, could possibly be read by someone who is watching information move around the Web. Although this isn't supposed to happen, it does. Think twice before saying something in a form that you may not want someone other than the recipient to read.

And while I'm at it, you should probably think hard about what you enter in a form with a company you don't know. As of this writing, no cases have been reported of companies using information from forms in a malicious fashion, but it's only a matter of time. When you submit a form, you don't know where it's going. (For example, a form on one Web site can point to a program on a different Web site.) Many people are, however, trying to implement better security for the Web.

Netscape and Internet Mail

Netscape's mail client, properly called *Messenger Mailbox,* is a reasonably good way to read and send email. The mail client in versions 1 and 2 of Netscape was downright awful (and I said so in the earlier editions of this book), but has greatly improved. I still think plenty of other good mail programs exist, but if you only use mail for simple things, you'll find that Netscape's mail is just fine.

To see your mail, you give the Communicator⇨Messenger Mailbox command, or click the second icon (the one that looks like a piece of mail going into a slot) on the component bar.

Figure 6-2 shows the Netscape mail window. It looks a great deal like the Navigator window, and most of the icons in the navigation toolbar are the same as they are in Navigator. The location toolbar is a bit different than Navigator, however; instead of a box that tells you the current URL, you get a pull-down menu that lists the different mail folders.

Before you can start using Messenger, you have to tell Netscape about where you get your mail, what your e-mail address is, and so on. Doing so is described later in this chapter in the section called "What More Could You Prefer?"

Having mail folders is actually quite a nice feature, one that has been adopted by most modern mail client software. New mail appears in the Inbox folder. After you read a message, you can put it into any of the folders in the Mail folders panel simply by dragging it from the Message list window. You can create new folders with the New Folder command in the File menu, and you can open and close the folders just by selecting them.

You cannot start reading your mail with Netscape until you tell Netscape some vital information in the Preferences command from the Edit menu. See the section later in this chapter on mail preferences for more information on the various options you must set in order to receive mail.

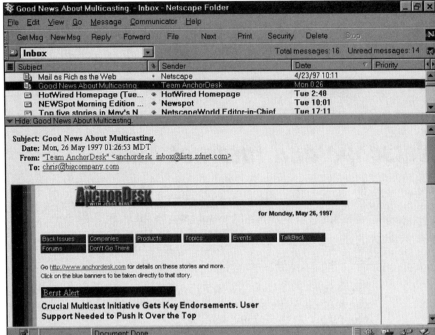

Figure 6-2:
The
Netscape
mail
window.

Creating new mail

If you select a `mailto:` link in an HTML document or you send mail from the Usenet or mail interfaces, Netscape opens a dialog box with the recipient's address already written into it. Figure 6-3 shows the dialog box for sending mail. The fields are probably somewhat similar to whatever program you are currently using for sending and receiving e-mail.

You can fill in the Subject field and the text of the message however you choose. If you are replying to a message, Netscape fills in some of the fields for you. Feel free to edit this text. In fact, you can even edit the "To:" field to change the intended recipient of the message.

Actually, the area around the "To:" field is fairly confusing. You can do several things here, but they aren't all that apparent. The three tiny icons that are stacked starting to the left of the "To:" field bring up three subwindows. The top icon, which looks like a tiny business card holder, brings up the window for entering addressing information. The second icon, the paper clip, brings up the window for allowing you to attach files to your message. The bottom icon, with the tiny check marks, brings up a window with assorted sending options.

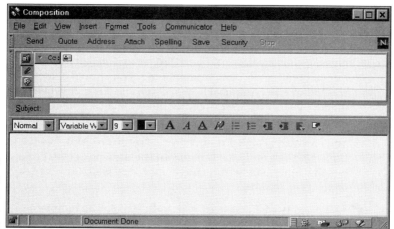

Figure 6-3:
Sending
new mail.

In the addressing options, you have already seen how to fill in the "To:" field. You can address mail in other ways, such as with the "Cc:" header. To add a "Cc:" header, go to the second line, click on the "To:", and you'll see a list of the other addressing headers you can choose. After you pick a header, you can fill in the rest of the line the same way you did the "To:" line.

When you are ready to send the mail, you simply click the Send button. If you decide to abandon the message without sending it, simply close the mail window.

Attaching files

Netscape can send a mail message with files attached to it. These attachments, sometimes called MIME attachments, can be any sort of file. Only those with MIME-enabled mail readers, however, can read these attachments.

To attach a file, click the Attach icon and choose "File." Netscape also lets you attach a whole Web page, in case you want to show someone a great page you found, or your address book card (also called your *vCard*). You can attach many items to a single mail message.

The assorted options are interesting, but you probably don't have to change them often. These options relate to a few different e-mail protocols; if you're just sending simple mail, you can ignore them.

✔ The "Encrypted" and "Signed" options give you ways of making your e-mail more secure, but only if you're sending mail to another person who is using a protocol called *S/MIME*. You must have an S/MIME certificate before you can use these features, and the procedure for getting one and for using S/MIME are beyond the scope of this book.

✔ If you are attaching a file to your message, and the recipient of the message has already told you that he or she can't read MIME messages, but can read *uuencoded* attachments, you should select the "Uuencode instead of MIME for attachments" option. Note, however, that this step doesn't guarantee that the attachment will be able to be read; it only increases the chance.

✔ You can also attach a request for a "return receipt," which is an indication that the person who received the message actually saw it. Few e-mail clients handle return receipts very well, however, so this system is not very reliable.

✔ The priority of a message is an indicator to the recipient of how important you think the message is. Generally, I always set everything to "normal" unless the message is really urgent, and I know the person whom I'm sending the message to will look at the priority.

✔ If you send a message that has both plain text and HTML-formatted text (which is described in Chapter 16), you can indicate this in the Format option. Otherwise, you should just let Netscape make its best guess about the format of your message.

Usenet News

Netscape revolutionized Web browsers by having a really useful Usenet client built into it. In fact, Netscape's interface to Usenet is better than those on many of the dedicated Usenet news readers available for the PC and Macintosh.

Before you can start using Usenet news in Netscape, you must tell Netscape where you get your news. You can do so with the Preferences command from the Edit menu (as described in the section "What More Could You Prefer?" later in this chapter). This might already be set up for you, such as if you got your copy of Netscape from your ISP or company.

You start Usenet news by giving the Communicator⇨Collabra Discussion Groups command, or by choosing a link that has a news: URL. You can also click the third icon, the one that looks like two cartoon word balloons talking, on the component bar. This opens up a window for the Netscape Message Center, as shown in Figure 6-4. After the list of your mail, you see the name of your Usenet news server, and under that and slightly to the right is the list of Usenet newsgroups you've subscribed to.

Server name

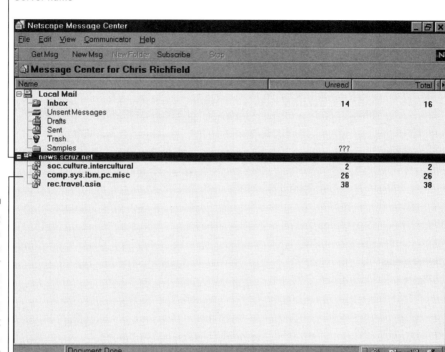

Figure 6-4:
The
Message
Center
shows you
your mail
folders and
Usenet
news.

Newsgroup name

You may be wondering, "What the heck does 'Collabra Discussion Groups'
have to do with Usenet news?" Good question, and the answer is kind of
silly. Netscape bought a company called Collabra a few years ago. Collabra
had a fairly nice product for business messaging, and this product was also
used for reading Usenet newsgroups. Well, Netscape thought that "Collabra
Discussion Groups" sounded much more business-like than "Usenet News
Groups" and therefore used this hoity-toity name instead of the one you
would have expected.

Reading the news

The Message Center isn't really where you want to be reading the news.
Instead, you want to get to the new window. The easiest way to do so is to
double-click on any of the Usenet news names below the name of your news
server. Doing so brings up the window shown in Figure 6-5. Note that this
window looks a lot like the main Netscape window, except that the content
area is split into two panes: the discussion list and the message window.

Navigation toolbar   Location toolbar   Discussion list   Message window

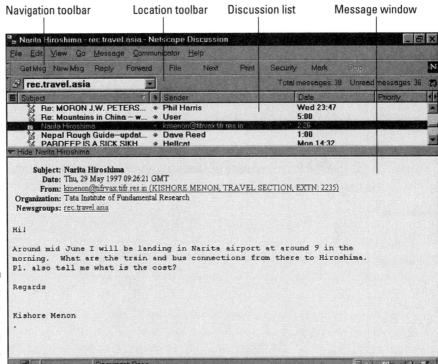

Figure 6-5:
The main
news-
reading
window.

The discussion list shows the current messages in the newsgroup. Messages in bold have not been read by you, while messages you have already seen are in plain text. When you select a message in the discussion list, the message is displayed in the message window.

The bar across the top of the discussion list lets you sort the order of the messages. The most useful choices are to sort by subject, the name of the sender, or the date.

The small icon with the lines on it next to "Subject" in the discussion list lets you show or hide *threads*. A thread is set of messages on the same topic. John sends a message, Jim and Jane each respond to John, Joe responds to Jane, and John responds to Joe. The whole group of messages, which will have very similar-looking subjects, is a single thread.

Subscribing to newsgroups

Of course, you don't have to only read the discussion groups that Netscape starts you with. You can choose from the thousands that are probably available from your news server. To see all the news groups, give the File➪Subscribe to Discussion Groups command. Doing so brings up the dialog box shown in Figure 6-6.

Well, maybe. Netscape has to get the entire list of news groups from the news server. At many sites, the list of all newsgroups is more than 300K, which means that it can take a long time to download, even with a fast modem. When the list finally gets there, Netscape has to then sort the list to show it to you in a reasonable fashion.

You subscribe to a newsgroup simply by selecting the group name and clicking the Subscribe button. However, finding the group that you want may take a bit of clicking around because Netscape shows you the hierarchy of groups, not all the groups at once. Thus, if you want to subscribe to the `rec.autos.antique` newsgroup, you must first select the `rec.` hierarchy listing, and then click the Expand All button to show the entire hierarchy. You can then find `rec.autos.antique` in the list.

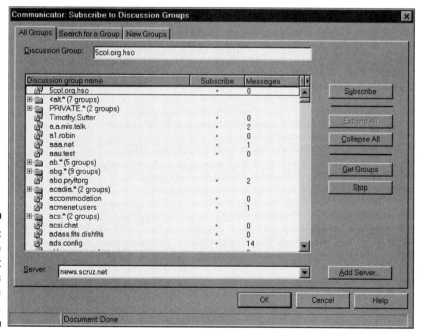

Figure 6-6:
All the
Usenet
newsgroups
in one
place.

If this method is too tedious, you can instead choose the "Search for a Group" tab in this dialog box and enter some of the text in the group name. For instance, entering "antique" brings up a list of all the news groups that have that word in the name, including `rec.autos.antique`.

After you subscribe to a newsgroup, it appears in the list in the location toolbar. If you later want to unsubscribe from the newsgroup, you can do so easily from the Message Center window.

The description in this chapter of how to use Usenet covers only the mechanics of Usenet, not the etiquette. Before you start merrily posting messages to newsgroups, you should read a bit about the basic manners, social customs, and so on of Usenet groups. *The Internet For Dummies* and *MORE Internet For Dummies* contain some good chapters on these topics.

Acting on messages

As you are reading a newsgroup, you will want to use the commands in the Message menu. You can use the buttons in the navigation toolbar.

The commands in the Message menu are as follows:

- ✔ Reply lets you reply to the message you are reading by posting to the newsgroup.
- ✔ Forward sends a copy of the selected message to someone through e-mail.
- ✔ Forward Quoted creates the message, starting each line with a ">" character.
- ✔ Mark As Read indicates you've read the message.
- ✔ Flag Message turns on the message flag.
- ✔ Add to Address Book adds the author of the message to your Netscape address book.

After you add users to the address book, you can use the address book window for creating new messages. Simply select the user's entry and click the NewMsg icon. Netscape opens a new message with that user's name already filled in for the To: field.

The Best Commands at Your Fingertips

Now that you've seen a slew of useful commands in Netscape, how do you remember where to find them all? Well, for many of them, you don't need to remember. If you press and hold the right mouse button, Netscape displays a pop-up menu of the most common commands you need (depending on the location of the cursor as you right-click and hold the mouse). Figure 6-7, for example, shows the list of commands that appears on the pop-up menu if the cursor is over a link. (Other commands appear on the menu if the cursor is elsewhere in a page.)

(Yes, yes, I hear the Macintosh users complaining that they have no right mouse button on their systems. The good folks at Netscape haven't forgotten you, nor do they require that you press and hold some odd combination of keys; simply press and hold down the usual mouse button for about a second or so without moving the mouse and the same menu appears.)

To select a command from this pop-up menu, keep holding the right mouse button down and then slide the pointer up or down the list. After you hit the command you want to execute, release the mouse button. If you realize that you don't want to use any of the commands, left-click in a clear area to make the menu disappear. (On the Mac, slide all the way off the menu and release the mouse button.)

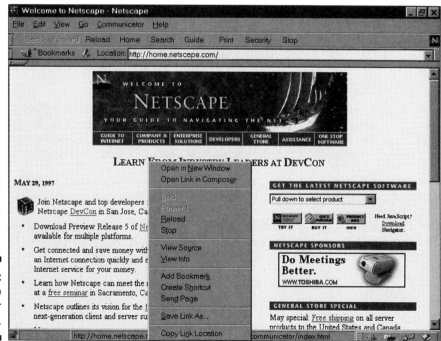

Figure 6-7:
The pop-up menu for links.

Finding Text

Okay, here's a small command that's not too thrilling but is useful in certain situations. The Edit menu's Find in Page command enables you to search for text on the current Web page. It works just like the Find commands in most word processors. You can specify the text you want to find, case sensitivity, and the direction to search in the Find dialog box.

Simple as it may be in function, the Find in Page command can be handy if you are looking through a long document for some specific information. It's particularly useful if you want to find where on a page an e-mail address appears (you simply search for the @ character).

Remembering Where You Have Been

As you meander around the Web, you often find places that you think are interesting. You can keep a list of those places by using Netscape's bookmark feature. Bookmarks consist of pointers to Web pages and the title of the pointer. They appear in the Bookmarks list in the location toolbar and in a separate Bookmarks window.

To add the current page to your bookmarks, open the Bookmarks menu in the location toolbar and choose the Add Bookmark command. The default name for the bookmark is the title of the page. Most of the bookmark action (other than adding the bookmarks) is generated by the Edit Bookmarks command in the Bookmarks menu. This brings up the Bookmarks window where you can edit bookmarks, add them, delete them, and so on. That window is shown in Figure 6-8.

To go to a bookmark in your list, simply double-click on it. To change the name or URL of a bookmark, select the bookmark and give the Edit⇨ Bookmark Properties command. You can also use this window to add a description of the bookmark; that description can be searched for later.

Of course, you will probably want to rearrange your bookmarks, such as by grouping related bookmarks together. To do so, create a new folder in the Bookmarks window with the New Folder command from the File menu. You can then drag bookmarks from the main list into the folder. Of course, you can create as many folders as you want and drag your bookmarks between them.

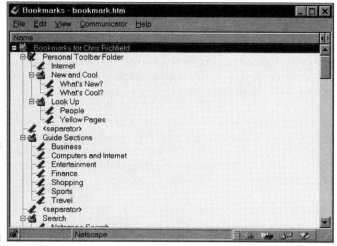

Figure 6-8:
The
Netscape
Bookmarks
window.

Bookmarks can be copied and pasted in the Bookmarks window. For example, you might want to have the same bookmark in two folders: Just copy it in the first folder and paste it into the second folder. You can also copy bookmarks from Netscape and paste them into other programs.

Customizing Your Toolbars

The toolbars at the top of the Netscape screen are pretty handy, but you may not always want to see them, or you may want them to be smaller at times. For instance, you'll notice that I've hidden them at times in the pictures of the screens in this book. That's so you can see more of the content window.

To hide or show toolbars, use the first three commands in the View menu. When the particular toolbar is shown, the command name starts with "Hide"; when the toolbar isn't shown, the command name starts with the word "Show." For example, if the personal toolbar is currently showing, the command is View⇨Hide Personal Toolbar.

You don't have to hide the toolbars if you just want to make them smaller, however. Notice the little gray area at the far left of the toolbar that looks like a small handle. If you click on this, the toolbar becomes just a few pixels tall but doesn't disappear altogether. You can then click on it again to make the toolbar reappear.

Getting More Personal

You may have wondered about the name of the personal toolbar. What's so personal about it? When you start Netscape, the items in the personal toolbar are what Netscape put there, not what you want. Fortunately, changing what's in the personal toolbar is an easy task.

At the top of the bookmarks window, you see an item called Personal Toolbar Folder. As you may imagine, these are the things that appear in your personal toolbar. You can change the items here just like the items in the rest of the bookmarks. You can add folders, get rid of the folders that Netscape started you with, and so on.

In other words, the items in your personal toolbar are treated like the items in your bookmarks list. The only reason why you'd want them in your personal toolbar is that they are a bit easier to get to than if they were in your bookmarks list. For my part, I don't use the personal toolbar and instead rely on the bookmark list. Consequently, I always hide the personal toolbar to give myself a bit more space on the screen for Web content.

What More Could You Prefer?

The final topic in this discussion of how to use Netscape is a big one: How to use the various commands in Edit⇨Preferences.

Fortunately, most (but not all) of the preferences that Netscape comes with are preset to work just fine. A few, however, you need to change before you can use certain Netscape features. Figure 6-9 shows the main window of the Edit⇨Preferences dialog box. Note that many of the categories have "+" signs next to them; this sign indicates that subcategories exist. To see the subcategories, click on the "+" sign.

Because you can change so many settings in Netscape, the Preferences dialog boxes consist of many pages. At the left side of the dialog box is a set of tabs from which you can choose which of its pages you want to work in. The names of these tabs describe the settings you can alter on the pages. The tabs for each command are as follows:

- ✔ Appearance
  - Fonts
  - Colors

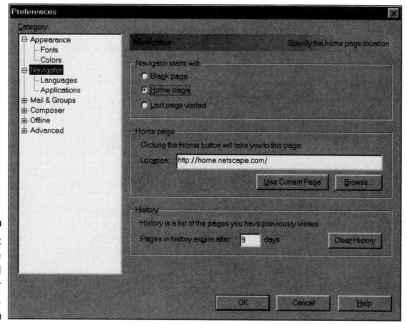

Figure 6-9:
One place
to make all
your
settings.

✔ Navigator

    • Languages

    • Applications

✔ Mail & Groups

    • Identity

    • Messages

    • Mail Server

    • Groups Server

    • Directory

✔ Composer

    • Publishing

✔ Offline

    • Download

✔ Advanced

    • Cache

    • Proxies

    • Disk Space

Appearance

Well, many people say that the Web is more about looks than content, so it's appropriate that Netscape's first preference category is "Appearance." The choices in this category let you tell Netscape what you want to see and how it should look.

The first set of choices let you specify which of the many parts of Communicator you see when you first launch the program. The default, Navigator, makes the most sense unless you mostly use Netscape for mail, in which case you should choose Messenger.

You can also specify how you want your toolbar to appear: as pictures and text, pictures only, or text only. In the screen pictures in this book, I've mostly chosen the text-only toolbars so that you can see more of the content area of the screen, but you are free to choose any of the three that best suits your visual tastes.

Fonts

Netscape has a small number of choices for applying fonts. These are clearly stylistic choices meant to make Netscape easier on the eyes as you use it. The choices available to you depend on the kind of computer you own, which fonts you installed, and so on.

The choices for fonts are shown in Figure 6-10. The first choice, "For the Encoding," affects the next two choices, the fonts to use. An *encoding* is a type character set, such as "Western characters," "Japanese characters," "Greek characters," and so on. Most readers of this book will just use the Western encoding.

For the Western encoding, you have two font choices: variable-width fonts (most of the text that you see), and fixed-width font (the typewriter-looking font you see in some lists). You can also choose the size. For example, I've made the font sizes 9 instead of the default of 12 and 10 so that I can see more text on the screen at one time.

Colors

Playing with the Colors subcategory is more fun than playing with fonts. Many modern Web sites come with their own sets of colors and backgrounds. If you select the Always use my colors, overriding document option, you will prevent these colors from being loaded. By clicking one of the color buttons, you can choose the color of the following elements:

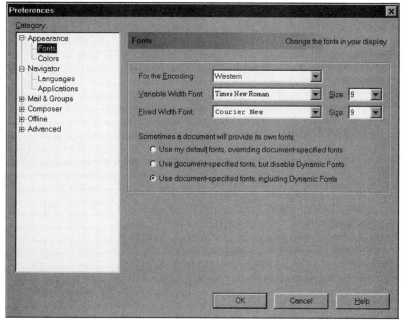

Figure 6-10:
Choosing
fonts for
various
encodings.

- Text
- Background
- Links you have not clicked on yet
- Links you have already visited

The defaults for these elements are usually okay, but you may, for example, want to change the text color to something other than black. If you choose not to underline links, you should certainly keep the link color something different from the text color; otherwise, you can't tell what is and isn't a link. Make sure, too, that you don't choose a background pattern that makes your text unreadable.

Navigator

With a name like that, you would think that the preferences in this category apply only to Navigator, not the other components of Netscape Communicator. But you would be wrong. I have no idea why Netscape named these choices this way.

In these choices, you can specify what you see when you first launch Navigator: a blank page, a home page that you specify, or the last page you saw before quitting Navigator the last time. If you want to always start with a particular Web page, you can enter that by hand. If you want to always start with a particular file from your hard disk, you can specify that by using the Browse button.

Language

Slowly but surely, some Web content is appearing in languages other than English. Netscape can tell Web servers what languages you are willing to accept for documents. That way, if a Web server has a document in a language you don't understand, it can tell you that instead of showing you the document.

You can add other languages to the list with the Add button. Netscape brings up a list of all the popular (and not-so-popular) languages, or you can even add your own.

Applications

Even though it is pretty versatile, Netscape cannot handle every kind of information on the Web. If you access data in a format that Netscape doesn't understand (for example, a movie), Netscape can launch another program or just save the data to disk for you to deal with later. The options in the Helpers tab specifies which programs Netscape launches in such cases.

Generally, you never need to change any of the settings in this subcategory because they come preconfigured for the best values. You may, however, want to change them if you consistently download a certain type of data and want Netscape to always launch a program that it doesn't currently know about. You might also want to change the values if you want to tell Netscape to always save certain kinds of files to disk without asking you what to do first.

Each kind of data on the Web has a file type, more accurately called a *MIME* type. These data descriptions consist of two words separated by a slash (/) character. Movies in the MPEG format, for example, have a file type description of video/mpeg. These types are defined in Internet standards committees, although some of them are temporary names until the committees get around to approving them.

For each file type, Netscape can take the following actions:

✔ For many formats, you can display the data in Netscape. This option works only for elements that Netscape knows about, such as simple text, HTML, GIF, and JPEG images, and for formats for which you have a plug-in.

✔ Netscape can just store some types of data on disk. You can open the file later with some other program.

✔ Netscape can start another program and give that program the data.

For each MIME type, you can tell Netscape what to do. Select the description of the type and choose the Edit button. You can also add new MIME types with the New Type button.

Mail and Groups

In order to use Netscape's e-mail or news features, you must change the settings in the Mail and Groups category. This category holds the addresses of both your mail server (for sending e-mail) and your news server (for reading Usenet news).

It is common for you to reply to messages that you see on the Internet, and you want a way to indicate that the information in your reply is a copy of the original message. Netscape allows you to automatically quote the original message, which begins each line with a ">" character.

Because you can get too much information on a single screen, Netscape lets you choose whether or not to open separate windows for each message you read, or to reuse the main mail or news windows to see the messages. I normally choose not to reuse the main window; this decision means that I have to switch back and forth between the main window and the message window, but I get to see more in each window. You should try both reusing and not reusing and see which best suits you.

Identity

Yes, you get to give yourself a real name, not just an Internet address. You can type whatever you want in the Your Name field, but remember that this name will be seen by anyone to whom you send mail or anyone who sees your Usenet postings. You must also fill in your Reply to address if it is different than your mail address.

If you want, fill in an organization name, although this is not a widely used feature. If you want to sign each outgoing mail message from Netscape with a standard signature, create a text file with the signature and specify that file with the Choose button.

You can also choose to always attach your vCard (described earlier in this chapter) to each message you send. While doing so may seem convenient, not that many people have vCard-enabled mail readers yet, so I would not recommend this option. Instead, you can attach your vCard on a message-by-message basis, sending it only to people that you know have Netscape or other vCard-enabled programs.

Messages

Netscape lets you specify how outgoing messages are formatted. This feature is important because some mail users have different capabilities than others, and you want to be sure to send messages that your recipients can read. For instance, the first choice is whether or not to send HTML-formatted messages by default. I suggest you *not* select this option because many people still don't have HTML-enhanced mail clients. You can still choose to use HTML formatting when you send individual messages.

You can also choose where to send copies of outgoing messages. This option lets you always send copies of the messages you post to yourself so you can keep them for future reference. You can also have Netscape copy all your outgoing messages into a mail folder.

The More Options button in the Messages subcategory brings up some interesting, if not obscure choices. If your message has "8-bit" characters, such as international characters, Netscape has to choose whether or not to send them directly. Your two choices are to send them as-is, which doesn't work with some mail and news clients, or to send them as "quoted print-able," which doesn't work with other clients. Unfortunately, I can't give you any advice here because no clear better choice exists.

Mail Server

This subcategory gives all the information that Netscape needs in order to get your mail for you. If you used Netscape's standard installation, the choices here are already filled in for you; otherwise, you need to get this information from your ISP. Figure 6-11 shows the choices.

The "Mail server user name" is the name you use to get your mail. This isn't necessarily the same name as you use in your return address, but most often is. The "Outgoing mail (SMTP) server" is the name of the server you

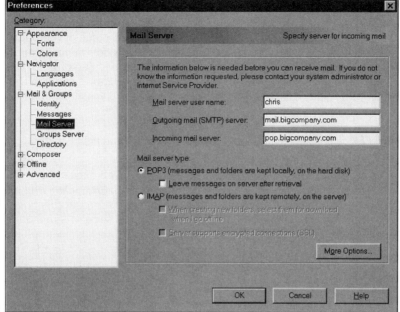

Figure 6-11:
Telling
Netscape
about your
mail
servers.

use for sending out e-mail. This is often, but not always, the same name as the name you use for your "Incoming mail server." Again, you should ask your ISP for each of the values that you should use here.

You also have to tell Netscape what kind of mail server you get your mail from. The two choices are POP and IMAP. *POP* is an older protocol for receiving mail, but it is still the most popular. *IMAP,* on the other hand, has many more nifty features than POP, but isn't as widely used yet. By the time you read this, I expect IMAP to be catching on much more widely.

Again, Netscape has hidden some important choices under the More Options button. If you don't want to type in your password each time you get your mail, you should select the "Remember my mail password" option. However, you should only do so if you're the only person with access to your computer; otherwise, someone else can cause Netscape to download your mail without you knowing about it.

Groups Server

The main thing in this subcategory is the address of your Usenet news server. Your ISP should tell you what this address is. In rare cases, your SP may also tell you a TCP port number to use, and you can enter that here as well.

Directory

Netscape lets you search for Internet users on some of the popular Web-based directories. This feature is handy if you don't know someone's address, but it often leads to wrong information. The directory services are getting better, however, so this option may be more useful in the future.

Composer

The preferences in this category are for the Web-page creator called Composer, which is covered in Chapters 16 and 17. Composer is pretty much a program unto itself and isn't covered in much detail in this book. You are probably safe leaving all of the options in this section alone unless you get deep into Composer.

Offline

The choices here affect how Netscape tells your computer to interact with the Internet. Some people are connected to the Internet all the time, such as on an office network, but most people are only connected to the Internet when they dial in to their ISP. This is important because you may want to read your old mail or look at pages on your hard drive without causing Netscape to start up your network connection.

It's dweeb time. Feel free to skip over this advanced category. It's really mostly for advanced folk, and even then, you don't find much of importance here. On the other hand, if you want to know something about how Netscape is more flexible than other Web browsers, feel free to read along.

The first set of choices are things that you may want Netscape to do, or not do, automatically. The items you can turn on and off are

> ✔ **Automatically load images:** If you are on a slow connection, you may not want to automatically load the images on Web pages.
>
> ✔ **Enable Java:** This item allows Java applications that you download to run automatically. Some people worry about how secure Java is, and therefore they would not want to automatically run Java programs from sites they don't know.
>
> ✔ **Enable JavaScript:** JavaScript is a language that can be used in HTML pages to perform certain tasks on a Web page. Like Java, it may not be as secure as you want, so you may not want to run JavaScript programs without being asked.

✓ **Enable style sheets:** The latest version of HTML has an experimental extension called "style sheets" that let Web designers make better-looking pages.

✓ **Enable Autoinstall:** This item allows automatic updating of Netscape over the Internet, and doesn't sound all that secure to me.

✓ **Send e-mail address as anonymous FTP password:** Most FTP servers force you to give an e-mail address when you log into them, but you may not want to give your real address, so Netscape gives you the choice.

The second set of choices tell Netscape whether or not to put up a dialog box before you either get a cookie from a server or before you submit a form by e-mail. *Cookies* (cute name, huh?) are items used to store information about your site when you visit a site. For example, cookies are often used to create shopping baskets, telling the server what you have ordered so far. More and more sites are using cookies, so getting an alert each time may be pretty annoying. On the other hand, if you're concerned about your privacy and the kind of information that is kept on you, you may want to disable cookies altogether.

Cache

A cache is an area to which Web pages and images that you have read are copied. Using a cache can increase the speed of access if you read the same page off the Web a second time, and it can also reduce traffic on the Internet (because you don't need to actually access the page from the Web a second time). Netscape includes two kinds of caches: memory caches and disk caches. The memory cache is kept in RAM memory, while the disk cache is kept on your hard disk.

The content of Web pages sometimes changes, so you don't want to always assume that the version of a page you have in one of the caches is the most recent. On the other hand, if you never trust the cache, you force Netscape to go out to a remote (and possibly slow) Web site every time you revisit a page.

The default sizes for the two caches are usually fine, but you can increase or decrease them if you think that may help. Decreasing the cache size means that fewer copies of pages are kept in memory or on disk, but it also means that Netscape is using fewer of your computer's resources.

You can tell Netscape whether to check the Web site if the document you are requesting is already in one of Netscape's two caches. These buttons function as described in the following list:

- ✔ "Once per session" means that, the first time during a Netscape session you choose a particular document that is in the cache, Netscape always obtains it from the remote server; after that, Netscape gets it from the cache (if it is still there).

- ✔ "Every time" means that Netscape always checks the remote server, even if the document is in the cache.

- ✔ "Never" means that Netscape does not bother ever to go to the remote server if the document is in the cache. Using this option may be a bit risky because the document may have changed since it got in the cache. On the other hand, this option gives you the best performance.

Proxies

Oh, my. Skipping this one altogether would certainly be nice. Describing proxies well in a book on this level is impossible. For that matter, few advanced Internet books do even a halfway decent job of describing proxies. They're a very dweeby, very confusing issue that you are best to avoid if you can; fortunately, most Web users can. Proxies don't relate to the Web per se; they relate to security and the Internet. Basically, proxies intervene between you and the Internet for the greater good of the people at your site.

Most people do not use proxies and therefore choose the "Direct connection to the Internet" option. If your ISP uses a proxy, you can hope that it lets you do automatic proxy configuration, in which case you only need to enter the URL of the configuration system. You may, however, have to manually configure the various proxies, at which point you'll need some very detailed instructions in how to set up Netscape for your proxy system.

Disk Space

If you have limited space on your hard drive, you can tell Netscape not to download large files in mail or Usenet news. To get you as much space as possible, you can also tell Netscape to clean up your mail and Usenet news folders more often that it would normally, which may free up a bit of space.

To access the security preferences, give the Communicator⇨Security Info command, or choose the Security icon from the navigation toolbar. The Security dialog box looks somewhat like the Preferences dialog box and is shown in Figure 6-12.

The first category, Security Info, tells you about what kind of security the current Web page that you're viewing in Netscape has. Most pages on the Web do not use any form of security, so this information isn't all that useful.

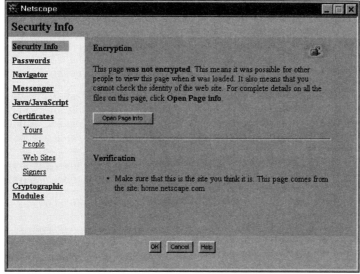

Figure 6-12:
The
Netscape
security
settings.

The Passwords category is useful if many people use the same computer. Each person can have her own Netscape setup, and you can make sure that no one uses your setup without knowing your password.

The navigator category lets you tell Netscape about how you want to handle security when you're moving around the Web. The first set of choices tells Netscape when it should warn you about changes in security.

Security Preferences

Security is quite rightfully a hot topic on the Internet. Because so few people understand how to keep themselves safe from snooping and tampering on the Internet, malicious people can do lots of damage without much risk of getting caught. Netscape gives you a few opportunities to avoid security problems, but you must assume most of the responsibility yourself.

Security Warnings may sound great, but they are often just a nuisance. These options open a dialog box whenever you enter or leave a secure or insecure area of the Web. Well, if you don't know by now, you'll find only a handful of secure areas on the Web; you can tell whether you are in one, however, by looking for the little key icon at the lower-left corner of the screen. If it's a full key, you're in a secure area; if it's a broken key, you're not. I doubt you'd like needing to respond to a dialog box every time you go from secure to insecure area, but if you do, you can turn on that feature here.

Two versions of the SSL security protocol are now on the Web. You can choose whether to use one or both of them; you're fine to leave both of these selected because both versions are quite good. You only need to use the Configure buttons if a particular site tells you to.

The Messenger category lets you specify how your Internet mail is encrypted and signed. These topics are covered earlier in this chapter. Before you can use this kind of security, you need to get an S/MIME certificate. After you have such a certificate, it appears in the "Yours" subcategory under the Certificates category.

The Certificates category lets you view all the certificates you know about. You can view, edit, and remove your own certificates, the certificates that other people may have sent you (such as in signed email), the certificates of secure Web sites that you've visited, and the certificates of the companies that sign certificates.

Personal certificates

As more and more people use the Web to perform financial transactions and to communicate about business, asking the question, "How do I know that you are who you say you are?" becomes important. Conversely, the people communicating with you want to know the same thing about you.

A *personal certificate* is somewhat akin to a driver's license: It is a form of identification that says that someone who everyone trusts (well, most everyone trusts) says you are who you say you are. If you trust the company that issued the certificate, you can trust the certificate holder.

If you don't already have a personal certificate, choose the Get a New Certificate button in the Yours subcategory and follow the directions. You can have more than one certificate, and you may get them from different certificate issuing authorities, for instance. In this case, you can specify the default certificate that Netscape presents to sites where you visit.

Personal certificates are just starting to be widely used. Because you need a personal certificate in order to secure your e-mail, many people are getting their first certificates as you read this. Within a year or two, they will probably be much more popular.

Site certificates

A *site certificate* is like a personal certificate, but you use it to be sure that a Web site is who it says it is. In order for a Web site to be trusted, a Web site has to have a certificate from someone you trust. Who do you trust? Well . . .

Signer Certificates

A *certificate authority*, or "CA" for short, is someone who vouches for the authenticity of someone else by giving them a signed certificate. You can find several public CAs in the world, and some companies act as their own CAs for certificates issued by the companies.

Netscape comes with a bunch of certificates for CAs that Netscape Communications trusts. If you trust Netscape, you should probably trust its list of CAs and therefore the certificates that those CAs issue. It's too early in the Internet security game to know which CAs are better than others, so I generally advise people to trust all the Netscape-trusted CAs until you hear otherwise.

Onward out to the Web!

Whew! You made it through all the preferences. I hope that you found many of them useful in your day-to-day use of Netscape. The next time someone tells you that "using a Web browser is so easy," you may want to point them to all the choices you had to make here.

Chapter 7

Searching High and/or Low

A few ways exist to find what you want on the Web. Because the Web is a collection of places and content at those places, you need to know where something is located on the Web before you can find that something. As discussed in Chapter 3, the Web's content is specified by URLs, and the URLs describe the content's location.

For example, `http://www.bigstate.edu/people/index` is a URL that points to some content; you know that this content resides on the computer that has the domain name `www.bigstate.edu`. You may find it helpful to think in terms of a library in which the book titles also include the shelf location indicators in them.

If you know the URL for the specific content you want to examine, this tactic is all well and good. What if you don't? If you were in a standard library with real books, you would probably look in a card catalog. In most libraries, the card catalog (which rarely contains cards these days) enables you to search by title, author, or subject for the books in the library. The subjects are all categorized in a standard manner, and searching is pretty easy.

Nothing even remotely like a card catalog exists for the Web. You won't find a complete listing anywhere of what's on the Web; some partial listings are available, but even they are not searched for information the same way a library card catalog is perused, usually for the following reasons:

▶ Pages on the Web often don't have terribly descriptive titles.

▶ The exact author of a Web page is often unclear.

▶ No standardized subject classification system exists.

Even worse, because it's impossible to know where everything is on the Web, you have no way to make sure that the search listing you are using is anywhere complete.

All is not lost, however. A few places do enable you to search parts of the Web; if you're looking for a fairly big topic, you can at least get a good start. Furthermore, some attempts are made to categorize topics on the Web, which are described in Chapter 9. This chapter describes some of the ways you may search for content for which you have no URLs.

Don't be surprised if your search for particular information comes up empty. Finding nothing (or finding information that isn't relevant) isn't necessarily a sign that what you want isn't on the Web. It's merely a sign that the Web search systems are still in their infancy. Five years from now, much better ways to look in one place on the Web and stand a good chance of finding a list of valuable pointers probably will exist; right now, however, it's all very hit and miss.

Web Catalogs

You may be wondering what good any sort of directory would be if it's impossible to catalog the entire Web. The answer is that you don't need to catalog the whole Web (or an entire library) for a directory to be useful. Many partial Web catalogs (like catalogs of just part of a library's collection) offer easy-to-use search features that, although incomplete, can often get you going on your searches.

You may find the way these catalogs work interesting. The person creating the catalog starts with a list of major and/or interesting sites on the Web and then launches a program that reads the home pages at those starting sites. The program starts following the links from those home pages to other sites, keeping track of where it's been. The program keeps looking around the Web by following these links, grabbing copies of whatever it finds, and using the links it finds as fodder for the giant index.

These programs are generally called *spiders,* an excessively cute term based on Web imagery. A better term for them is robots because they perform their tasks much like classical mechanical robots would; people, however, seem to like the spider imagery.

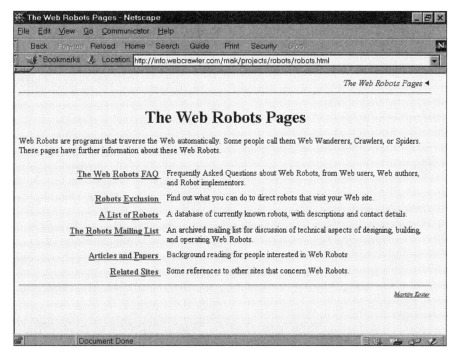

HotSpot 7-1: http://info.webcrawler.com/mak/projects/robots/robots.html
This page is an excellent resource if you want to create your own Web catalog service.
It tells you how to construct a robot or a spider, describes important things not to do, and
mentions the other catalog services already on the Web.

Spiders have many problems, but given the imperfection forced on those
trying to catalog the Web, they also have many nice features. The problems
include the following:

✔ New Web sites are added slowly to the catalogs because few links to
  them exist.

✔ Pages that have been viewed and then later updated often are not
  looked at again, meaning the updates aren't reflected in the catalog.

✔ The kind of material that appears in the catalog is heavily based on the
  pages it started from.

Some of the big advantages of using spiders instead of catalogs are as
follows:

✔ Pages near the top of a site hierarchy are favored. Those pages usually contain more general information than the ones farther down the hierarchy.

✔ The spider can be modified to emphasize certain link chains. This capability makes the catalog better for certain kinds of information that interests the person putting the catalog together.

Very few Web spiders do anything other than index HTTP content. Almost all of them completely ignore the other important parts of the Web, such as Gopher and FTP sites. So if you are searching the Web for something and you don't really care whether it comes to you in HTML, you also must use Veronica and Archie (described later in this chapter) if you want to search a bigger chunk of the Web. With luck, this situation will improve in the future.

Many places offer lists of Web catalogs. Experienced Web users have their favorite catalogs, but their preferences are usually not based on quantitative criteria such as biggest or fastest. Instead, they generally choose their preferred searcher based on the user interface, the perceived quality of results they got the day they needed to find something fast, and so on.

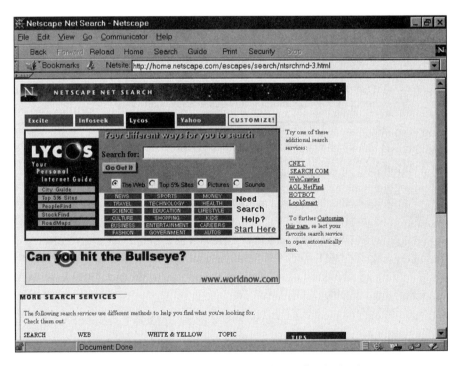

HotSpot 7-2: http://home.netscape.com/escapes/search/ntsrchrnd-3.html
This page shows the list of Web search spots maintained at Netscape Communications. It contains links to the most popular search sites and a brief description of each.

Brian Pinkerton, for example, created one of the more popular searchable catalogs, called WebCrawler. WebCrawler, as shown in Figure 7-1, is kept up to date by a sophisticated spider that does much more than just wander the Web. The folks who run WebCrawler can add in new Web sites, tweak the way the spider moves around the Web, and so on to accommodate the creation of the best catalog possible.

Guessing How to Get What You Want

Sometimes searching by using indexes is not enough. If the search sites in this chapter don't help you find what you need, check through the many resources discussed in Chapters 9 through 14. Many of the sites in those chapters offer lists of links to other sites on the Web. Some of the larger sites can even be searched.

If you can't find what you're looking for directly, however, you may find helpful some indirect methods that advanced Web users have been using. Many of these methods lead nowhere, but they only take a few minutes at most to try and sometimes yield results.

Figure 7-1:
Main page
of
WebCrawler.

One of the most common site-searching methods is creative name guessing in a URL. Suppose that you are looking at the Web page for a department at a university, and you want to see the page for a particular professor. The department's page lists some professors, but not the one you want. You notice that all the URLs from that page look like `http://www.bigstate.edu/polisci/smith` and `http://www.bigstate.edu/polisci/yu`. If the name of the professor you want is Sugarman, you can enter the URL `http://www.bigstate.edu/polisci/sugarman` as a guess. To do so, use the command in your Web browser (such as the Netscape Open Location command) that enables you to specify a URL not located on a Web page.

More often than not, this method yields only an error. If you do get where you wanted, however, you may find it worth the attempt. Remember that generating errors doesn't have a significant effect on Web sites or on your browser. Sometimes, the error itself can even be helpful in your guessing. (You may, for example, receive a message saying that the URL you gave is too busy, which at least means that the server you asked for exists.) Errors are described in much more detail in the next chapter.

Chapter 8

It May Be Broken

In This Chapter

▶ Figuring out error messages

▶ Staring at a blank screen

▶ Avoiding problems

*B*rowsing the Web isn't always fun and flowers. You are bound to encounter some problems in your travels, and you may find it difficult to figure out what is wrong. But then, what would a computer be without aggravating error messages and weird results?

The kinds of errors you see, and the amount of help you get in figuring out the problem, depend to a large extent on your Web browser software. Some browsers send you cryptic error messages that don't give you much help; others, such as Netscape, give you as much help as possible. Even the best programs, however, can't always give good advice on what went wrong and how to prevent it from happening again.

This chapter describes the most common problems you may come across on the Web. Most of the problems occur regardless of the Web browser you are using. The error messages described in this chapter, however, are for Netscape, for the following reasons:

✔ This book is about Netscape.

✔ Netscape has some of the most helpful error messages available.

 Whenever your Web browser gives you an error message that you don't understand, or whenever something really weird happens while viewing the Web, the first thing to do is remember to breathe. Yes, that sounds like simple advice, but you'd be surprised how many people stop breathing or breathe very shallowly if something goes wrong on their computer. If you see an error message or if you realize that something's not working, remember to breathe. Breathe again, slowly. Think, "It's just a piece of software; it's just a computer network. It's not worth not breathing."

The Errors of Your Ways

In a chapter about errors, starting with the easy ones — the ones that come with reasonable error messages — is best. These errors also happen to be the most common ones you see as you wander around the Web.

Sometimes very busy and very dead look the same

The number-one, most-common, happens-all-the-darn-time error you get while roaming the Web is a server that is too busy to accept your request. This error can happen because you are trying to access a very popular site, such as a server that has downloadable software or pictures, or because the server at the site is set up to handle only a few users at a time.

Figure 8-1 shows the error message Netscape displays after you try to access a server that is too busy. The wording in the dialog box is a tad vague for a good reason. The first sentence explains all that Netscape knows is definitely true: The connection was refused by the server. This problem, however, can exist for a number of reasons. The following are some of the causes of this message:

✔ The server may really be too busy. Your browser sends the query to the server, but the server takes too long to respond.

✔ The server may not be accepting requests on the port to which you sent the message. If, for example, the URL you sent has a port number indicated by a colon and number after the site name (such as www.acompany.com:8012), the server may not be accepting messages on that port.

✔ The server may be temporarily or permanently off the Internet because of technical problems.

✔ The path on the Internet from your computer to the server may be so clogged that the message or the return is delayed for longer than your browser permits.

As you can see, many different symptoms can lead to the same diagnosis — nothing came back from the server, so who knows what's wrong? You can sometimes get a clue, however, if the message comes back immediately. An immediate return indicates that the server is up, but it really is too busy. Or you may have tried to access an incorrect port.

Figure 8-1:
The
dreaded
"too busy"
error
message.

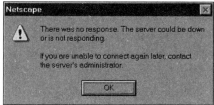

URL doesn't exist

The next most common error is usually seen in your Web browser's content area, not as a separate error message. The *404 error,* as shown in Figure 8-2, means that you have tried to access a Web page that doesn't exist. You see this message if the server exists and is accepting requests, but the requested page doesn't exist on the server.

This error is most commonly caused by following a link that used to exist but no longer does. If you link from a page you found on a not-too-busy Web site, for example, the page maintainer may no longer be keeping that page up to date. The link may have been fine months ago, but it has since moved or changed names.

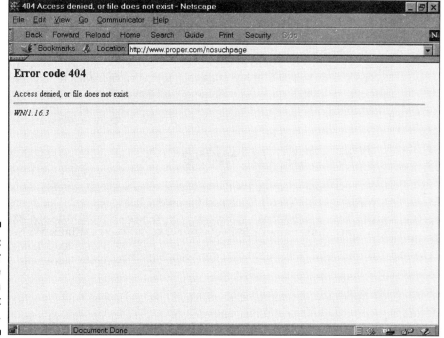

Figure 8-2:
The error
message
for a
nonexistent
Web page.

The message you see on the screen after you get a 404 error is different from server to server. Some servers give you polite explanations, but most give you terse messages with very little helpful information.

Typing the URL incorrectly is another common reason for getting the 404 message. If you see a link in a book such as this one, for example, and you enter it into your Web browser, you may miss a letter or transpose a pair of letters, resulting in a URL that doesn't exist.

If the URL you are giving is for a directory, not a document, some Web servers require a / at the end of the URL. Assume, for example, you are entering the following URL:

```
http://www.bigstate.edu/candle-making
```

If you receive a 404 error, you may next want to try the following URL instead:

```
http://www.bigstate.edu/candle-making/
```

(Notice the added / at the end of the URL.) This change works only if the URL is for a directory, not a file. So you wouldn't try this trick on an URL that ends in .html or .txt or other endings that indicate that the URL is that of a file.

Errors such as the 404 error come from the server software and are sent back to your browser. Many such errors can come from servers that follow the HTTP standard correctly. If you really want to know, the list of all error messages can be found in the full specification for HTTP, which can be found at ftp://ds.internic.net/rfc/rfc2068.txt on the Web. You certainly don't need to know about the other HTTP error codes to use the Web. Errors other than 404 are very uncommon, and even if you do get other error messages, a bit of explanatory text usually comes with them.

Wrong server name

You may see an error similar to the one shown in Figure 8-3. This error indicates that your URL is bad for a very basic reason: The domain name of the host is wrong. Again, this error is most likely caused by a typing mistake because host names rarely disappear completely (although it has been known to happen).

Figure 8-3:
The error
message for
a bad host
name.

Hmmmm, Nothing Happened

The worst errors are those you can't tell are happening. Something's wrong, but you receive no error message, no problem indicator, nothing. All you can do is wait to see if something happens after a while. These errors are all too common on the Web.

The "nothing happened" errors occur mainly due to the slowness of the Internet. Of course, the entire Internet isn't slow at the moment, just the connection between your computer and the Web site you are trying to access. As more and more people start using the Internet, the pathways for messages get more and more crowded. Conveniently, the Internet is well equipped to handle slowness, so crowded message pathways aren't usually a serious problem.

Sometimes, however, a pathway becomes more than slow — it gets completely clogged. Actually, any one part of the pathway between your computer and the Web site can cause you to get nothing on your system. This situation is much like traveling across town on surface streets to attend a meeting: One congested block can make you miss the meeting entirely. That you eventually get to your destination doesn't matter if the meeting is over by the time you arrive.

Clogging isn't the only problem you can encounter: The link can actually be completely dead, forcing all the information to go some other route to get around the broken data pipe. Web clients don't enable you to follow the path of the messages on the Internet, so you can't tell where a dead link occurs. That's actually okay because you can't change the path of your message anyway. You just have to sit and wait for the network folks to fix the broken link or start rerouting messages around the broken link more quickly.

Fortunately, programs such as Netscape can give you clues in cases such as these. If using Netscape, watch the bottom line of the window, in which the status messages appear. The messages you see after you connect to a system appear in the following order:

 ✔ **Looking up host.** Netscape translates the domain name in the URL to the IP address of the host. It must perform this translation before it can communicate with the host computer. This translation usually goes fairly quickly, but it can sometimes take a long time if the host is in a different country or if traffic problems occur on the Internet.

 ✔ **Contacting host.** Netscape has sent the request to the host computer but hasn't heard anything back yet. This step is usually where you get stuck the longest because the Web host must accept the request before you can proceed. If the host computer is very busy, this process can sometimes take a while.

 ✔ **Host contacted. Waiting for reply.** This message is a good sign. It means that the host computer has accepted the message and is thinking about it. Web hosts usually process the requests reasonably quickly after they get in, so you rarely get hung up in this stage for very long.

 ✔ **Transferring data.** You're almost home free. You are receiving the information from the host, and you can watch Netscape as it renders the information you are receiving on your computer's screen.

You can still lose the connection during the last step. The Web browser is merrily getting data and then — nothing. It stops dead. Many problems can cause this failure but, unfortunately, you can't do anything about them. If you're sure that nothing is coming from the server anymore and want to abort the connection, most browsers enable you to do so. (In Netscape, for example, you use the Stop icon on the toolbar.)

Netstorms

In the past few years, as more and more servers were added to the Internet, some other major problems started to appear. These problems aren't caused by the increased number of Internet users. Instead, they are caused by the Internet's system software having to manage so many host addresses and routes between systems. The term *netstorm* means bad weather on the Internet, and the symptoms of these storms usually manifest as mysterious errors.

One all-too-common type of netstorm is caused by bad routing tables. *Routing tables* are used by the large nodes on the Internet to determine how to pass information around. Assume that you sent a Web request to the site www.bigstate.edu. After your browser determines the address of www.bigstate.edu, it sends the request out on the Internet with that address. Remember that addresses tell only the address of the destination, not how to get messages from your computer to their destinations.

Each stop holds your message while it looks up the destination address in its routing table to determine the next hop on the route. Ninety-nine percent of the time, the routing tables are fine. If a routing table is bad, however, all hell breaks loose. Messages going from one computer to a nearby computer can actually go all the way across the country and back. Worse yet, some messages can go bouncing around the Internet indefinitely, never arriving at the destination computer. (After a while, however, these messages are killed by the Internet's system software.)

Sometimes major nodes on the Internet go down for a while, which is another cause of netstorms. If minor nodes experience breakdowns, the data flows around them without much difficulty. If a major node goes off-line, however, the redirection of traffic can be incredibly disruptive because significant amounts of data suddenly must be rerouted.

The symptoms of netstorms are hard to pin down, but the following are some typical ones to watch out for:

✔ Requests that have been taking about two seconds suddenly start taking 20 seconds.

✔ Sites that you know exist on the Internet disappear, and your Web browser tells you that no such domain exists.

✔ You are receiving a 50K file and, after 30K has arrived with no problems, it just stops.

In all these cases, the best thing to do is just accept that this sort of thing happens on the Internet, that it will happen next year just as it is happening this year, and hope that it gets fixed within an hour or so.

Broken Pictures

One last all-too-common problem you may find on the Web is that of broken pictures. *Broken pictures* are inline images that are unreadable because they contain bad or missing data. Netscape illustrates these images by a broken picture icon, as shown in Figure 8-4.

Fortunately, broken pictures are fairly easy to fix: Simply click the icon, and Netscape downloads the picture again. Unless the picture is broken on the host system, it probably downloads fine the second time you try it. If the host does have a messed-up graphics file, the only thing you can do about it is to send a message to the Web site maintainer and point out the problem.

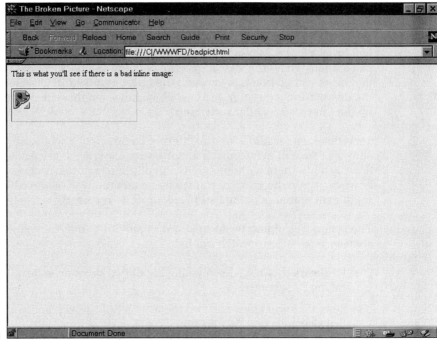

Figure 8-4:
The broken
picture
icon in
Netscape.

Part III
Who's Webbing Now?

In this part . . .

The best part of the Web is its content, and these chapters show you dozens of Web sites of interest to almost everyone. You can find all sorts of fun places; you can make — or lose — money; you can read online magazines; you can meet computer geeks; you can even learn more about your government. This part offers more than a bit of everything!

Chapter 9

Starting in the Library

· ·

In This Chapter

▶ Looking at places that attempt to organize the Web

▶ Discovering the best catalogs

▶ Poking around other collections

· ·

The first two parts of this book show you what the Web is and the tools you need to explore it. Now's the time to start exploring. This chapter and the five that follow it are full of examples of the best and brightest spots on the Web. Something for everyone can be found here; with luck, you'll find dozens of "somethings" in these chapters.

Notice that these examples are not simply "good places to go." In fact, you may spend only a minute or two at a site before moving on to another one. Thus, many sites are often "good places to start."

This difference is important, particularly on the Web. Some of the best Web content doesn't really contain very much content. Instead, much of the content consists of pointers (links) to other good content. This setup is one of the ways in which the Web differs from other electronic media, such as television and radio. Web sites that are high-quality collections of pointers to other Web sites are, in fact, quite valuable locations in and of themselves. A television station, for example, that runs only listings for other stations may not be so valuable.

Getting In When There's No Front Door

People who come to the Web after using a service such as CompuServe or America Online are often confused because the Web doesn't have a hierarchical structure. To find information about Windows programs on America Online, for example, you must first go to the Computer area and then to the PC area under the Computer area and, finally, to the Windows area under the PC area.

No surfing allowed

A short note on vocabulary. By now, you may have noticed that this book uses terms such as *explore, traverse,* and *wander* to describe your movement around the Web, but never the term *surf.* In fact, *surf* is probably the most inaccurate and overused metaphor for the Web to date — worse even than calling the Web the "information superhighway."

Think about it for a moment: What do surfers do? They go to one place; they paddle out; they ride in; they paddle out; they ride in; and so on. Their movement is limited to about 100 yards, always going back and forth.

Now think about how you use the Web. You start in one place. You read a bit and find a link to somewhere else. You find a link somewhere else again. Maybe you return to the second place to go out again to a fourth place. Or you go all the way back.

Notice the difference?

The *surf* metaphor also breaks down in what makes surfing fun versus what makes using the Web fun. For most surfers, a really wild ride in which they barely hang on for dear life but get some great action is the goal. (Actually, the goal is a day full of such rides.) For a

Web user, the ride itself shouldn't be wild. Maybe you want the destination to be wild, but getting there should be relatively painless.

The differences go on and on:

✔ Most surfboards look nicer than Web clients.

✔ No Web-inspired clothing is anywhere to be found (well, at least none you'd want to wear in public).

✔ You don't need to wash your feet off after exploring the Web.

✔ Surfing causes your thighs and ankles to hurt; wandering the Web hurts the wrists and eyes.

✔ You don't get blonder by using the Web.

✔ So far, surfing has inspired many more songs than has the Web.

✔ People don't usually go "oooh, ahhh" while watching you use the Web.

So the next time you hear people saying something about "surfing the Web," you can assume either that they haven't used the Web that much or that they have never gone surfing.

The Web has no "ceiling" and no single, agreed-on beginning location. A few Internet providers would like you to believe in a Web top — namely the home page they give you with their Web browser. By now, however, you know that ain't so.

But don't get the impression from this lack of a Web ceiling that you have nowhere to start. Almost all Web browsers include a function that enables you to type in any URL you want; on Netscape, it's the File menu's Open Location command. This command enables you to start wherever you want by entering a URL you see in this book, in a magazine article, in an advertisement, and so on.

Almost every Web browser also enables you to specify your *home page* —
the page displayed when you first run the browser. Few home pages, however, have everything you'd want on them. Most Netscape users use the
File⇨Open Page command liberally (this command used to be called
File⇨Open Location in earlier versions of Netscape). The term *home page*
can be somewhat confusing because some people also call the first page you
see after you enter their Web site a "home page." Thus, two different things
are called home pages: the first page you see after you start your Web client
and the first page you see after you enter a particular site.

Collecting because it's there

People who collect lists of pointers often have many motivations. Some
people may need to have good collections of pointers for their jobs. If your
job concerns forestry, for example, you may want access to all the information about forests on the Web that you can get. If you have such a list and
you publish it on the Web, you are assured to get mail from people who
appreciate your effort but want to point out that you forgot a particular Web
site. What a great way to do research!

Other people who publish lists of pointers do so because they just love to
have lots of information. These people are often the same people who
collect antique encyclopedias, who get excited if they find a reference book
on a subject they don't already have, and who would rather hang out in a
university library than at a university sporting event. These folks are good
to have around if you're doing a difficult crossword puzzle.

Both kinds of people do in fact perform a valuable service for the Web
community. Well-organized people produce well-organized lists that can
make the difference between finding the information you want and missing a
great resource. Not-so-well-organized people produce lists that may not be
so well organized but often contain nuggets that you can't find in other
places.

Picking the best

"I'm busy," you may be saying. "Just tell me which list of lists is the best."
Nope. There's no such thing. Good ones certainly are there to be found, but
none is "the best" in all circumstances, just as no one television channel is
best to watch for all kinds of shows.

For some people, "the best" is the biggest. (Texans are often said to have
this belief.) But even for these people, no single best Web pointer site can be
specified. Which is "bigger": the site with the most pointers in a few categories or the one with the most categories of pointers?

Virtual Libraries

Some of the major starting point sites are organized loosely as libraries by subject. In other words, the pointers are grouped by topic, just like the books on the shelves at most libraries are grouped by topic. Of course, the method for grouping by category is different for each site, just as it is for the various library cataloging methods.

The term *virtual library* indicates that these libraries don't actually contain much content. Virtual libraries are sets of *pointers* (links) organized by category, like a real library's card catalog. It's almost as if you went into a building marked "Library" and found a catalog where the cards just pointed to the contents of other libraries. At first, that doesn't sound so useful, but if the card catalog is really complete and well organized, you can still benefit greatly from it.

World Wide Web Virtual Library

```
http://www.w3.org/vl/
```

One of the first major attempts to organize the Web was the World Wide Web Virtual Library. In fact, it is still one of the best places to look for a categorized view of Web sites. Each subject is maintained by a different volunteer, usually a specialist in the area. As you can see in Figure 9-1, the categories are listed alphabetically. The library currently has more than 100 categories, and new ones are being added all the time.

People use the Virtual Library for starting their search for all sorts of topics. In a recent survey, the most popular places people went to from the Virtual Library, in decreasing popularity, were the following:

- Museums
- U.S. Federal Government Agencies
- Latin American Studies
- Association Football
- Non-Profit Organizations
- Art
- Writers' Resources on the Web
- Telecommunications
- Communications
- Sports

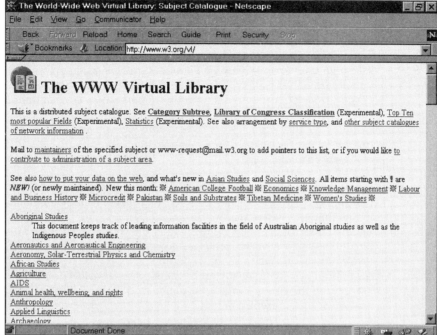

Figure 9-1:
The top
level of the
World Wide
Web Virtual
Library.

- Fish

- Secular Issues

- AIDS

- Astronomy and Astrophysics

- Physics

- Asian Studies

- Architecture

- Education

- Audio

Of course, this list changes as different topics become more and less popular and as topics are added to the library.

As with the other libraries described in this chapter, you can search the top level of the World Wide Web Virtual Library for words and phrases. Other libraries that contain more information kept at a single site usually have better response to searches. Most of the individual libraries pointed to by the World Wide Web Virtual Library, however, are individually searchable, which usually is sufficient if you know which topic you want to look in first.

ElNet Galaxy

http://galaxy.einet.net/

Although the World Wide Web Virtual Library is made up and categorized by volunteers, ElNet Galaxy is organized by a for-profit company that helps corporations set up and maintain their company networks (among other things). Most of the sections of Galaxy are moderated by volunteers, but the overall structure comes from ElNet. Many people find ElNet Galaxy better organized than the World Wide Web Virtual Library, although it is less complete in some areas.

Figure 9-2 shows part of the top level of the Galaxy. Each of the links below the top is edited and formatted at ElNet, making Galaxy much easier to follow than the World Wide Web Virtual Library. The maintainer of the World Wide Web Virtual Library controls only the top-level listings; after you go into a particular subject, other authors take over. On the other hand, all the levels of ElNet Galaxy are controlled by ElNet. Thus, Galaxy is more like a traditional card catalog sorted by subject; the World Wide Web Virtual Library, on the other hand, is more like a collection of reference magazines published by different companies.

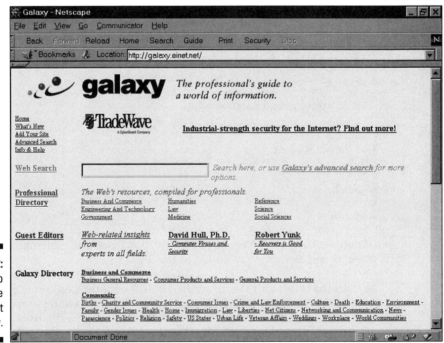

Figure 9-2:
The top level of the ElNet Galaxy.

Unfortunately, many of Galaxy's topics are fairly shallow, with only a few pointers. Some of the topics, however, are very long and give you many other places to look. If you are trying to do an exhaustive search for sites related to a topic, you should probably visit the World Wide Web Virtual Library, Galaxy, and probably a few of the other sites described in this chapter.

Clearinghouse for Subject-Oriented Internet Resource Guides

```
http://www.clearinghouse.net/
```

If you like libraries because they are organized by librarians, you'll probably love the Clearinghouse for Subject-Oriented Internet Resource Guides. (That's quite a mouthful; from here on, it's just called the Clearinghouse.) It was originally from the University of Michigan and organized by the University Library and the School of Information and Library Studies. Figure 9-3 shows the top level of the current Clearinghouse.

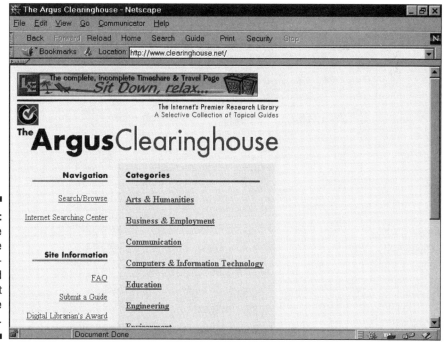

Figure 9-3: Entering the Clearinghouse for Subject-Oriented Internet Resource Guides.

As you may imagine, it's about as much like a university library as you can get on the Web. Many of the subtopics are collected by librarians; the others, mostly by academics. As such, it has a very academic slant to it, making it different from the other large pointer sites. The pointers in the Clearinghouse tend to be to universities, although plenty of non-university pointers are there as well.

As you use the Clearinghouse, you'll probably discover that some of the information is in Gopher and not HTML. For people who are very Web-oriented, this fact may be a bit disconcerting because Gopher menus aren't nearly as easy to use as good Web lists. Remember, however, that many universities still use Gopher rather than the Web as a publishing medium, and older material that is still valuable is still cataloged in Gopher.

Figure 9-4 shows a typical listing from the Clearinghouse.

Inter-Links

```
http://www.nova.edu/Inter-Links/
```

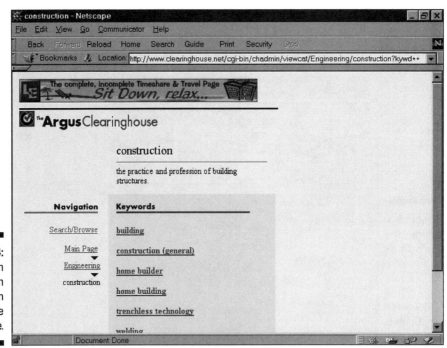

Figure 9-4:
Information on construction in the Clearinghouse.

Previously known as NovaLinks, Inter-Links is more of an overview of the Internet, particularly the Web, than are the other virtual libraries. The intent of Inter-Links is to help beginning users get a feel for all that is on the Internet. In that, it isn't as complete as some of the other libraries. The simple introductory page is shown in Figure 9-5.

The tradeoff of designing a Web site for beginners, compared to trying to be complete, may be lost on some people, particularly if you forget how overwhelming it is to be presented with dozens of pointers when you first start using the Web. The links in Inter-Links are generally of higher quality than those on the "we-list-everything" type of sites.

Yahoo!

```
http://www.yahoo.com/
```

Some of the best libraries start off as whims or short-term projects and then take on a life of their own. Yahoo! is such a site. Containing more than 30,000 links, Yahoo! has quickly become one of the most popular libraries on the Web. Figure 9-6 shows the top of the hierarchy, but don't be fooled by the lack of listings: Each level has many levels beneath it, and the maintainers are adding dozens (and sometimes hundreds) of links every day.

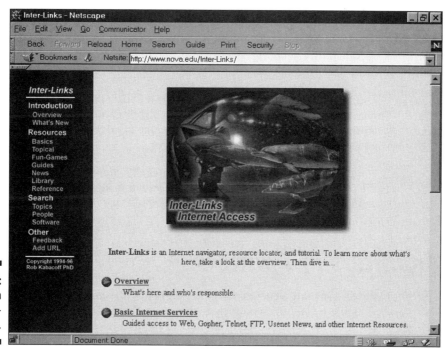

Figure 9-5:
Introduction
to Inter-
Links.

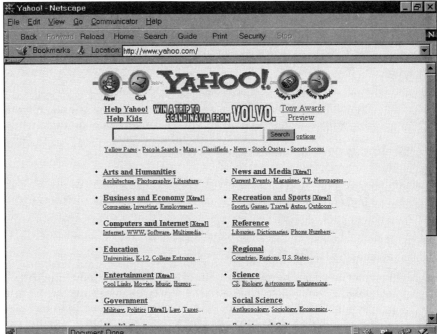

Figure 9-6:
Just the tip
of the
iceberg in
Yahoo!

The folks who run Yahoo! actively solicit new links from people on the Internet. They supplement those links with ones that they get from their own worm that crawls in various parts of the Web. This two-pronged approach to collecting resource pointers has helped Yahoo! grow to an incredible size in a very short time.

And, yes, there is a silly story behind the name. *Yahoo!* stands for (are you ready for this?) *Yet Another Hierarchically Organized Oracle.* Yeah, right. It's more likely that the name appeared before the decision about what the name stood for.

I find Yahoo! to be one of my favorite sites. It's more complete than most of the other libraries, it has a much nicer feel to it, and something new is always going on there. If you're looking for a "first library," I recommend Yahoo!.

Anointers of Pointers

Beyond the large libraries are dozens of smaller collections that are very valuable for people wondering what's out there on the Web. Most of these libraries are created by individuals or companies hoping to convince people coming to their sites looking for pointers to check out the other services they offer.

As described in Part IV of this book, anyone who learns a bit of HTML can create Web lists. Not all lists, however, are created equal. If you are not terribly thorough, for example, you could be doing a disservice to someone searching for information by pretending to have a complete list on a particular subject. To be helpful, these kinds of lists need to be both complete at the time they are created and updated often with new pointers as they arise.

Good lists also must include all kinds of Web resources, not just ones on HTTP servers. It's easy to lapse into the mentality that "it must be hypertext to be good" and ignore lots of good but older information (called *legacy information*) that is still on Gopher and FTP servers. The best lists in this section are quite multifaceted, pointing to all sorts of resources.

Yanoff's List

```
http://www.spectracom.com/islist/
```

Another venerable list of pointers on the Internet is Yanoff's list, shown in Figure 9-7. Yanoff's list seems to have been around forever and was certainly popular before the Web was. In fact, the text version of Yanoff's list is still much more popular than the HTML version.

Figure 9-7:
Yanoff's list,
in HTML.

The story behind Yanoff's list is similar to the story of some of the best home pages on the Web. Scott Yanoff started the list in 1991 for his own research. He started sharing the list with a few people, and then more people wanted it, and so on until it became one of the most popular lists of lists on the Internet.

Net-happenings archive

```
http://www.mid.net/NET/
```

One of the better mailing lists for keeping up with what's new on the Internet, particularly on the Web, is the Net-happenings list run by Gleason Sackman. The list is not inclusive; it lists only things that Gleason thinks are interesting. His bent is clearly toward computing for the K-12 teaching community, but he lists new Web sites, new mailing lists, new software, and so on that should interest most Web users.

The list sometimes gets 50 messages per week, which is too much for some people to handle. Thus, the archive of the mailing list, as shown in Figure 9-8, is the most convenient way for some people to scan and find what they want. Of course, the archive is searchable, so you can look for announcements on particular topics.

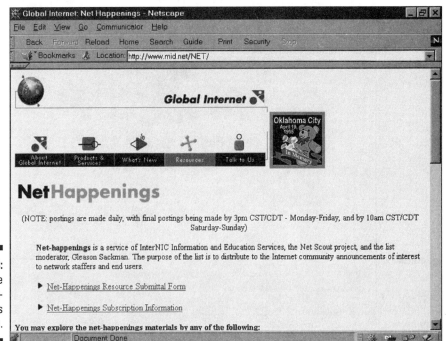

Figure 9-8:
The archive of Net-happenings postings.

New Web sites

```
news:comp.infosystems.www.announce
```

If you want to know what's new on the Web, the best place to look is the `comp.infosystems.www.announce` Usenet newsgroup. It is a moderated newsgroup in which anyone can post an announcement of a new Web site, Web software, and so on. As shown in Figure 9-9, the group catches a bit of everything.

Even though it is moderated, you can find a very wide range of announcements here. Following the group for a few weeks gives you a good sense of how the Web is growing, who's putting up new information, and how Web users are helping to change the Web.

Business Web

```
http://www.bizweb.com/
```

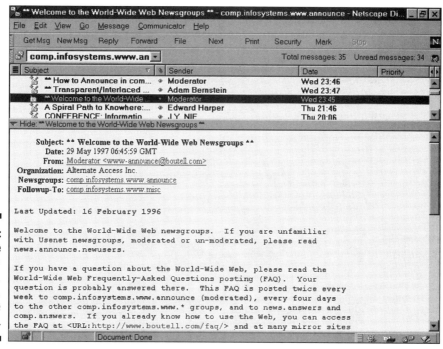

Figure 9-9:
The
comp.info-
systems.
www.
announce
newsgroup.

BizWeb is an attempt to organize the business side of the Web. Although it is not terribly large, it is probably one of the best listings of products and services on the Web pulled together in one place. Figure 9-10 shows some of the categories on BizWeb.

BizWeb is far from perfect, mostly due to companies not registering with BizWeb. As more and more companies find out about BizWeb, however, it should become even more useful for searching for products and services.

Microsoft Library

http://library.microsoft.com/

Since Microsoft entered the market for selling information and not just software, it has done an admirable job of collecting data on all sorts of computer-related topics. It sells some of this data in various Microsoft CD-ROM packages but also gives lots of it away free. The Microsoft Library, shown in Figure 9-11, is an example of the latter.

The Microsoft Library provides lots of great references, including a very complete list of library-related sites that should be of interest to most teachers and parents. Its list of computer magazines is also pretty impressive, given how many of those magazines are not overly fond of Microsoft.

Figure 9-10: BizWeb covers many categories of businesses, particularly shops and malls.

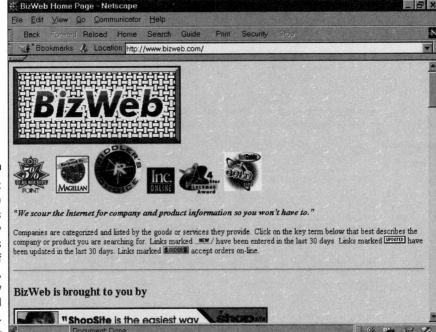

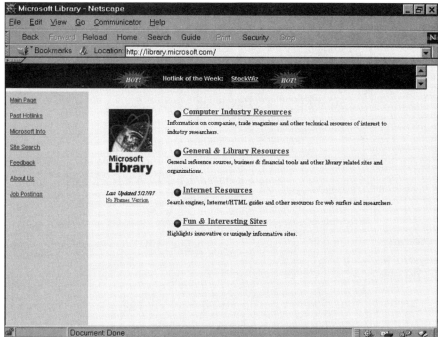

Figure 9-11:
Microsoft's
free library.

Larry's InfoPower Pages

```
http://www.clark.net/pub/lschank/home.html
```

Some librarians can't get enough of the library at work. Larry Schank is one
such librarian. His InfoPower Pages are an excellent source of pointers on a
small list of topics. The top level of his pages is shown in Figure 9-12.

His set of resource lists is pretty impressive for a single person. Among the
topics for which he has collected pointers are the following:

- ✔ Behavioral sciences
- ✔ Library and librarians
- ✔ Business and economics
- ✔ Law and legal resources
- ✔ Humanities
- ✔ International and country studies
- ✔ Education

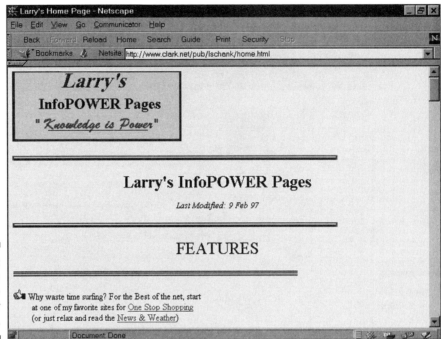

Figure 9-12:
The base
for the
InfoPower
Pages.

✔ Geography and environment

✔ Health and medicine

✔ Internet and computing

✔ Government and political science

Figure 9-13, for example, shows part of his political science resources.

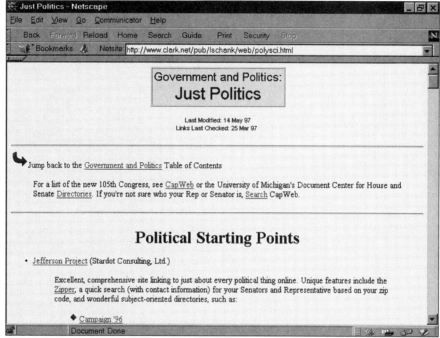

Figure 9-13:
The
InfoPower
Pages' list
of political
science
resources
available on
the Web.

Chapter 10
Finding Fun, Fun, Fun

● ●

In This Chapter

▶ Finding people on the Web

▶ Exploring Web game resources

▶ Humming along with Web music resources

▶ Using the Web to help turn into a couch potato

● ●

*A*s many of the Web pages in this book show, the Web is more than research, business, and commerce. People create the content on the Web, and people tend to act like, well, people when they get creative. Thus, many of the best Web resources are not all that serious or high-minded.

All This and People, Too!

If you're a people person, you probably like to see what people on the Web are doing when they're not being so serious. Some are just trying to make contact with other people out there in the universe; others are trying to keep themselves amused; and others are trying to hide. (Of course, the ones trying to hide should probably not create Web home pages.)

You can find people being people at hundreds of places on the Web. This section shows just a few, but finding many more is easy. Much of Usenet consists of people trying to make one-to-many contacts; in fact, Usenet is a good place to do people-in-public watching.

Who's who on the Internet

`http://people.farfan.com/`

Chapters 15 through 18 discuss how to create your own Web pages. Of course, people have been doing this for quite some time, with varying degrees of success. Many people can get the hang of HTML but may miss the mark with respect to, shall we say, interesting content. Others have good content but need a few lessons in design or even basic HTML use.

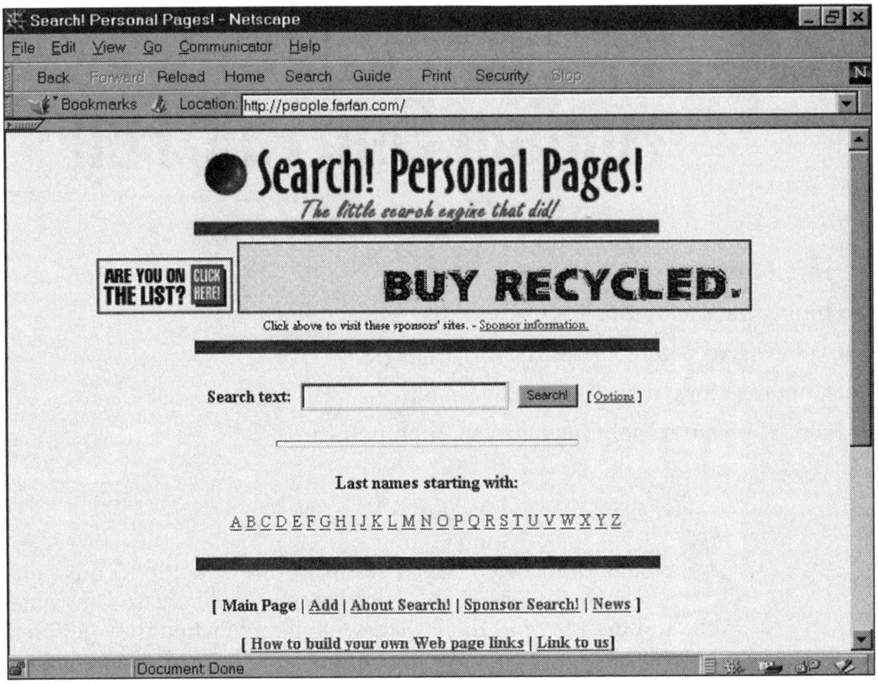

Figure 10-1:
Finding
everyone on
the Web,
made easy.

Still, you may want to take a look at what ordinary Web folk have for home pages. Figure 10-1 shows the Farfan personal pages Web site. Here, thousands of people have registered their home sites with short descriptions of what kind of content they offer (if any). Anyone can register for free, so it's quite the egalitarian listing.

A surprisingly high number of these pages are published by ordinary folk who freely admit that they don't have much to say on their home pages. They're mostly there to watch, but they may pipe in every once in a while. If you end up creating your own home page, even if it isn't anything special, you should probably register it with this site so that other people can find you, giving them the same browsing opportunities that you are taking advantage of; that seems only fair in the people-watching game.

Going other places

```
news:rec.travel.misc
```

If you like to travel, the newsgroups with names that start with rec.travel (such as rec.travel.misc) are a great place to chat with other people who travel and who live in the places where you want to go. Figure 10-2 shows some of the articles in rec.travel.misc. You can find many travel groups, including the following:

✔ rec.travel.africa

✔ rec.travel.air

✔ rec.travel.asia

✔ rec.travel.australia+nz

✔ rec.travel.caribbean

✔ rec.travel.cruises

✔ rec.travel.europe

✔ rec.travel.latin-america

✔ rec.travel.marketplace

✔ rec.travel.misc

✔ rec.travel.usa-canada

The kinds of conversations you see in the Asia, Europe, and USA-Canada newsgroups often fall into either the "have you been to so-and-so before" category or the "when you go to so-and-so, be sure to see such-and-such." These kinds of conversations are good ways to see what people find important when they travel and what natives find important to show others. The other newsgroups are good places to talk about bargains and warnings, but the main discussion groups are excellent for people who like to get around.

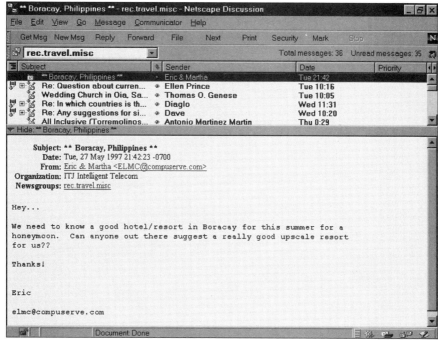

Figure 10-2:
Chatting
about
traveling.

Making things

```
news:rec.crafts.misc
```

If you are interested in crafts, you can probably find a newsgroup that interests you. Of course, not everyone has a craft to play with, but those who do tend to want to tell others about their favorite finds, what they've made recently, the best stores for supplies, and so on. Figure 10-3 shows the `rec.crafts.misc` newsgroup. Many craft-related groups are around, including the following:

- ✔ rec.crafts.beads
- ✔ rec.crafts.brewing
- ✔ rec.crafts.carving
- ✔ rec.crafts.dollhouses
- ✔ rec.crafts.glass
- ✔ rec.crafts.jewelry
- ✔ rec.crafts.marketplace
- ✔ rec.crafts.metalworking
- ✔ rec.crafts.misc
- ✔ rec.crafts.polymer-clay
- ✔ rec.crafts.pottery
- ✔ rec.crafts.textiles
- ✔ rec.crafts.winemaking

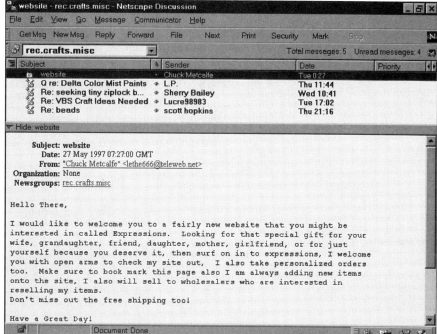

Figure 10-3:
Craft topics
in
rec.crafts.
misc.

The newsgroups with names that start with `rec.crafts.` are usually much easier to read and follow than many other Usenet groups. You will certainly run into fewer flames and inappropriate postings here than on other newsgroups. However, because many of the newer users of these groups haven't the faintest idea of what Usenet is or how to post messages, you will see fewer messages in these groups than you might expect for popular hobbies. People-watching is easy here, and you may actually find yourself picking up a new hobby. For example, Figure 10-4 shows some of the kind of talk you'll see on `rec.crafts.metalworking`.

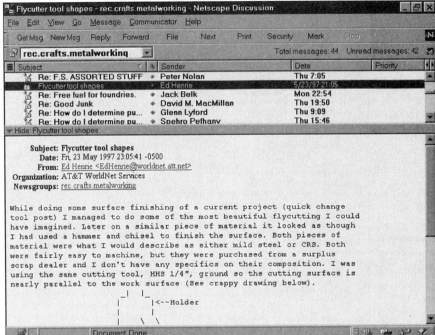

Figure 10-4:
The folks
who love to
work with
metal.

Four11 Directory

`http://www.four11.com/`

You may not be as interested in watching random people chat as you are in finding specific people. For that, the best service is SLED's Four11 Directory Services, as shown in Figure 10-5. Four11 is a free service, although for a small amount of money you can sign on for premium service that enables you to list your Web page, a *public encryption key* (a security mechanism that a few people on the Internet use), and so on.

Using the search function is easy, and you can specify as much or as little as you know about the person. If you want to find a person who has an uncommon last name, for example, knowing the last name should be sufficient. SLED makes its money from people signing up for the premium service, which is becoming more popular as people want to publish their public encryption keys.

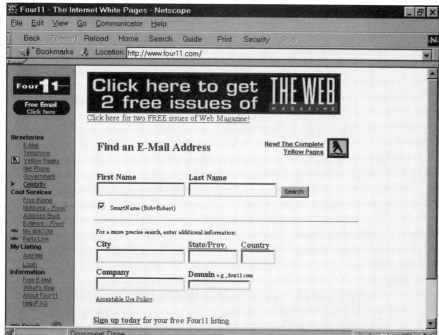

Figure 10-5:
Finding
folks using
Four11.

Names of the Games

The non-work activities that take up most people's attention are often sports and games. In the U.S., many more people are interested in sports as a spectator event than in actually participating in them, but tens of millions of people still play basketball, baseball, and golf. Multiplayer games such as bridge and Scrabble used to be much more popular than they are today, but millions still enjoy them.

Both sports and games have given way in the past decade to electronic games and video games that are for one or two people. Many people believe that the prevalence of Nintendo and Sega systems in homes, as well as the rise of similar computer games, has largely sapped the popularity of participant games and sports. Many Web sites cover all sorts of games and sports, including the now-popular video and home games.

Games Domain

http://www.gamesdomain.com/

By far the most complete Web site that covers games (but not sports) is Games Domain, shown in Figure 10-6. Games Domain has a worldwide view of the games realm. It covers all types of games, including video games and computer games, as well as traditional games such as chess and Go that can be played with a computer.

One of the best features of Games Domain is its collection of Usenet newsgroups and their affiliated FAQs. Games Domain was an early proponent of converting FAQs to HTML so that they could be easily viewed through the Web, and it now includes pointers to dozens of games-related FAQs (as well as, of course, to the Usenet newsgroups themselves). If you haven't encountered them yet, FAQs are files that contain the answers to many frequently asked questions; they can be an incredibly valuable resource.

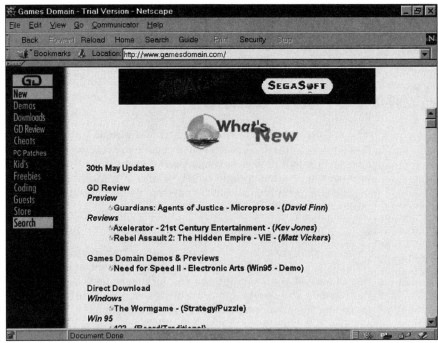

Figure 10-6:
The top
level of
Games
Domain.

Games and Recreation Virtual Library

`http://www.cis.ufl.edu/~thoth/library/recreation.html`

As virtual libraries go, the Games and Recreation Virtual Library, shown in Figure 10-7, is one of the best. It is not as slickly put together as Games Domain, but it covers more ground, particularly for outdoor recreation that is not strictly classified as sport. For example, it offers pointers for canoeing, kayaking, and skydiving.

Many of the activities described in the Games and Recreation Virtual Library have commercial sites associated with them. Many of those sites are, in fact, the only Web sites that cover particular recreational activities and are thus fairly valuable, even to people who aren't interested in the sponsor.

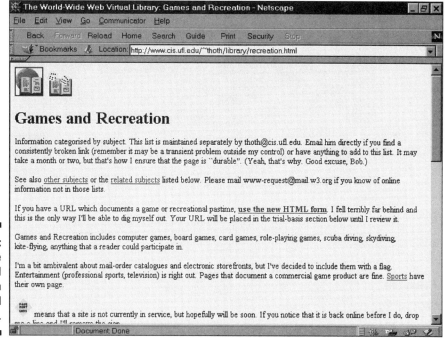

Figure 10-7:
Fun with the
Games and
Recreation
Virtual
Library.

Sport Virtual Library

`http://www.justwright.com/sports/`

Leave it to the British to come up with the consummate sports site, one that not only is complete but fairly funny as well. The Sport Virtual Library, shown in Figure 10-8, puts most American sites to shame by having more of an international view (no surprise there) and less of an "all sports are good" attitude. The Web site also has an impressive set of pointers to information about international sporting events such as the Goodwill Games and the Olympics.

The sports are categorized loosely by the devices used in the sports, such as ball sports, wheel sports, and water sports. The topic headings also give a flavor of the prejudices of the authors; for example, the soccer section is entitled "The Mother of All Sports." A few topics that should otherwise probably go on the Games and Recreation Virtual Library, such as juggling, also appear on the Sport Virtual Library.

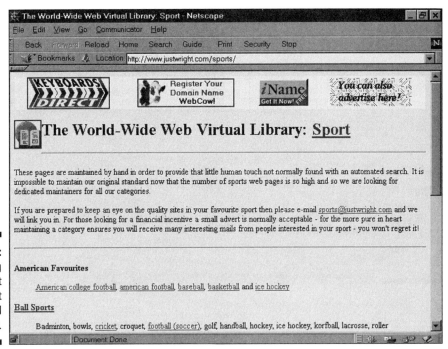

Figure 10-8:
Playing around at the Sport Virtual Library.

Games on Usenet

news:rec.games.misc

For a bit more interactivity around games, you should certainly check out the many Usenet newsgroups in the rec.games hierarchy. You can find dozens of these newsgroups, including ones for the following games:

- ✔ Backgammon
- ✔ Board games in general
- ✔ Bridge
- ✔ Chess
- ✔ Chinese chess
- ✔ Game design
- ✔ Diplomacy
- ✔ Empire

Figure 10-9 shows the rec.games.misc newsgroup. The FAQs in this newsgroup point you to the other newsgroups of interest. Many other Usenet newsgroups also relate to games; most of these can be found at the Games Domain Web site discussed earlier in this chapter.

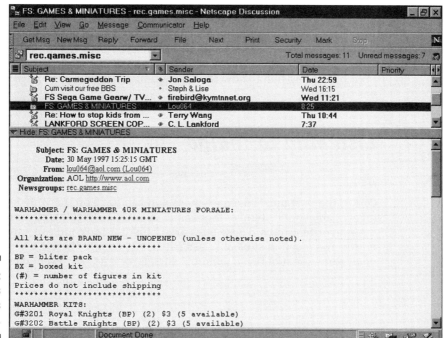

Figure 10-9:
Messages
in a games
newsgroup.

Funky Web Groove Thang

The Internet was a center of musical chatter well before the Web came into existence. The multimedia aspect of the Web, largely unrealized as it is, makes the Web a bit more enticing for music lovers, but it is still in its infancy. That said, the music-based areas of the Internet have pretty much moved over to being Web-specific, with the exception of the dozens of fan mailing lists that still thrive.

Internet Underground Music Archive

http://www.iuma.com/

For the last 20 years, the modern music scene has always relied on bands starting small, getting local coverage, and growing slowly to national and international presence. Many bands and artists spend their hard-earned cash on making tapes and CDs, trying to get them distributed in local stores, and so on. Independent music labels usually have between only one and ten bands on them and often fold as fast as they arrive.

The folks at the Internet Underground Music Archive (IUMA), shown in Figure 10-10, started their career by letting bands publish songs, promotional literature, and so on for free. Now they charge a small amount, but the purpose of IUMA is still the same: to enable unknown bands to promote themselves on the Internet.

The IUMA site has hundreds of artists in a variety of genres, although most would be classified as rock and roll. Some artists are selling CDs and tapes; others are just trying for a bit of recognition. If you want to sample music from bands you don't know (and have time to download large files), IUMA has the variety.

Listening to Indigo

http://www.u36.com/james/indigo.htm

One of the best musical experiences you can have on the Web doesn't involve any sound. Tens of thousands of sites are created by music fans for their favorite groups. These sites aren't just for rock and roll superstars, either: You can find sites for classical music, country, world music, and folk of all sorts. Most of these personal sites have a homey, excited feel to them.

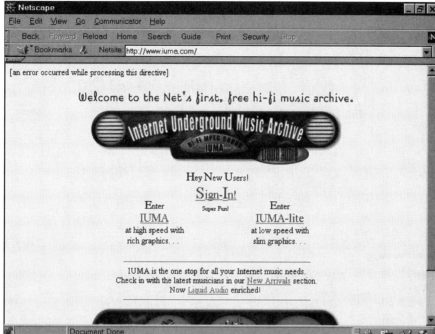

Figure 10-10:
Internet
Underground
Music
Archive's
introductory
page.

If you're a fan of the Indigo Girls like I am, you are fortunate to have over a dozen Web sites that cover all aspects of this folk duo's career. For example, Figure 10-11 shows Listening to Indigo, a typical fan site. Here you can find tour dates, what songs they played at earlier concerts, pictures, e-mail addresses of other fans, and so on. The Indigo Girls' music has had a big impact on many of our lives, and being able to keep in touch with other fans (or just see what you missed at recent concerts) is great. Of course, the same is true for fans of the thousands of other bands who have also inspired unofficial Web sites.

TeeVee via TCP

The Internet may be a haven for music lovers, but it's also a haven for couch potatoes who want to chat about their favorite television shows. Dozens of Web sites have (usually unauthorized) picture and script archives for the most popular shows. As you may imagine, science fiction shows are over-represented among these sites, but you can also find Web sites for everything from soap operas to Saturday morning cartoons.

Figure 10-11:
A personal
view of the
Indigo Girls.

Star Trek: Voyager

http://www.paramount.com/tvvoyager/

Many sites on the Web come and go, and it's always a risk publishing the addresses of such sites. Television shows come and go even more quickly, however, doubling the risk. The newest series in the Star Trek universe, *Star Trek: Voyager,* has its own site that is sponsored by its producers (see Figure 10-12).

You can find summaries of story lines, look at biographies of the characters, download pictures, and so on. The site is set up to keep current fans interested, although it is also a good model for how future television and movie promotions may appear on the Web.

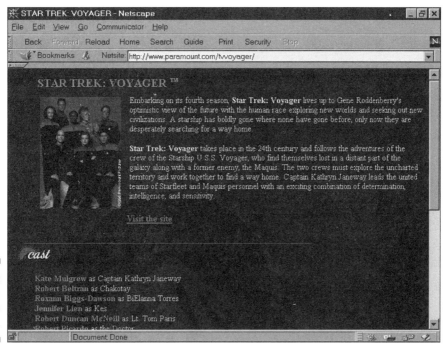

Figure 10-12:
Entering
the starship
Voyager.

The Tonight Show

http://www.nbc.com/tonightshow/

The Tonight Show with Jay Leno, shown in Figure 10-13, is another example of an official Web site that is supposed to keep people's interest in a particular show. Of course, the fans of *The Tonight Show* are quite different from fans of *Star Trek: Voyager,* so its Web site is much more low key.

The Tonight Show Web site lists who's going to appear in upcoming shows, a few of the recent jokes, and so on. It also has quick video clips of some of the sight gag spots. In all, it's a pretty sedate Web site for a pretty sedate television show.

Figure 10-13:
The home
site for *The
Tonight
Show.*

Chapter 11

Web Ways to Shop

A few years ago, barely any real commerce existed anywhere on the Internet. Sure, a few companies had their advertising available by FTP or by mail response systems, but by and large, there wasn't much reason to have your wallet handy when you were on the Internet.

The Web has changed all that. As the Web became a popular medium for publishing, some people saw the dollar signs appear and wanted to make parts of the Web safe for shopping. All other media had advertising; and as the goal of advertising is to entice people to spend their money, why shouldn't the Web do the same?

So far, the reality of the Web as a shopping medium is not nearly as grand as merchandisers had hoped for. The speed of the Web prohibits catalogs from having very many full-color pictures in them, and many people still prefer to buy from a human, even if it is a disembodied person in the middle of who-knows-where at the other end of a toll-free 800 number.

The commercial side of the Web, however, is still in its formative stages. Television advertising took decades to get into a profitable pattern, and newspaper advertising is still hit and miss; no one should expect to understand how best to sell things on the Web for at least another few years. Plenty of early adopters of Web advertising have made an incredible variety of things (also known as "stuff") available for purchase on the Web.

Doing the Mall Crawl

Many early Web entrepreneurs had the idea that, by making the Web seem like a place, people would want to come to a part of it to do their shopping. Parts of the Web could be like suburban shopping malls, in which people go wandering around from store to store for all their shopping needs.

This picture, of course, doesn't work well with the Web. Clicking a link that is supposedly "in" a mall could just as easily take you to another mall — maybe on a different continent. The early attempts at making malls on the Web failed for lack of tenants for the malls and lack of desire on the part of Web users to stay in one place. (Maybe the lack of frozen yogurt shops had something to do with it as well.)

Dealernet

```
http://www.dealernet.com/
```

One kind of mall that is having some success is the Web commercial site where every store sells similar items. This setup seems to work well if the mall also offers free, noncommercial information that Web users find attractive enough to justify putting up with the commercial aspects of the stores, or if the stores sell merchandise that is so compelling that people will come just for the merchandise.

Dealernet is such a mall, specializing in car dealers. Figure 11-1 shows Dealernet's main entry point. From there, you can look for a car by manufacturer or see what particular car dealers who are participating in Dealernet have to offer. You can also get information on various new cars, repairs, and other car-related subjects.

The Internet Mall

```
http://www.internet-mall.com/
```

One mall that survived the early Web mall shakeout is, appropriately enough, The Internet Mall, a project of Dave Taylor. The mall lists people and companies for free, making it a much better deal than many of the other malls. It is supported by commercial sponsors and Taylor's other publishing enterprises. The Internet Mall is different from many other Web sites in that it lists many companies who have no Web presence, just electronic mail addresses.

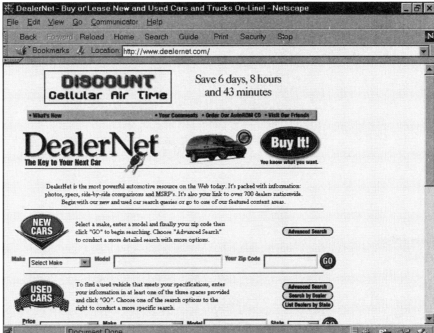

Figure 11-1:
The main
showroom
for
Dealernet.

The entrance to The Internet Mall is as shown in Figure 11-2. Taylor has organized the mall as if it were a multistory department store; you can almost hear the elevator operator saying "Fifth floor: clothes and sporting goods." You can also find a complete list of all the companies in the Internet Mall, which also provides you with a description of each company as well as other companies in the same category.

MarketNet

```
http://mkn.co.uk/
```

Malls can be found in many countries other than the U.S. MarketNet, for example, shown in Figure 11-3, is a similar mall idea from England. Although it has many of the same features as the American malls, many of the shops have a particularly local appeal to the British.

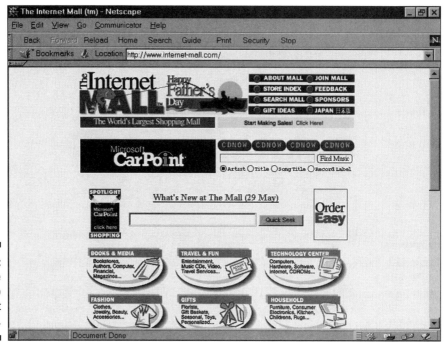

Figure 11-2:
The entrance to The Internet Mall.

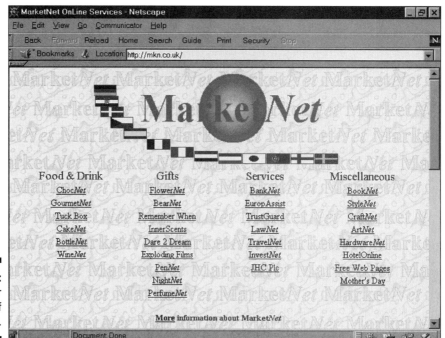

Figure 11-3:
Center court of MarketNet.

Malls such as MarketNet show one of the features of the Web that is both a strength and weakness of the idea of commerce on the Web. As at American Web malls, many of the shops in MarketNet sell by mail order. Few, however, list postage rates for outside the U.K. Many banks also add large surcharges to credit card orders outside the merchants' countries. Problems such as these may get addressed as the Web gets more popular outside the U.S., but it could take years to get everyone to understand that it is just as easy for someone to link to a shop halfway around the world as it is to link to a shop in the same city.

One Shop Towns

In most places off the Web, finding a shop to spend your money is easy. Finding a place on the Web to spend your money may be a bit more difficult, particularly if the places are competing with other kinds of stores. If shopping on the Web is tedious, the merchants quickly lose your business.

Today, most stores on the Web compete directly with mail-order catalogs that offer toll-free 800 numbers for ordering. On the other hand, many of the best stores on the Web are mail-order stores that are experimenting with the Web as an additional way to get customers.

Music Boulevard

```
http://www.musicblvd.com/
```

CD shoppers fall into two categories: those who know what they want and those who don't. For those who don't, record stores are great. For those who already have a good idea of what they want to buy, mail-order CD stores offer lower prices and usually have a larger selection. Music Boulevard has made quite a reputation as a leading Web discount CD dealer.

Music Boulevard's site, shown in Figure 11-4, is meant to attract some of the buyers who like to browse in the record store, looking at albums one at a time. Most of the albums display complete song lists; some have additional information. As you browse and order albums, its Web page tells you how much you've already ordered so that you don't get out of control. In this way, the experience is somewhat of a cross between going through a catalog and browsing in a record store.

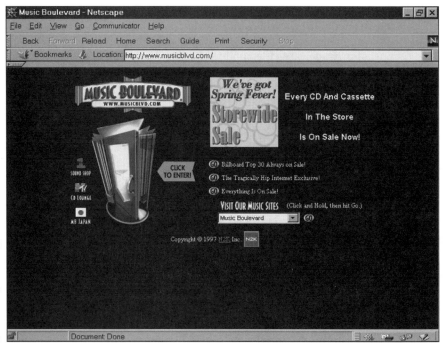

Figure 11-4:
The top
level of
Music
Boulevard.

Internet Shopping Network

```
http://www.internet.net/
```

If it's computer hardware and software you're shopping for, the Internet Shopping Network (ISN) may be the place you want. It is a discount mail-order store with tens of thousands of items, categorized and easier to find than in any paper catalog. Figure 11-5 shows the "member's entrance" of ISN.

ISN has big plans, particularly to branch out beyond the computer market. In fact, the shop-by-television HSN cable channel bought ISN as a way for it to get more into the Web world. ISN started with more funding than many other Internet stores, and it has a good chance of growing into many areas where large volume can lead to lower prices.

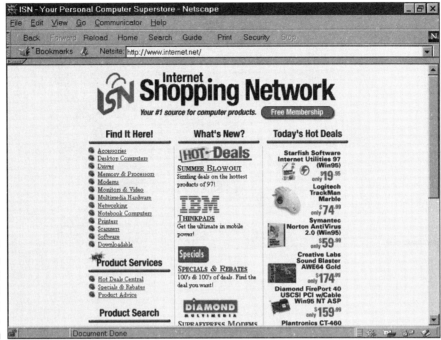

Figure 11-5:
Shopping at the Internet Shopping Network.

Computer Literacy Bookshops

`http://www.clbooks.com/`

Computer users like computer books, and no store anywhere is quite like Computer Literacy. It has an incredibly huge collection of books and magazines on computer topics and has a very active mail-order department. Visitors to Silicon Valley often make trips to Computer Literacy on their way to the airport, leaving with many hundreds of dollars of books that can't be found in the regular bookstores in their home towns.

As part of its mail-order business, Computer Literacy has a Web site, as shown in Figure 11-6. Because so many computer books have similar titles, being able to search for a particular word in a title or for an author can make all the difference in finding a specific computer book. After you select a book you are interested in, Computer Literacy's search feature also enables you to search for all books on the same topic.

Figure 11-6:
Computer
Literacy's
starting
page.

Amazon.com

`http://www.amazon.com`

If a regular bookstore is more your style, you can find many from which to choose on the Internet. One recently popular bookstore is Amazon.com, which is shown in Figure 11-7. It has a wide selection of books in many categories. Although it offers many computer books, its strength is in its "regular" books and audio tapes.

Like shopping for records, shopping for books online is not as pleasing for most people as is browsing in a bookstore. On the other hand, online bookstores can have a much deeper depth of stock than normal bookstores, and searching for a particular book that you want can be much easier. The trick is to find a Web bookstore (or record store, and so on) that matches your desire for convenience with reasonable additional features, in exchange for the desired feel of a real-life bookstore.

Figure 11-7:
The main
entrance to
Amazon.com.

DomeSpace

`http://www.branchmall.com/dome/`

The Web is an excellent way to sell information-intensive products, ones that take many pages of a printed catalog to sell. For example, before you buy plans for a home or an entire kit including all the lumber, you probably want to see more than a small brochure.

Figure 11-8 shows the home page for DomeSpace, a company that sells plans for alternative-style buildings. Their Web site goes into much more detail than a simple brochure could, probably enough to give you a good idea of whether the plan is right for you or a bit too far out.

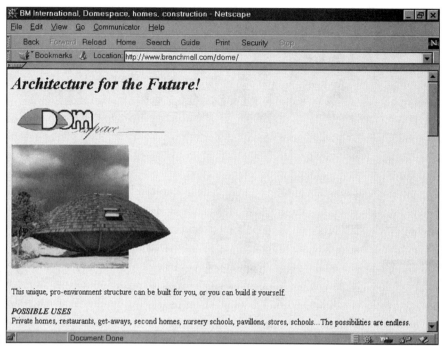

Figure 11-8:
DomeSpace's
description.

Wits' End Antiques

http://www.tias.com/stores/witsend/

Even small stores have Web pages. In fact, it's almost impossible to tell the difference between a small store and a big one just by looking at their Web pages; you must look at what the stores carry. Small stores that understand the culture of the Web and understand their customers can do well on the Web.

Wits' End Antiques, shown in Figure 11-9, for example, could exist anywhere. It has the kind of merchandise that is usually bought in person but can be bought by mail order. It's added a few nice touches to its Web page, such as pointers to other antique dealers and Web sites that cover antiques, resulting in a feel that a plain "buy from us" style Web page lacks.

Services with a Smile

When you think of shopping, you may think of getting stuff you can hold in your hand or put in your garage. You can buy many other types of things, however, including services. For example, many people spend more on services such as insurance and financial advice than they do on merchandise such as CDs and books.

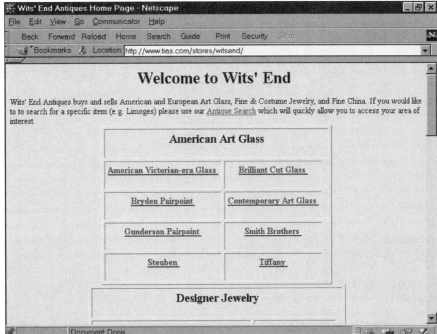

Welcome to Wits' End

Wits' End Antiques buys and sells American and European Art Glass, Fine & Costume Jewelry, and Fine China. If you would like to to search for a specific item (e.g. Limoges) please use our Antique Search which will quickly allow you to access your area of interest.

American Art Glass

American Victorian-era Glass	Brilliant Cut Glass
Bryden Pairpoint	Contemporary Art Glass
Gunderson Pairpoint	Smith Brothers
Steuben	Tiffany

Designer Jewelry

Document Done

Figure 11-9:
Wits' End
Antiques.

The Web offers an opportunity for service companies to give lots of free information to prospective and current customers, thereby seeming like the good guys of the Information Superhighway. It also enables them to transact business in a way not allowed by telephones and regular mail. Service companies are far behind merchandise companies in using the Web for commerce, but they will probably be catching up soon.

Infoseek

```
http://www.infoseek.com/
```

Sometimes you don't have time to do the kind of research that you need. Although the Web enables you to find many things, you certainly can't find everything yourself. If you want to pay to have someone else research small or large questions for you, you can usually find a research service firm to help. Of course, most of these firms have access to the Web to help them with their searches.

One of the best places to look for things is Infoseek, shown in Figure 11-10. Infoseek offers a few different levels of service, starting with a very capable free service. For a small monthly fee, you can also have it cull information of interest to you and retrieve articles from many sources for you.

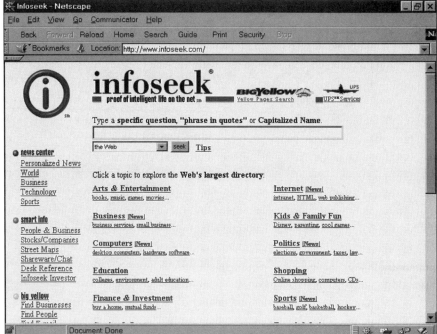

Figure 11-10:
Search
Infoseek for
free or at
low cost.

Homebuyer's Fair

http://www.homefair.com/

Many people spend thousands of dollars using real estate agents. In any town, you can often find dozens of agents, and choosing one who meets your needs is often a hit-or-miss proposition. Of course, no one would buy a home just from looking at its Web page, but the Web is a good way to choose an agent, find an area to move to, or preview homes in a particular area.

Homebuyer's Fair is a general marketplace for people looking at homes. Its Web site, shown in Figure 11-11, gives lots of good advice about finding homes and also has many commercial listings. It has many collateral sections, including information about mortgages, finding apartments, and so on.

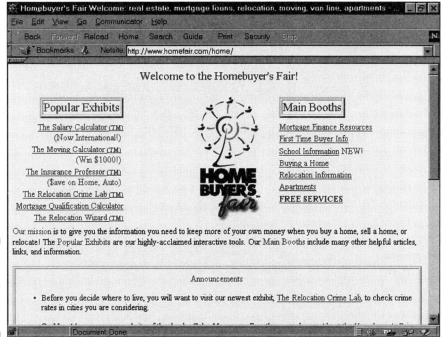

Figure 11-11:
Starting
location for
Homebuyer's
Fair.

BookWeb

```
http://www.bookweb.org/
```

Another type of service becoming popular on the Web is that of trade organizations. These groups often provide lists of all their members, give background in what the groups do, and so on. The Web is a good medium for trade groups who normally don't get much coverage. For example, the American Booksellers Association (ABA) has a Web site called BookWeb, shown in Figure 11-12.

BookWeb enables ABA to do more than just list the location of its members, which for bookstores isn't all that interesting because most people know where a local bookstore is located. For example, BookWeb highlights recent bestsellers, trends in book selling, and so on as an inducement for Web users to go to their local bookstores more often. Another feature, the lists of author tours, also has the same effect: get people to go to bookstores more often.

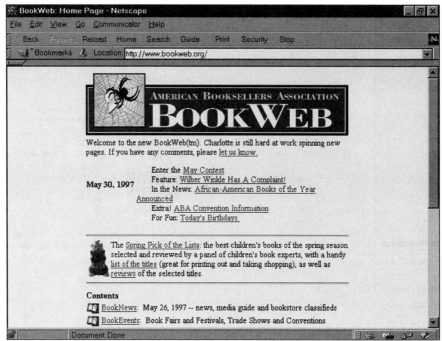

Figure 11-12:
The
entrance to
BookWeb.

The Business of Business

Given that commerce is fairly new to the Internet, and particularly to the Web, many companies are just now feeling their ways through the maze of challenges. Some are trying to emulate other companies; others are trying new things to differentiate themselves from their competitors. The goal for most of these companies, however, is the same: attract customers by using the technologies available through the Internet.

CommerceNet

http://www.commerce.net/

CommerceNet was one of the first business groups to get publicity for bringing together commercial interests on the Internet. Its charter, "to develop, maintain, and endorse an Internet-based infrastructure for electronic commerce in business-to-business applications," pretty much means that it wants the Internet to be safe for commerce. At the same time, it is investigating ways to promote commerce on the Internet by looking at how to publicize commercial vendors.

CommerceNet's Web site, as shown in Figure 11-13, describes its goals as well as its progress. You can also find a list of pointers to the Web sites of its members and subscribers. Like many other business groups, CommerceNet's work moves forward slowly, but its Web site has also been a place where Web-phobic companies can start to look at the methods they will be using in a few years to collect money and promote themselves on the Web.

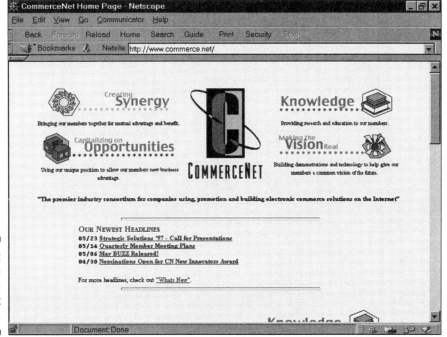

Figure 11-13:
The top
level of the
CommerceNet
Web site.

Chapter 12

The Real World Meets the Web

Some find humor in watching those who've had no interaction with computers discover that parts of the computer world mimic parts of the real world. Many folks who have never laid hands on a keyboard assume that the computer experience is so completely different from ordinary reality that they need a brain transplant to understand what's going on.

Most of us have experienced hearing someone say something along the lines of "And then I saw stuff from a magazine on her computer!" or "It was just like typing on a typewriter!" or "He showed me mail he got from this other person — just like regular mail!" Early computers, circa 1975, were very different from real life. For about the last decade or so, however, computer engineers have been trying to create computers that mimic real life to get you to use them more often.

This chapter shows examples of many Web sites that use aspects of regular life but put a Web-like spin on them. All the sites give information or services that your computerphobic friends can obtain without a computer or a modem but that have some advantages in their electronic form. Of course, mail is the best example of such an electronic experience that also occurs out in the real world, but until e-mail becomes a tight part of the Web, these other sites can better give you an idea of just how normal the Web can be.

Magazines on Your Monitor

The immediacy of words on paper is very important for some people. Picking up a book, feeling it, and so on is part of the entire reading experience. Other people are magazine people: They like design, timeliness, portability, and the consistency from month to month of their favorite titles.

Given how new the online medium is, you can read two distinct types of magazines on the Web: those converted or condensed from their print equivalents and those designed to exist only online. After they get online, magazines that are normally print magazines take on a very different feeling. That feeling is also evident in the online-only magazines, which are designed by people who have been reading print magazines most of their lives and want to create something new.

Boardwatch

```
http://www.boardwatch.com/
```

In the online world, few magazines garner the respect that *Boardwatch* does. *Boardwatch* has been around almost ten years, and for most of its life, it has concentrated on the BBS world, mostly from the *sysop's* (system operator's) perspective. In the past few years, the content of *Boardwatch* has shifted some to include the major online services (which can be viewed as giant BBSs) and the Internet, which many BBS operators want to hook into.

The Web version of *Boardwatch* is pretty much the same as the printed version, with a fancy table of contents. Figure 12-1 shows the main *Boardwatch* home page, from which you can access recent issues or subscribe to the print version. So as not to lose subscriptions to the print version, however, the Web site usually lags at least two issues behind the print version. Even with this delay, *Boardwatch*'s content is well worth exploring, particularly if you want an in-the-trenches view of the online world.

One of the great features of the *Boardwatch* Web site that you can't get in the paper-based magazine is the online map of all the Internet Service Providers (ISPs) in the U.S. Figure 12-2 shows the map. Click on any region and you get a list of all the ISPs near where you clicked.

Figure 12-1:
Boardwatch's
introductory
page.

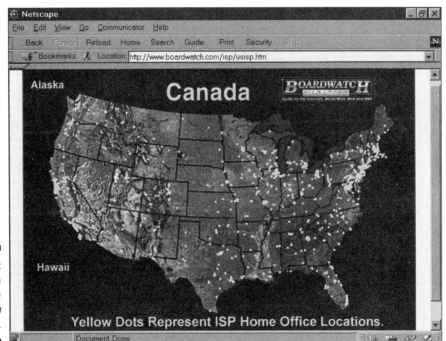

Figure 12-2:
Finding an
ISP on the
Boardwatch
site.

Mercury Center

http://www.sjmercury.com/

The dream of getting your entire daily newspaper online is still just a dream, but a few newspapers are experimenting with putting more and more of their content on the Web. The *San Jose Mercury,* the local paper for Silicon Valley, has its own Web site known as the Mercury Center web. The "front page" of a typical day's paper is as shown in Figure 12-3.

So far, no major paper has gone fully on the Web. For example, Mercury Center carries only some of the major stories from the daily paper, and the coverage is much more tilted to national news and sports than the paper is. In fact, the version of Mercury Center on America Online contains more content than the Web version does, which probably reflects the fact that content providers on the major services such as CompuServe and America Online receive money if users spend time in their areas. Attracting advertisers for Web sites often is hard, too, and advertising rules most newspapers.

Mercury Center is split into a small free area and an expanded for-cost area. The for-cost area is much less expensive for people who subscribe to the paper edition of the newspaper than for other Web users. Again, most publishing companies view the Web as an experimental medium that hasn't proven itself one way or another, and they try all sorts of different things before settling on how to best use it. Some make their sites free, others partly free and partly for cost, and others for subscribers only. The large daily newspapers will probably be behind other publishers in figuring out what they really want to do with the Web.

Personal Finance

If one field seems to encompass an intense addiction to data and timeliness, it's that of personal finance. Given that most people pretend to budget and plan their savings and retirement funds with time frames of five years or more, it's a tad odd that some of these same people read the stock market listings in their papers every day.

Even if you think that you can beat the stock or bond market with day-to-day timing, most shifts on which you can make money take place on an hour-to-hour basis. However, people still want daily (or hourly) stock quotes, company profiles, industry analyses, and so on. Plenty of companies are willing to sell this kind of information, and a few companies have realized how attractive the Web is for this sort of information distribution.

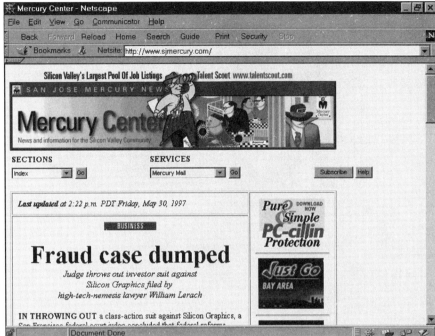

Figure 12-3:
The *San Jose Mercury* Web edition.

NETworth

```
http://networth.quicken.com/
```

The hot item for most individual investors in the past decade has been mutual funds. These funds have grown phenomenally as investors decided (or were convinced) that they could not pick individual stocks well. Mutual funds are advertised everywhere and are fairly easy and inexpensive to buy.

NETworth is a free information service that specializes in mutual fund investing for individuals (but does not exclude other types of investments); their home page is as shown in Figure 12-4. NETworth is supported by advertisers who promote their funds on the service, although NETworth carries information, including daily price listings, for nonadvertisers as well.

Figure 12-4:
The
entrance to
NETworth.

QuoteCom

http://www.quote.com/

If you are not as interested in news and are more inclined to get just stock quotations, market information, and so on, QuoteCom is probably right up your alley. Unlike NETworth, QuoteCom has a monthly service charge. On the other hand, it has many more features that are tailored to those who already know what they are doing, such as the capability for automatic alerts and quotations by e-mail.

For Web users, QuoteCom's Web page, shown in Figure 12-5, is a quick way to get current stock quotes and keep up with other items in your portfolio. For example, QuoteCom can automatically copy for you any news items about the companies in which you've invested. You can also get copies of recent experts' investing advice (however valuable that is) and other types of information.

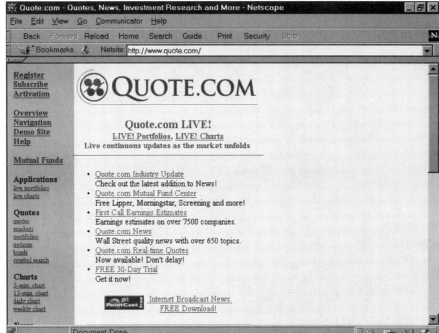

Figure 12-5:
Services
offered by
QuoteCom.

The Finance Virtual Library

`http://www.cob.ohio-state.edu/dept/fin/overview.htm`

People subscribe to magazines such as *Money* so that they can keep up on the latest information about finance. Many resources on the Web, however, have much more timely information and are usually not slanted toward the interests of advertisers. The Finance Virtual Library, as shown in Figure 12-6, contains pointers to many of these Web-based resources.

As you follow links from the Finance Virtual Library, you must be careful to notice where you are before you take any financial advice. (Actually, that's true any time you meander around the Web.) Many Web sites are commercially sponsored, and you may plop into the middle of an advertisement without knowing it. The Finance Virtual Library also points to the many Usenet newsgroups that cover personal finance; remember that some of the postings are also from people who have a vested interest in getting you to buy something that they sell.

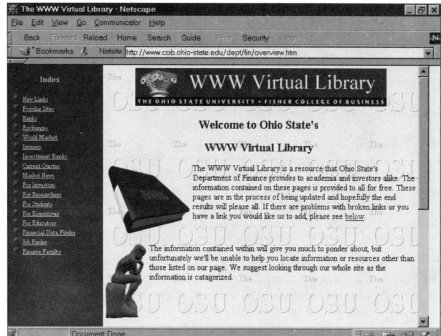

Figure 12-6:
The top
level of the
Finance
Virtual
Library.

K through 12 through the Web

Home computers are widely touted for their capability to help kids in school. Whether or not you believe that computers can be used to enhance education (and plenty of folks don't), you can find plenty of resources for parents and students on the Web — everything from lesson plans to science project ideas to homework helpers.

Many of the K through 12 resources you find on the Web are pretty much the same as you find in magazines and books aimed at kids and parents. The advantage of the Web is that you don't need to go out and search for the magazines and books; the content on the Web is often more up to date, and it's almost always free.

Web66

`http://web66.coled.umn.edu/`

A few Web K through 12 sites are aimed specifically at parents; many more, however, are aimed at teachers. In the current educational funding environment, parents are often helping teachers with everything from buying computer equipment to staffing computer labs in schools. Thus the Web sites aimed at teachers are usually quite appropriate for parents as well.

Web66 is a new service that is meant to help teachers work with the Internet in general and the Web in particular. It is a service of the University of Minnesota College of Education. The folks at Web66 advocate that K through 12 schools set up their own Web sites so that schools can share information with other schools.

The Web66 site, shown in Figure 12-7, contains lots of good information about how to set up a Web server, how to structure pages so that kids can share and get good information, how to deal with appropriate use of computers, and so on. It also includes links to all the known K through 12 schools that have Web pages. Some of these are cute, and some are barely usable, but many look better than some of the commercial Web sites you encounter. Figure 12-8, for example, shows a typical school site.

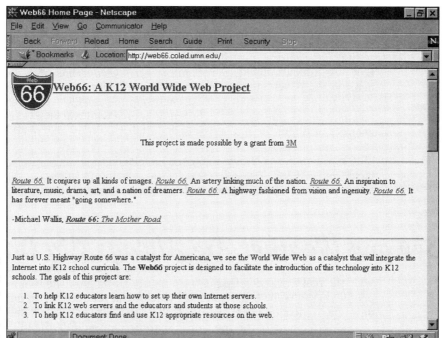

Figure 12-7:
The
entrance to
Web66.

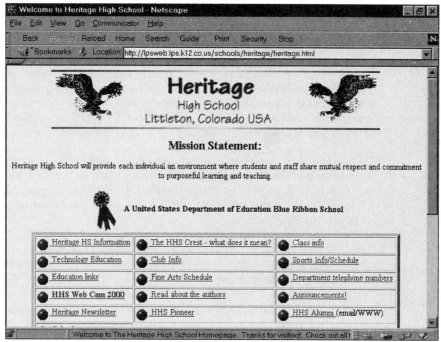

Figure 12-8:
A typical
home page
at a high
school.

ERIC

http://eryx.syr.edu/

ERIC, the *E*ducational *R*esources *I*nformation *C*enter, has been around for many years, providing information to teachers about how to deal with computer and technology issues. Their popular AskERIC service enables teachers to ask questions of a board of people who can give personalized answers or direct them to existing materials that they may need.

ERIC's Web page, as shown in Figure 12-9, leads to all of ERIC's services, including AskERIC. The collection includes pointers to many other Web sites as well as lists of conferences, publishers, and so on.

Sex and Weather Are Always Big Draws

Well, the real world covered in this chapter so far isn't the real world that people on the Web seem to want. If you look at the most searched-for words on some of the search services described in Chapter 7, you'll see somewhat of a pattern. Some of the top words searched for include the following:

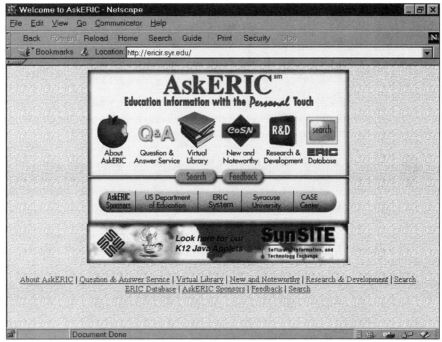

Figure 12-9:
A section of
the Web
page for
ERIC.

✔ Sex

✔ Erotica

✔ Adult

✔ Supermodels

✔ Pornography

✔ Porno

✔ Nude

✔ Penthouse

✔ Playboy

If you look at the number of queries, most search services report that far more than half are for sex-related words and phrases. (One search service reports that the misspellings *eroctica* and *erotiga* sometimes appear in the top 100 words, well ahead of some other words that you may have hoped people were looking for — or could at least spell.)

Penthouse

`http://www.penthousemag.com/`

Yes, *Penthouse*. And, yes, you can download pictures of unclothed women from the magazine at its Web site, which is shown in Figure 12-10. And, yes, the photos are just as (take your pick) realistic/fake, exciting/boring, and marvelous/appalling as the ones you can see in the magazine.

You can, of course, also do more than just look at the pictures. *Penthouse* has put some of the text content on the site as well. Of course, *Penthouse* doesn't place all the content from each issue on the Web; if it did, most readers of *Penthouse* may find the experience of downloading 50K pictures to be a bit different than that of reading the paper magazine. Clearly, *Penthouse* sees the Web site as an advertisement for its series of magazines, and the site helps prove how little it costs for some companies to publish Web sites that bring in good publicity for their commercial projects.

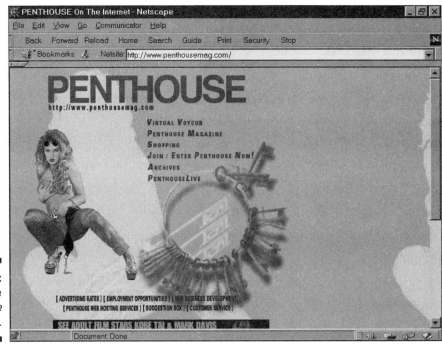

Figure 12-10:
The
Penthouse
Web site.

Blowfish

http://www.blowfish.com/

Companies that sell "adult" books, magazines, and devices have a quandary: They all sell pretty much the same merchandise; they advertise in the same places; and they're almost indistinguishable from each other. This is somewhat similar to the quandary that many insurance agencies, stock brokers, and medical doctors have. A few of these companies have discovered the Web as a place where they can advertise in a way to give themselves a bit more of a personality.

One company that has differentiated itself is Blowfish, whose Web site is as shown in Figure 12-11. Its site is more than just an online catalog of what it sells; it contains health information, political advocacy, and even self-publishing tips. Blowfish's catalog also offers many mini-reviews of what it sells, and the general tone is that Blowfish wants you to know plenty about what you are buying before you actually buy it.

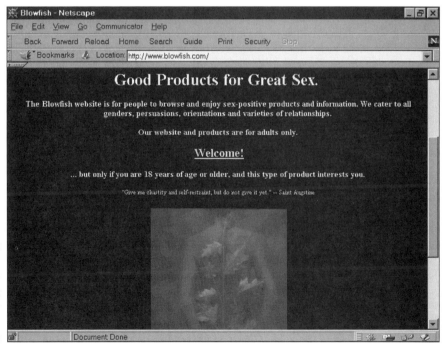

Figure 12-11:
Not your basic adult mail-order store.

alt.sex and non-alt sex

```
news:alt.sex
```

and

```
news:alt.binaries.pictures.erotica
```

The most popular, yet least discussed, Usenet newsgroups almost all begin with `alt.sex`. In those groups, you can read (and post, if you dare) messages about everything and anything having to do with sex. Some of the new groups come and go, but many have been around for years, such as the somewhat central `alt.sex` newsgroup. Other popular newsgroups in the hierarchy discuss various sexual desires, practices, humor, locations, and so on.

Another set of newsgroups, the ones with names that begin with `alt.binaries.pictures.erotica`, contains downloadable erotic pictures. Most of the pictures here are scanned from magazines without the publishers' permission and are clearly copyright violations, but that doesn't keep these groups from being more popular than almost any other groups on Usenet.

The Weather Channel

```
http://www.weather.com/
```

Sexual matters aren't all that people want to read about (and stare at). Some of the busiest Web sites are those that cover the weather — particularly those displaying up-to-date weather maps. Seems like folks can't get enough immediate news about rain, snow, and sun.

As proof of how popular a topic the weather is, look no further than the Weather Channel on most cable systems. People demand it more than many other news channels. The Weather Channel also has a pretty good-looking Web site, too, as shown in Figure 12-12. This is one of the more popular sites for people living in weather-bound parts of the U.S., or who are traveling and want to know the forecast in other parts of the country or the world.

Weather Underground

```
http://www.wunderground.com/
```

Another popular spot for a quick weather map is the Weather Underground, shown in Figure 12-13. This site has local weather for most cities around the U.S., even very small ones. You can, of course, get world weather as well.

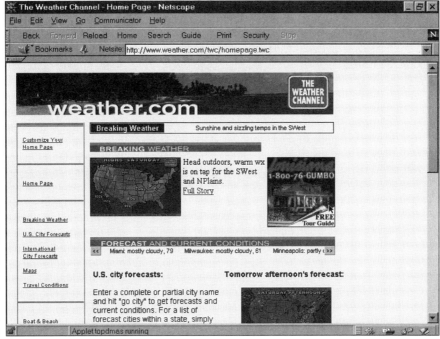

Figure 12-12:
Find out if
it's raining
or blazing
on The
Weather
Channel.

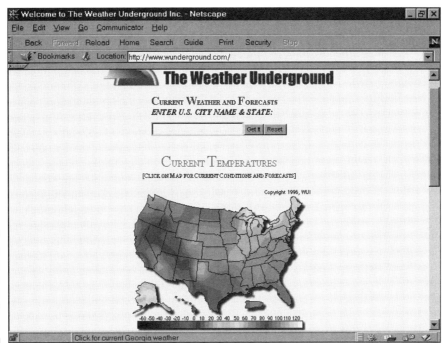

Figure 12-13:
The
Weather
Underground
has lots of
local maps.

The site isn't as flashy as The Weather Channel or some of the other weather sites, but it is much easier to navigate. Because it is friendlier, the Weather Underground is often used by children in classrooms for learning about weather in their city and the nearby vicinity.

Chapter 13

Self-Reference: Computers on Computers

● ●

In This Chapter

▶ Getting help when you need it most

▶ Talking to the big companies

▶ Doing the dweeb thing

▶ Reflecting on the Internet

● ●

*E*verybody on the Web has a computer. This may seem a tad obvious, but it also means that everybody on the Web has something in common: computers. Although not all computers are alike, their commonalty has led to large areas of the Web being devoted to discussions of computers.

Actually, people on the Web certainly have more than computers in common, but people don't seem to want to talk about the nature of the human condition, spirituality, impending death of the body, and so on as much as they want to talk about computers. Maybe next year. . . .

Emergency Road Crews for Your Computer

Every computer user is familiar with becoming dependent on a computer and then having it fail at the wrong moment. For some people, such failures are a nuisance; for others, they are nerve-wracking. If my computer doesn't work, I want help, and I want it *now*.

Of course, you can always refer to the manual or the books (such as this one) that you have bought to help you. However, if none of these printed materials have what you need to fix the problem, you can turn to online resources. The Web is still a bit weak in this area. Commercial services such as CompuServe and America Online have much better forums for getting problems resolved quickly. Some places, however, do exist on the Web where you can search for answers and even ask questions if you cannot find what you need.

Capital PC User Group

http://cpcug.org

Many local user groups have Web pages. Calling the Capital PC User Group a "local user group" is a misnomer, however. The group is an international support organization that just happens to have a location in its name. The CPCUG is one of the biggest computer groups in the world.

The most interesting part of the CPCUG Web site (and for many people, the most interesting part of the CPCUG) is the myriad user groups that are part of CPCUG. Figure 13-1 shows this part of the Web site. Some of these groups consist of just a few people who share a specific interest; other groups have hundreds of members.

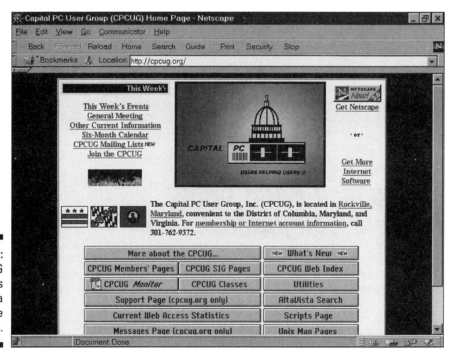

Figure 13-1:
CPCUG user groups cover a wide range of interests.

PC questions

`news:comp.sys.ibm.pc.misc`

Usenet is not a good medium for getting instant response in an emergency, but thousands of people have gotten help from other users in some of the newsgroups. One of the most active groups is `comp.sys.ibm.pc.misc`, the catch-all group for questions about PC systems. Figure 13-2 shows a few of the messages that go by every day.

Because of the often overbroad range of topics at this site, one of the dozens of other Usenet newsgroups that also discuss the PC may be the best place for specific queries. For example, more than a dozen groups have names that start with `comp.sys.ibm.pc`. Similar Usenet newsgroups that relate to parts of the PC, such as `comp.os.ms-windows.misc` (which covers Microsoft Windows) also are available.

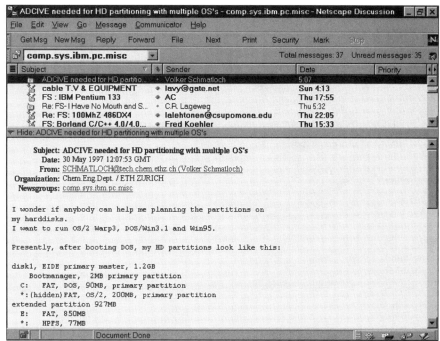

Figure 13-2: This PC newsgroup often gets hundreds of messages per day.

The Well Connected Mac

`http://www.macfaq.com/`

Macintosh users can tap a different set of resources. The Well Connected Mac site, maintained by Elliotte Harold, is a superb collection of all the Web resources about the Macintosh. Figure 13-3 shows the top level of the site.

To many people, the Macintosh community seems more tightly knit than the PC community, and this Web site has been able to grow well based on suggestions from people visiting it. The list of Usenet newsgroups is particularly good because it contains a good introduction to the differences between various types of newsgroups.

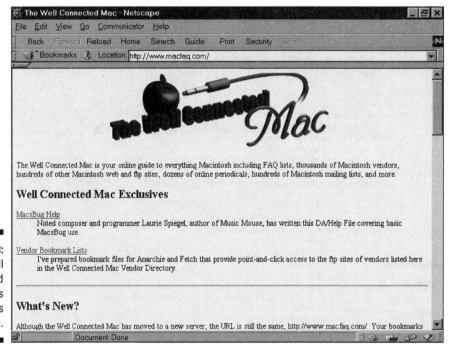

Figure 13-3:
The Well Connected Mac covers all things Macintosh.

Support in Your Court

Calling the tech-support department of most companies is an exercise in frustration. Wait on hold for, typically, ten minutes. Pray that the hold music they have isn't horrible. Get used to the horrible music or, worse, a constant stream of advertising for the product that isn't working.

A few companies have started to put much of their product-support information on the Web in hope of keeping customers off the phone and happy. Of course, lots of questions that can be answered by humans at the company can't be answered by the material at the Web site. On the other hand, the Web site is free, it's available after hours and on weekends (which is when products seem to break, isn't it?), and it has no hold music.

If you are a company, putting up your support database on the Web isn't really technical support; it's more like *presupport*. Presupport is a good way to reduce the number of people who need to call you, and it enables you to keep your customers happy for a very small price. The sites shown here are for the largest manufacturers, although dozens of other smaller companies also have presupport sites on the Web.

Microsoft

```
http://www.microsoft.com/
```

They're big. They're bold. They own the market. And, in a nice twist, they have one of the best tech-support Web sites you can find anywhere. Even before it became The Monopoly that Ate the Software Industry, Microsoft published its database of tech support information on many services such as CompuServe. Now that database and gigabytes of support information are available for free on the Web. Figure 13-4 shows part of the Microsoft Web site.

Microsoft's Web site mixes technical support with sales, marketing, and news. The tech support part of the Web site is under its Knowledge base section, which is a set of searchable databases. The searches return information on bugs, common problems, "workarounds," and so on. Of course, the material is written by Microsoft, so don't expect the reports of bugs to be at all apologetic.

Microsoft also maintains a huge collection of files that you can download from its Web site. These files are updated device drivers, sample code for its programming packages, fixes for some software, and so on. Again, all these are free; and for most people, finding these files is easier than waiting on the phone to Microsoft.

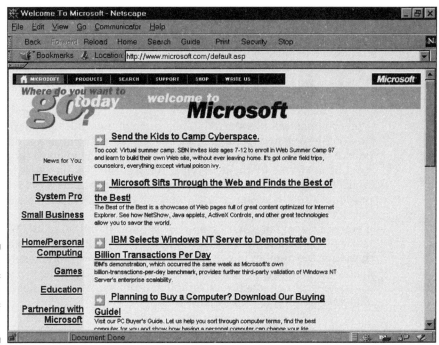

Figure 13-4:
A portion of
the wide
world of
Microsoft.

Apple

```
http://www.info.apple.com/
```

Macintosh users also have a very good Web resource for them: the Apple
Web site. Like the Microsoft site, the Apple site offers a plethora of software,
fixes, and so on. Figure 13-5 shows the top level of the Apple/ Web site.

Like many other companies, Apple is somewhat of a bureaucracy, and many
divisions have overlapping responsibilities. Thus finding the best place on
the Apple Web server to look for answers to specific questions is not always
easy. On the other hand, Apple is very familiar with presenting information
in a variety of fashions, so you can often find what you're looking for in more
than one place.

Figure 13-5:
Apple's
Web site.

Novell

http://www.novell.com/

If you work on a LAN that operates using Novell's Netware or Internetware products, you're familiar with the problems that a network crash can bring. And because so many manufacturers sell software that works on Netware, finding conflicts and problems is almost easy. Novell's Web site, as shown in Figure 13-6, can be an answer to many of your problems.

Because network problems are notoriously hard to track down, Novell has worked hard to make the technical support database easy to search. People who support Netware networks report that they have found incredible nuggets of information looking through the support database, and regular users should feel reasonably at home as well.

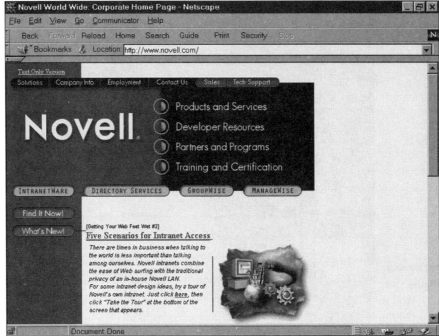

Figure 13-6:
Novell's
support
Web page.

Dweeb Talk

If you like computers, you probably like to talk to other people who like computers. For the first decade, the Internet consisted of almost nothing other than people talking to each other about computers or sending each other files that related to (you guessed it) computers.

Like the rest of the Internet, the Web is full of computer talk. Some of the talk is idle chatter, but the best of it is very helpful to people who rely on their computers for their work or, um, their pleasure. This section shows a few places that you may find interesting if you want to know just what people who talk computers talk *about*.

Seidman's Online Insider

```
http://www.clark.net/pub/robert/
```

Because the growth of the online world has been so quick, many print magazines try to make sense of BBSs, major services, and the Internet. If you are already using an online service or the Internet, however, these magazines are mostly full of things that you either already know or have no interest in. Another problem with monthly magazines about the online world is that they are out of date by the time you get them in your hands.

Seidman's Online Insider is a free, weekly electronic magazine that you can get sent to you through e-mail. The magazine is written by Robert Seidman, who has a very eclectic view of the online world. It covers all the major services as well as the Internet. Figure 13-7 shows the home page for *Seidman's Online Insider,* where you can also look at back issues and find subscription information.

The *Seidman's Online Insider* page also has pointers to the home pages for the major services such as CompuServe, America Online, and Prodigy. Keeping in the spirit of the Web, *Seidman's Online Insider* also provides pointers to the home pages of the magazines that *Seidman's Online Insider* competes with.

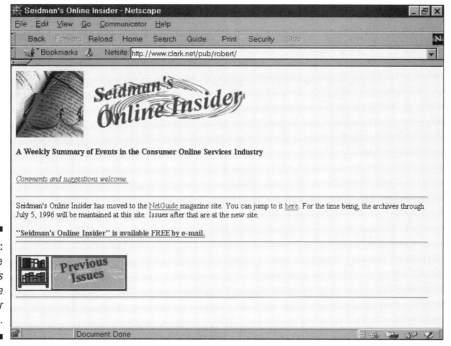

Figure 13-7:
The
Seidman's
Online
Insider
home page.

HotWired

```
http://www.hotwired.com/
```

If you crossed *People* magazine with *Rolling Stone* with *BYTE* and put it online, you'd get *HotWired,* the online sister to the oh-so-hip *Wired* magazine. *HotWired,* shown in Figure 13-8, is free, but you must use a Web form to subscribe to it. This means that you can read *HotWired* only if you have a Web browser that supports forms and security.

The content on *HotWired* is all over the map. Different areas of *HotWired* include the following:

✔ Large multimedia files, such as music and pictures.

✔ Computer industry news overlaid with life-style coverage.

✔ Technical posturing about the future of the Internet.

✔ Advertising.

✔ Discussion about the articles.

✔ Interactive entertainment.

The feeling on *HotWired* is cutting edge (possibly *over* the cutting edge), immediate, and trendy. For example, Figure 13-9 shows another, typically overstimulating page on HotWired.

If that's what you like, *HotWired* is certainly an interesting Web site to visit over and over.

Perl

```
http://www.perl.org/
```

Programming languages are not everyone's cup of tea. People who don't use computers much often look at programming languages as if those languages were forms of black magic that they could never learn. Even if you're a regular computer user, you may feel more than a bit of trepidation if you are asked to learn a programming language such as C or Basic. I'm quite fond of Perl, enough so that I have written *Perl 5 For Dummies*. It's a great starting point for learning Perl, in my not-so-humble opinion.

Perl is a relatively new programming language that has many features that make it particularly attractive to people writing quick-and-dirty programs that can process text. Learning Perl is fairly easy: Perl is between Basic and C in difficulty. After you learn even a bit of Perl, however, using it is a breeze.

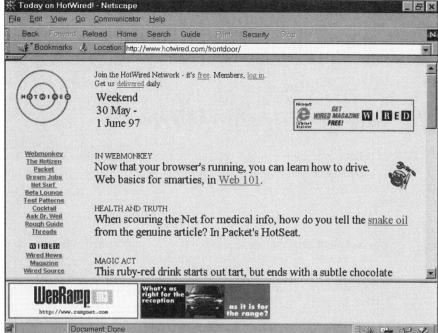

Figure 13-8:
The starting
page for
HotWired
subscribers.

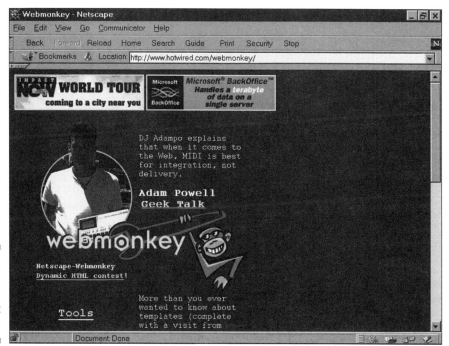

Figure 13-9:
Design
gone mad
at
HotWired.

Best of all, Perl is completely free. Most Perl programmers use it on UNIX systems, but versions for MS-DOS, Windows NT, and the Macintosh also are available. Figure 13-10 shows one of the best sites, which contains lots of pointers to other Perl resources. Perl has garnered a near-fanatic following of users, and a great deal of sample source code is available.

The Internet in the Mirror

What could be more self-referential than using computers to talk about computers? Using computers on the Internet to talk about computers on the Internet! Does life get any better?

Actually, the Internet can evolve in no better way than through online discussions about what is happening, what people want, and so on. For example, Usenet news was started as an experiment. As the experiment succeeded, Usenet also became the medium for discussion about itself. Almost every new Internet service has come out of heavy discussion, followed by experimentation, followed by revision based on feedback.

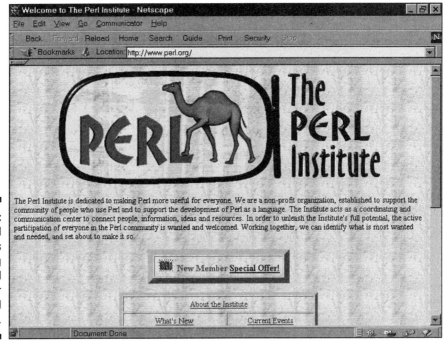

Figure 13-10:
The Perl
Institute is
the leading
professional
group for
Perl
programmers.

IETF

http://www.ietf.org/

The main group who coordinates the standards on the Internet is the *IETF* (*I*nternet *E*ngineering *T*ask *F*orce). The IETF is a voluntary group that meets only three times per year. Almost all the work of the IETF is done through the mailing lists of its Working Groups.

Figure 13-11 shows the IETF's home page. It leads to Working Group lists, descriptions of upcoming meetings, and the archives of documents and standards called *RFCs* (*R*equests *F*or *C*omments). RFCs are the written understanding of the underpinnings of the Internet. They have no force of law, but everyone on the Internet pretty much agrees to try to abide by them.

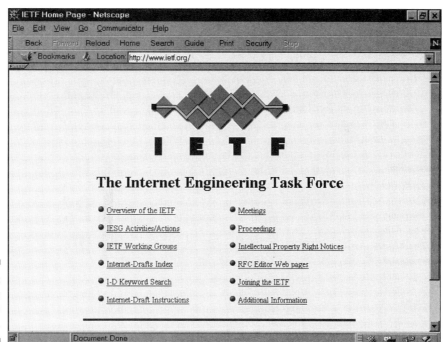

Figure 13-11: Here is the gateway to the IETF.

If you're interested in the human side of the IETF, you should look at some of the Working Groups. Figure 13-12 shows the Working Group area of the IETF server. Each Working Group has its own mailing list, and many of the Working Groups have Web sites that have collected all the old mail from the mailing lists. The Working Groups are also where RFCs originate.

Because people don't need to do anything to join the IETF other than participate, the number of people in the IETF is unknown. On the other hand, IETF's loose structure has served the Internet and the Web well so far, and there is no need to change it now.

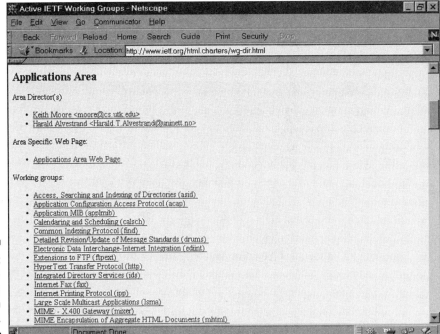

Figure 13-12:
Some of the
Working
Groups in
the IETF.

Usenet Info Center

http://sunsite.unc.edu/usenet-i/

Usenet has become so large and diffuse that finding out what's new and what's happening in the Usenet world is hard. Kevin Atkinson has put together an excellent Web page, shown in Figure 13-13, that pulls together a wide range of resources about Usenet, such as a searchable list of all newsgroups.

The Center's list of FAQs (documents with answers to frequently asked questions) concerning Usenet is particularly useful. If you are new to Usenet or want to go a few levels farther into it than you already are, these FAQs are excellent places to start. Also check out the descriptions of the various Usenet news readers. If you are a Netscape user, you'll find the description of some of the older news readers particularly humorous, given their arcane syntax and rules.

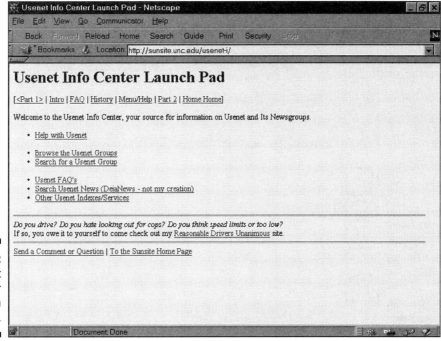

Figure 13-13:
The Usenet Info Center Launch Pad.

Security reference index

`http://www.telstra.com.au/info/security.html`

The Internet is not all fun and games. You've probably heard about some of the more notorious break-ins that have happened on the Internet, but you probably haven't heard about the hundreds of others that happen all the time. Security is a big issue for administrators and users everywhere on the Internet.

Telcom Australia has put together an excellent Web page that covers almost every aspect of security on the Internet. The site, shown in Figure 13-14, actually covers more than just the Internet; many of the pointers lead to LAN security discussions as well. For an overview of what's being discussed and done about security on the Internet, however, this is an excellent place to start.

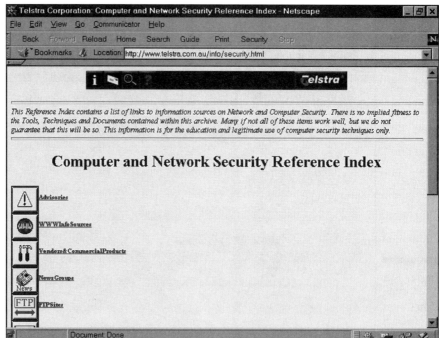

Figure 13-14: Telcom Australia's security Web site.

Consummate Winsock Apps List

`http://cws.iworld.com/`

If you use a Windows system and TCP/IP, you are probably aware of the myriad choices you must make. First, you need to choose a Windows TCP/IP driver, commonly called *Winsock,* of which there are more than a dozen. Then you must choose all the TCP/IP applications, such as your Web browser. The choices go on and on. Fortunately, a single Web site collects information on all the known Winsock drivers and applications. The Consummate Winsock Apps List, shown in Figure 13-15, is a godsend for system administrators and end users who just want to know what is available. The pages have links to the manufacturers or, in the case of freeware or shareware, links to the programs themselves. Lists of helper programs, such as HTML editors, also are available.

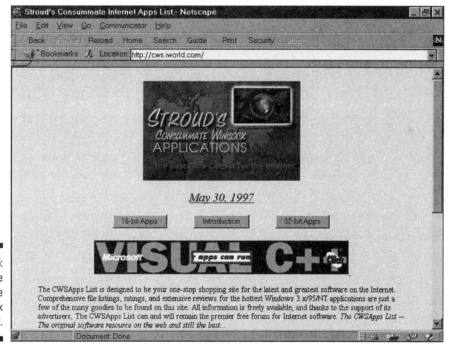

Figure 13-15:
The
Consummate
Winsock
Apps List.

Chapter 14

Your Government: At Work?

*A*lmost everyone has a love/hate relationship with the government. We love it when it provides services we want and need; we hate it when it charges us for those services or charges us for services that we don't want or need. As Thoreau put it, "Government is at best but an expedient; but most governments are usually, and all governments are sometimes, inexpedient."

More and more governments are using the Web in the same way as many companies are. These governments and their agencies use it as an advertising medium, a way of giving out information, and a method for keeping their clients (that's us, the citizens) happy. People have responded by setting up Web sites that are based around either supporting current laws or changing them, much like normal political activities are organized.

The Feds Are Ahead

In the U.S., few people think of the federal government as being at the forefront of communications technology. In fact, few people believe that they can communicate at all with their elected representatives or most parts of the federal bureaucracy, such as the IRS or the Social Security Administration. Many federal agencies, however, have recently latched onto the Web as a way to tell the online world about themselves.

The U.S. federal government has zillions of departments, many of which are still stuck in the paper era. Now that funding cutbacks are becoming more common, many of these departments are getting on the Web as a way to protect their turf, letting the taxpayers know what the agencies actually do with their tax dollars.

U.S. House of Representatives

http://www.house.gov/

The most direct way to affect federal legislation is by contacting members of Congress. Most newspapers list the addresses of all the local congress-people, but few citizens ever write to their representatives about the issues that are important to them. The small but vocal minority then gets the most say with the representatives.

Congress has taken steps to reverse this trend by making more information about itself available free on the Web. Figure 14-1 shows the House Congressional Web site, a central repository of information on such things as the name of every representative, what committees they serve on, and the internal congressional bureaucracy. Don't expect to find a lot of creativity here, but at least the information is up to date.

Federal legislation

http://thomas.loc.gov/

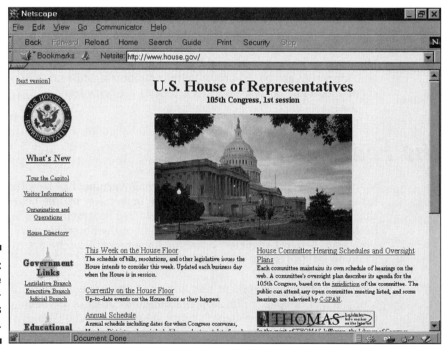

Figure 14-1:
The House
of Repre-
sentatives
Web site.

If you are more concerned about legislation that is moving through Congress than the people moving it, the THOMAS system run by the Library of Congress is probably for you. THOMAS, as shown in Figure 14-2, tracks all laws as they are amended and passed through the two houses. (The name "THOMAS" always appears in all capital letters even though it doesn't stand for anything; the system is, in fact, named for Thomas Jefferson, a strong believer in open public debate.)

The Library of Congress, which is traditionally thought of as the place where you send books to copyright them, has taken a much more activist role in enabling people to find legislation in which they are interested. The search feature of THOMAS enables you to access the text of legislation by searching for the bill number or words that appear anywhere in the bill. You can also quickly find out where in the congressional process the bill is, who has sponsored it, and so on.

FedWorld

```
http://www.fedworld.gov/
```

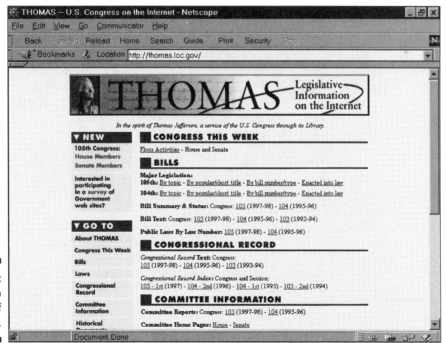

Figure 14-2:
The top level of THOMAS.

Congress isn't the only one getting into the Web. Many agencies of the Administration have Web sites. FedWorld, shown in Figure 14-3, is the best central spot to look first if you want to see which part of the Administrative branch is doing what on the Web. FedWorld usually has the most up-to-date pointers of any Web site.

The main part of FedWorld is a list of topics. Under each topic is a list of all the federal Web sites that relate to the topic. For example, Figure 14-4 shows a way to search for federal government jobs. A few of the topics have dozens of pointers, although many have only one or two. Many of the pointers are to telnet sites, which are much harder to use than HTTP, Gopher, or FTP sites.

National Science Foundation

```
http://www.nsf.gov/
```

The National Science Foundation (NSF) has always been on the forefront of Internet use. For many years, the NSF paid for many of the main Internet links so that scientists around the country could pass data quickly, thereby helping their research. Although the NSF is now much less involved with the Internet itself, it is still very active in sponsoring scientific research.

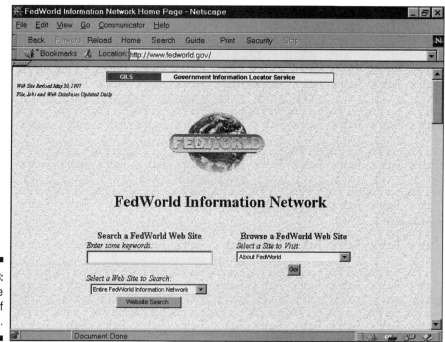

Figure 14-3:
The beginning of FedWorld.

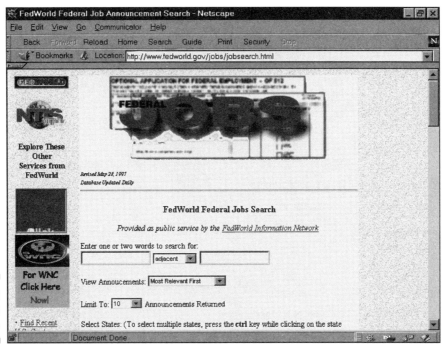

Figure 14-4:
Searching
for a job.

The NSF's Web site, shown in Figure 14-5, is one of the best you can find in the U.S. government. Part of this, of course, has to do with NSF's Internet legacy, but another part has to do with making sure that NSF projects continue to get funded. The NSF does an excellent job of promoting its funded projects, particularly the expensive ones, to reduce the chance that they will lose congressional funding.

U.K. Government Information Service

http://www.open.gov.uk/

The U.S. federal government isn't the only national government on the Web. Many European countries, as well as the European Union itself, are starting to publish Web sites for pretty much the same reasons as those of the American government.

Figure 14-6, for example, shows the central Web site for the federal bureaucracy in England. A surprising number of federal agencies there have set up their own Web sites, many of which are better designed and have more information than their American counterparts. This site also has pointers to federally supported agencies such as museums and research labs.

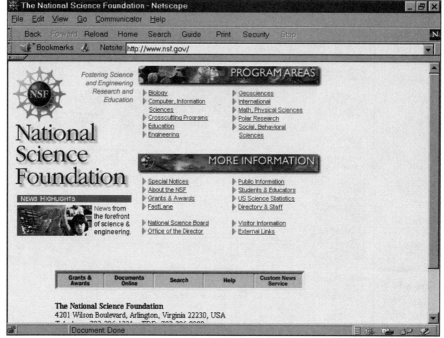

Figure 14-5:
The central
Web site for
the National
Science
Foundation.

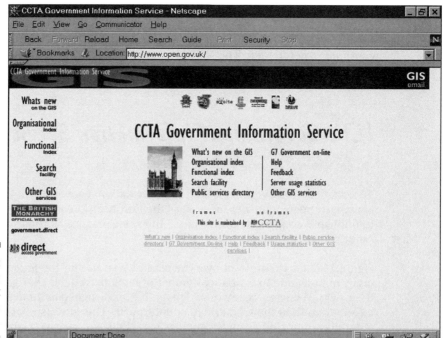

Figure 14-6:
Finding
government
information
in the U.K.

State and Local Folk

If you move down from the federal level, you find many fewer Web sites. A handful of states have systems, some of them as extensive as FedWorld, but most states with a Web presence have only one or two experimental pages that don't say much other than "Come visit our state; we need the tourism."

On the other hand, state bureaucracies have the same need for advertising and information distribution that federal bureaucracies do. In fact, with the current trend in Washington toward canceling federal programs and giving the money to the states, many state agencies will probably start promoting themselves more so that people within their states know more about them.

California departments

```
http://www.ca.gov/
```

California has one of the more online governments. With so many computer activists living in the state, the legislature and executive branches have had little choice but to put much of its most important information online. Figure 14-7, for example, shows the list of state departments that have Web servers.

In many ways, the California government is trying to make the Web part of its daily affairs. Election results are now reported on the Web as they appear on election night, and the state legislature has the text of many of its bills available online.

North Carolina

```
http://www.sips.state.nc.us/
```

Other states also have Web sites that contain a great deal of public information. North Carolina, another computerphilic community, has a very complete Web site, as shown in Figure 14-8.

The North Carolina server is a good example of how state Web sites often grow from disconnected servers into a central site. Many of the locations listed in Figure 14-8 are very rudimentary Gopher servers that probably existed for a few years unconnected to the central hub. A single central agency can help bring all these together into one Web page and still let each of the agencies run their own servers and manage the information on them. This setup differs from many company's Web sites, in which the entire server is run by one person, usually a system administrator or other technical person.

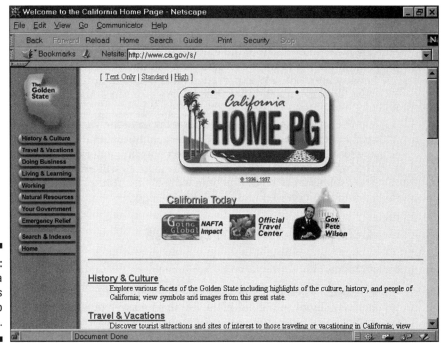

Figure 14-7:
California
agencies
with Web
sites.

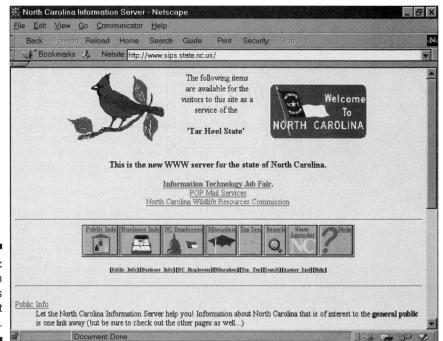

Figure 14-8:
North
Carolina's
government
site.

Change That Law: Advocates Get the Word Out

You may have heard how the power of the Internet has helped prevent bad laws from being passed. For example, a legislator introduces a bill with some extreme changes; people on the Internet hear about it; a flurry of e-mail and postings to various Usenet newsgroups results; and many people then get in touch with their legislators, who put the kibosh on the bill. The press then notes how the Internet has changed things.

Unfortunately, this scenario is still relatively uncommon and usually has little to do with the Web because most of this type of action occurs in mailing lists and Usenet newsgroups, which are usually not available to people who aren't already participating. Face it: Hundreds of bad laws are passed every year, and only a handful get the kind of publicity described here.

The Web is quite useful for groups of people who want to make long-term political statements and to track the laws that affect them. Oddly, it is not yet being used much for these purposes, but that will probably change as the Web grows in the next few years.

NRA and NOW

```
http://www.nra.org/
```

and

```
http://www.now.org/
```

The National Rifle Association, commonly called the NRA, was one of the first major political groups to put up a Web server. This site, as shown in Figure 14-9, looks pretty much like what you would expect. It includes information about current legislation, how to join, group benefits, and so on. Figure 14-10 shows a similar kind of site, this one for the National Organization for Women, better known as NOW.

In many ways, the NRA and NOW Web sites look like the Web sites for a company selling products. Political groups have products just as commercial organizations have products. They want you to stay interested, to feel like you want to keep in contact with them, to give you a sense of urgency about their products, and so on.

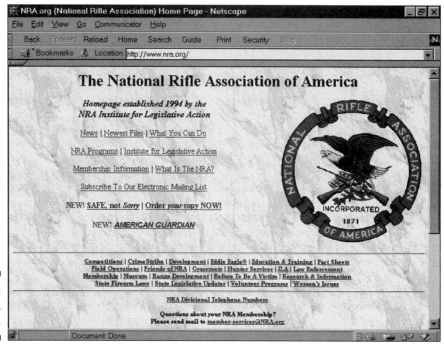

Figure 14-9:
The NRA
Web site.

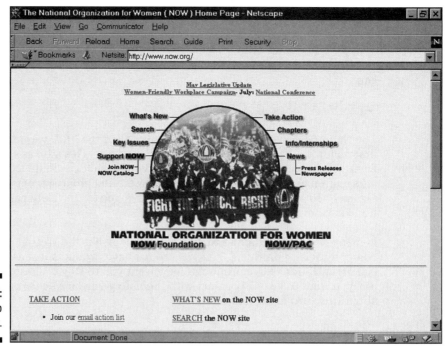

Figure 14-10:
NOW's Web
site.

Tibet liberation

```
http://www.manymedia.com/tibet/
```

To many people, the NRA is part of the right wing of a "left-versus-right" debate, and NOW is part of the left wing. These people try to shoehorn local and national issues into the Republican/Democratic membership division or the liberal/conservative conceptual division. Issues such as social welfare, national defense, governmental power, and so on all get split up along these imaginary lines.

Many political groups and struggles lie pretty much outside of the left/right spectrum. For example, millions of people from all political persuasions have been trying to pressure China into allowing Tibet to exist as an independent country ever since China invaded Tibet in 1950. Figure 14-11 shows the home page for a group that is trying to keep the debate about Tibet alive.

Computer Professionals for Social Responsibility

```
http://www.cpsr.org/home/
```

Figure 14-11:
The Free
Tibet page.

Many other political groups also fit outside the left/right spectrum. Some groups, such as Computer Professionals for Social Responsibility (CPSR), are mostly concerned with educating people about their current rights so that those rights are not taken away. Figure 14-12 shows the CPSR Web site.

Like many political groups, CPSR's interests revolve around more than a single issue. For example, CPSR is using the Web to publicize privacy issues that the growth of the Internet affects. The Web site also has pointers to other computer-affiliated political groups.

Advocacy in the Usenet realm

```
news:alt.activism
```

and

```
news:alt.politics.media
```

Usenet is still the most interactive part of the Web, and people tend to get interactive when they are discussing the things near and dear to their politics. Many Usenet newsgroups have a fair amount of political content to them. One of the most active is appropriately called `alt.activism`. A similar group is `misc.activism.progressive`.

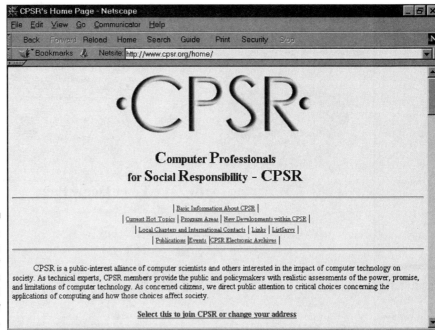

Figure 14-12: The Computer Professionals for Social Responsibility Web site.

Another group of politically oriented newsgroups have names that start with `alt.politics`. These groups cover the gamut of political discussion (and diatribe). Most of the discussions are about U.S. politics, but some groups are global or at least national outside the U.S. Figure 14-13, for example, shows a bit of the `alt.politics.media` discussion.

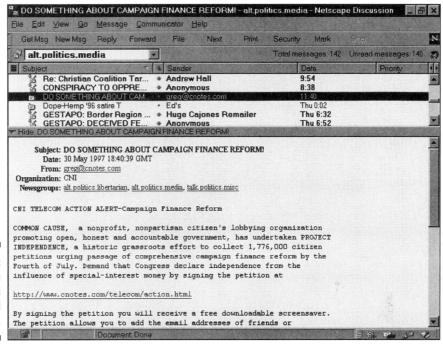

Figure 14-13: Views from all across the political spectrum.

Part IV
Your Name in Lights

The 5th Wave   By Rich Tennant

"What do you mean you're updating our Web Homepage?"

In this part . . .

*I*f you're one of those people who isn't content to just sit back and read what's on the Web, these chapters are for you. They explain how you, too, can publish your own Web pages, with guidelines on exactly how to do it as well as a solid grounding in the technical stuff you need to know. Beyond all that, they give you advice on how to publish content that is not only attractive, but compelling.

Chapter 15

So You Want to Be a Producer

In This Chapter

▶ Deciding to publish on the Web

▶ Exploring individual and business publishing on the Web

▶ Finding a Web provider

*U*p to this point, you have pretty much been reading about other people's content. You have seen dozens of pictures of places on the Web that have interesting things on them: fascinating ideas, humorous snippets, and so on. If you're like most people, you have probably said, "Hey, I can do that!" Of course you can.

As discussed way back in Chapter 2, to browse around the Web, you need a Web client; and to put your content on the Web, you need a Web server. That last part isn't completely true: You must have *access* to someone who has a Web server. That is, each site on the Web needs to have a server, but each user at the site needs only to be linked into the site's content to have something published.

This chapter and the following three chapters cover how you can become a Web publisher. Putting your content on the Web is similar to putting your content on paper. In the print world, publishers range from people who photocopy a few pages to massive publishing houses. On the Web, you may publish a hundred words, or you may create a huge site consisting of thousands of pages. No matter how much or little you add, you need the same technology, the same design choices, and the same talent for figuring out what to say and how to say it.

Home Sweet Home Pages

Don't be put off by the highfalutin' sound of the word *publishing*. At its simplest, putting content on the Web is no more like publishing than typing up a page of some of your thoughts, printing a dozen copies, and sending them to a bunch of friends is like publishing. Publishing can be simple, cheap, and low-key.

If you have explored some of the sites shown so far, particularly those mentioned in Chapter 10, you've probably come across some areas that seemed incredibly minor, leaving you to wonder why someone bothered to create those pages. On the other hand, you've probably also come across other areas that seem a bit rough but quirky in a way that *you* like, but that you know most other people may not like.

In other words, Web pages can be like the people who create them. If you're lucky, you can publish Web pages that are a great reflection of yourself. Millions of people wish that they could write a book with a title such as *The Way Things Ought to Be* (that is, the codex of their views on life, the universe, and everything). Unfortunately, that title has already been used by Rush Limbaugh, but you get the picture. Every year, almost every book publisher receives proposals (or entire manuscripts) that consist of little more than "I think this way, and I want to tell the world about it."

Not everyone can write a full book about his thoughts and views. Maybe you hate writing, but you really want to communicate one special idea, and you can summarize this special idea on one or two pages. Or you want some songs that you wrote to be published, but you think that only three or four are worth sharing. Or you are a painter, but you have only a dozen or so paintings that you think the whole world deserves to see.

Imagine how many trees would be killed in an effort to publish one- or two-page books, three or four songs, or a dozen or so paintings. Imagine how many of these books would remain unsold because buyers would be forced to choose among too many books. (Today, many books already lose money for their publishers.)

Think about the gas used to truck the books from the publisher to the bookstore, back to the publisher, and finally to the grave. Look at all the time lost at the publishers and at the bookstores. If everyone thought their ideas should be turned into books, imagine how much greater the waste would be.

Now look at the Web.

Personal Webtop Publishing

The cost of publishing content on the Web is essentially $0. No paper is involved, and no transportation costs are charged. You can create the content on your PC and spend a few cents uploading it to your Internet provider; after that, the electrons just float around the Internet. If your intent is simply to have your words available to the world, or at least the part of the world that has a Web account, the solution is incredibly simple: create Web content.

Of course, creating Web content is different from getting your book published and making it available in bookstores. In most parts of the world, many more people have access to bookstores than have access to the Web. But face it: How many people buy books that aren't best-sellers or that aren't on topics that they are particularly interested in? The next time you're in a bookstore, look at the shelves of novels and think about how many of them no one will buy.

Publishing on the Web is quite different from publishing books in that the Web's possible audience is smaller. (A few tens of millions can access the Web, while hundreds of millions or billions of people can read books.) On the other hand, today's typical Web users are much more curious than today's typical book buyers. Web users poke around more. They look into places that may lead them nowhere on the off chance that something interesting may pop up. Of course, this is true for some book buyers, but not in the same proportion as Web users.

The teeny cost of gigantic storage

The economics of publishing on the Web are really amazing. Suppose that you've written what you think is a terribly interesting book, but you haven't found a publisher for it. You decide to put it out on the Web for free, forgoing the chance to get rich in exchange for the chance to be appreciated (and maybe courted for your next novel).

Typical novels run from around 80,000 to 100,000 words, which translates roughly to 500 kilobytes (half a megabyte) of hard disk space. Today, the folks running Web sites can buy hard disks for roughly $100 to $200 per gigabyte, meaning that the space your novel takes up on the hard disk costs them about 5 cents. (If the Web site is smart enough to store your story in compressed format, squeezed into a teensier disk space, we're talking a penny or two.) And the cost of disk storage goes down every year.

Of course, not everyone is a writer. You may be an artist, and pictures certainly take up more disk space than words. Moderate-sized photos, however, usually take less than 1 megabyte each, and a good collection of photos rarely runs to more than 100 megabytes, which is about $20. If you're a musician, full stereo, CD-quality music takes up about 10 megabytes per minute, so a few songs for your sampler shouldn't run more than the same 100 megabytes.

Compared then to standard publishing, storage on a Web site isn't a significant expense. In fact, it is almost trivial relative to just the beginning costs of publishing a book or a CD. Of course, storage isn't the only cost for Web sites, but it is often one of the major costs that book and CD publishers must deal with.

Communications cost more than storage

The communications cost for an Internet provider is usually quite low. Of course, the cost depends on the location of the Internet provider, the provider's overhead, the number of other people like you who want to publish Web pages, and so on. For most Web providers, however, the communications cost is less than $1,000 per month, and for many, this cost is less than $250 per month.

At first, communications cost may seem like the biggest part of the costs of being a Web provider: If a Web provider has only ten people who are publishing on its service, it must charge each of them $25 to $100 per month just to cover its communications cost. Very few companies, however, are just Web providers; they are also general Internet providers, which enables them to spread the communications cost over a much larger number of people.

Administration can be cheap or expensive

One of the hardest things for Web providers to predict is the cost of getting you, the novice, on the Web. If you read this and the following three chapters, you can learn almost everything you need to know about putting your information on the Web in a well-formatted manner. Your Web provider won't need to help you much at all.

On the other hand, if you tried to publish your content right now without having read these chapters, you'd probably have a zillion questions; and the chances are good that you'd take up a great deal of the Web manager's time. Web providers need to factor the amount of hand-holding you may need into the cost of the service; and hand-holding time is usually quite difficult to predict, so providers often guess high.

If you aren't actually changing any of your Web content, don't pay money to the Web providers that charge you a monthly fee for maintaining your Web content unless the rate is very low — for example, about $5 per month (although even that is somewhat high). To maintain a static Web site takes no effort. You should be charged a monthly fee only for those months in which you add or change your content — and even then the fee shouldn't be very high.

You may get it for free

As a potential content provider, you probably want to go with a Web provider that has many, many people already using its service so that the communications cost to you is low. If you read and absorb the next few chapters, you also want to choose a Web provider that won't charge you much for administration and training because you'll already be better trained than most beginners. So how do you find such a Web provider?

Many Internet providers let you publish on the Web for free as long as you have an account with them and as long as you don't bug them for too much help in your Web publishing. Today, hundreds of providers offer this kind of arrangement; soon, thousands will.

This arrangement makes a fair amount of sense. An Internet service provider already pays the communications cost and probably has loads of disk space just sitting around. The Internet service provider may limit the amount of space you can take up on the disk to 5 or 10 megabytes, but you're unlikely to fill that up with text, and the provider probably will let you run over the maximum for a small amount of money.

Web providers can be found in many ways. (Any list we put in this book would be out of date before you got a chance to read it.) You should also ask your own Internet provider if they offer Web services.

Business Publishing on the Web

As you have seen from the many HotSpots throughout this book, the Web is much more than a personal publishing medium. Companies big and small have been posting Web pages for a few years, and more are rushing to the Web all the time. You may even be reading this book because your company wants to be part of the stampede.

Putting a company's advertising or content on the Web is quite different from publishing an individual's content. Individual publishing usually aims at letting anyone look at an individual's work for free; businesses trying to sell their content clearly want to be paid somehow, so they need to induce Web users to buy their product. And individuals usually don't advertise on the Web as companies do.

The differences between Web pages for companies and Web pages for individuals often boil down to the following three areas:

- ✔ Style and design
- ✔ Payment
- ✔ Promotion

That professional look

A business is much more likely than an individual to spend time, and possibly money, getting the look of its Web content just right. Most companies, even small ones, pay designers and artists to create advertising for them. Designers and artists have a good understanding about what does work and what doesn't work in ads, and they know how to avoid the cheesy look of some ads you see in places such as the telephone yellow pages.

For a business with lots of competition, the particular "look" that business presents to the world can be everything. For individuals who are merely publishing their writing or some art they have created, the presentation isn't nearly as important because their competition all looks pretty much the same.

Think for a moment about how you would select an insurance salesperson by looking in the yellow pages. A badly designed ad, a blurry photo, or awkward wording in the listing can easily make you pass over one salesperson's listing in favor of any of the other zillion listings.

Selling it

The Web is promoted as the future of retailing, enabling people sitting in their homes in front of their PCs to buy things they see on-screen. Actually, the home shopping cable channels use the same scenario, and guess which medium has the larger market? Face it: For most people, sitting in front of a TV is a great deal more fun than sitting in front of a computer.

This is not to say that you can't make money selling products on the Web. In our consumer culture, you can sell products almost anywhere. The Web has the advantage over most other mediums in that the user can buy something without leaving the medium (by using Web forms illustrated in many earlier chapters). Even TV home shopping channels force you to pick up the phone to place an order; on the Web, you're only a click away from ordering.

Businesses that want to achieve direct sales through the Web must make on-line ordering as easy as possible for people, or else shoppers will continue to shop the old, familiar ways — such as by calling toll-free numbers. Furthermore, because most people don't enjoy doing too many new things, businesses must make ordering on the Web easier — or at least more fun — than ordering on the telephone.

So far, they haven't done this. Ordering items on the Web is just getting out of the novelty stage. Ordering items by using a Web form is usually slower and more confusing than to simply pick up the phone and call a toll-free number and speak with a human. The Web is fine for giving things away, and a great deal of effort is being put into using it as a sales tool, but it doesn't work well quite yet for bringing in the sales.

Getting people in the front door

Even if you are trying only to advertise on the Web, not to sell directly to consumers, you still want your Web area to be seen by as many people as possible. Advertising is notorious for *not* being seen. If you keep your finger on your television's remote control, for example, you are likely to see far fewer ads than someone who just sits and watches one channel for longer periods. All those ads you miss by zipping through the channels are failing to sell you whatever they were designed to sell you.

Many businesses on the Web are trying to get people to see their advertising by having it mentioned in the many lists of commercial Web sites. Those lists have become increasingly crowded, however, and their value has been decreasing lately because they contain just too much information. Other businesses are sponsoring some of the free newsletters on the Internet so that their URL appears in each issue of the newsletter. Others are paying to be part of the many Internet malls in hopes that people who visit the mall site see the business' site and check it out.

Still, having people find you is one of the most difficult tasks of any business. Only so much money is available for advertising; if getting listed in the "better" Internet lists and malls costs you, you can spend only so much on other forms of advertising.

In this way, business Web sites have some of the same desires as individuals who publish on the Web — namely, to get noticed. If you've published your collection of short stories for anyone and everyone to see, you want the collection located in a place where people will see your short stories or can at least find them through other means. The question is whether you are willing to pay for more and better exposure for your Web presence. For both businesses and individuals, the answer is based on their budgets and how much they believe that the service will actually increase their exposure.

Where to Hang Your Shingle

If you were reading a book on how to start up your own Web site, this would be the section that would contain all the nasty details about buying a computer, setting up the communications connection to another Internet provider, setting up the Web server software, and so on. Be thankful that none of that tedious technical detail is found here.

Most individuals who want to publish on the Web, as well as most companies that want a small Web presence, have absolutely no reason to set up their own Web server. The hardware costs are high, a huge amount of technical savvy is necessary to set up the software and hardware, the communications costs are great, and on and on. This isn't to say that you should never consider setting up a Web site — just that you can probably save a great deal of time and money by going with an existing Web provider.

The definition of a *Web provider*, by the way, is a bit shaky in this context. In essence, anyone who lets you put *your* content on *his or her* Web server is a Web provider. Many companies, and some individuals, charge for this service, while others offer it free to people who use their other services (such as their Internet connectivity). Hundreds of such Web providers are scattered throughout the U.S., and many international ones can be found as well.

The Web providers that charge for their services offer myriad price structures. Some charge a flat fee based on how many pages you have; others charge based on how frequently people access your content; and still others charge a flat monthly fee. Most of these structures are geared toward businesses and are way too expensive for the individual who just wants to put up a page or two of political views or sports predictions.

The free services usually don't offer you any help in creating a good looking Web area, but some offer this kind of help. If you are going to publish your own work, you should check with your Internet service provider about whether you can publish through its service, if it charges you anything for publishing, and how much (or how little) the service provider is willing to help you make a good looking Web area. If the Internet service provider indicates that it doesn't allow any Web publishing, you need to look around for a different Web provider, which may entail having to establish a second Internet account.

Chapter 16

HTML 101

● ●

In This Chapter

▶ Discovering the basics of HTML

▶ Figuring out HTML's structure

▶ Formatting text in dozens of fashions

● ●

*T*he preceding chapter describes how to get started creating your own Web pages. The next step in the process of creating your own Web content is to learn enough about HTML, the hypertext language used on the Web, to make your pages attractive and useful. For many people, HTML isn't the easiest thing to learn because it is certainly more than just a few commands. If you have never used a text markup language before (most people haven't even heard of them, much less used one), getting the hang of HTML may take a while.

By the way, in case you have forgotten, HTML stands for *H*yper*t*ext *M*arkup *L*anguage. You'll see what the markup language part means very soon; see Chapter 17 for the hypertext part.

The next few chapters of this book give you enough of a grounding in HTML to create your own Web pages. If you want a much more in-depth lesson in HTML, however, check out IDG Books' *HTML For Dummies,* 3rd Edition, by Ed Tittel and Steve James.

Using the Tools Given to You

Some people would say that you don't have to learn any HTML in order to create Web pages because Netscape Communicator comes with a very capable Web page creator called Netscape Composer. In addition, there are dozens of other Web page creation packages, and most work pretty much like Composer. Netscape advertises Composer as a simple way to create Web pages that prevents you from having to learn HTML.

However, I partially disagree with Netscape here. Composer, which I discuss throughout this and the next chapter, is a good way to *start* creating Web pages, but if you don't understand HTML, your pages are not going to look very good. Thus, I believe that you both need to learn to use Composer and understand the HTML that Composer creates in order to make reasonable Web pages. Regardless of the package you use, you need to understand HTML if you want anything more than a rudimentary Web page.

Thus, this chapter and Chapter 17 help you understand HTML and also describe how to use Composer. Some books separate these two, teaching Composer first and then describing HTML in later sections "for more technical readers." I think this does a disservice to the reader because it means that you're going to end up creating Web pages that don't really convey what you want.

It's Just Like a Word Processor — But Completely Different

If you've worked with computers at all, you're probably at least somewhat familiar with using a word processor to perform such tasks as formatting text. These days, most people use (or have at least seen) word processors that display the formatting as the text is entered. For example, most people have used a word processor such as Microsoft Word or Corel WordPerfect.

Programs that show formatted text as you enter and change it are humorously referred to as *WYSIWYG*, which stands for *What You See Is What You Get*. (Consider yourself an old-timer if you remember which character on the late-'60s hit television show *Rowan and Martin's Laugh-In* made that line popular. *Hint:* She was played by Flip Wilson.)

Each word processor is different and has different user interfaces, but almost every modern word processor has certain capabilities in common. They all can add formatting attributes (such as italics and boldface) to characters, they can indent paragraphs, and so on. Even simple word processors such as the Write program in Windows offer these capabilities.

Assume, for example, that you create the following sentence in your word processor:

```
The second word in this sentence is emphasized.
```

Then assume that you want to make the word *second* appear in your text in boldface characters. In most word processors, you select the word and issue a command (probably the Bold command.) Again, word processors differ, so the act of selecting a word and the act of giving a command can entail different actions on your part (such as choosing a menu command, pressing a key combination, clicking an icon on a button bar, and so on). The result of selecting the word and giving a command, however, is a sentence with the word *second* in boldface. The sentence on-screen now looks like this:

```
The second word in this sentence is emphasized.
```

Word processors differ even further from one another if you format entire paragraphs. To indent a paragraph in one program, for example, you may need to specify the indentation by using a Paragraph command; in another, you move markers on a ruler; in still another, you may press the Tab key.

In many ways, Netscape Composer is like a word processor. You type plain text in, and you can select and format that text in many ways. What you see on the screen is the formatted text with the boldface, underline, paragraph formatting, and so on.

HTML: WYSLCDTWYG (Say What?)

Okay, now forget all that stuff about formatting text in word processors. Documents created with HTML look completely different from how they appear on the Web (*ergo*, the heading for this section: *What You See Looks Completely Different Than What You Get*). HTML documents are created by using *text editors* or HTML creation programs like Composer, not word processors. A text editor enables you only to add, delete, and change text; unlike a word processor, text editors do not enable you to change the formatting of the text you enter or edit. The Windows Notepad program, for example, is a text editor because it uses no formatting commands. If you have a character-based interface to the Internet, you may be familiar with a text editor on your host system.

Netscape Composer is a glorified text editor. That is, what Composer produces are HTML files, which are really just text files. Composer actually does a bit more than this, but its basic product is text files.

HTML enables you to convert or create documents by using a plain text editor that Web clients then display as nicely formatted pages. The formatting consists of two parts: the formatting commands you put into your HTML documents and the interpretation of these commands by the particular Web client that someone uses to view your document.

Every HTML document has two kinds of things in it: *content* and *HTML commands*. The content consists of most of the words that you type. (Chapter 17 describes how to add pictures and hypertext links.) The HTML commands are also text, but they are labeled in a special way so that a Web client reading the document can say, "Oh, an HTML command; I'm supposed to do some formatting."

The correct term for HTML commands is *tags* because they aren't really commands in the same sense as, say, Windows commands. Instead, these commands mark areas of your text where the Web client performs some formatting or takes some other action. You can imagine these tags as markers that "hang on" the text to tell the Web client what to do.

You really need to understand the difference between content and HTML tags before you delve farther into learning HTML. Your HTML document itself doesn't look nice after it's complete. In fact, it may be barely readable. That's why Composer (and other Web site creation packages) exist: to make it easier to create HTML documents by hiding the ugliness unless you want to see it. If that document is accessed by a Web client, however, the Web client knows how to read the HTML part and then interpret it as formatting commands. This action alters the appearance of the text by formatting it with fonts, boldface, blank lines between paragraphs, and so on.

What it looks like

If you're still confused, here's a short example. Remember that sentence from the section on "Formatting with Word Processors"? If not, here it is again:

```
The second word in this sentence is emphasized.
```

HTML tags consist of the character <, the text of the tag, and the character >. (The < character is also known as the *left angle bracket* or the ever popular *less than symbol*. The > character, as you can probably guess, is called the *right angle bracket* or *greater than symbol*.)

Now, to start making your text bold, you use the HTML b tag; to stop the text from being bold, you use the /b tag. Adding the HTML tags to your sentence make it appear as follows:

```
The <b>second</b> word in this sentence is emphasized.
```

If you view this sentence by using a Web browser, the browser removes the <b> and the </b> and formats the text between them, the word *second,* as boldface type.

Now you can see what the *ML* in HTML stands for: HTML is a *markup language* because you use the language to mark up regular text with tags. If you look at a document and you don't see any tags, it isn't marked up and, therefore, isn't an HTML document.

HTML documents

Again, you need to remember that HTML documents are text documents with no inherent formatting. All the formatting you see on the Web is done by using HTML tags that are imbedded in those text documents. Without the formatting, the document would be a plain text file.

The difference between a standard HTML document and its formatted view is quite striking. Figure 16-1 shows a typical HTML document. Notice how many tags are in the document relative to the amount of text. (Many of these tags are described later in this chapter.) If you view this same document by using Netscape, you see something more like the screen shown in Figure 16-2.

You can create HTML documents with a text editor two ways: You can start with a complete text file and add HTML tags, or you can add the tags as you enter the text. Many people prefer the first method because they can see

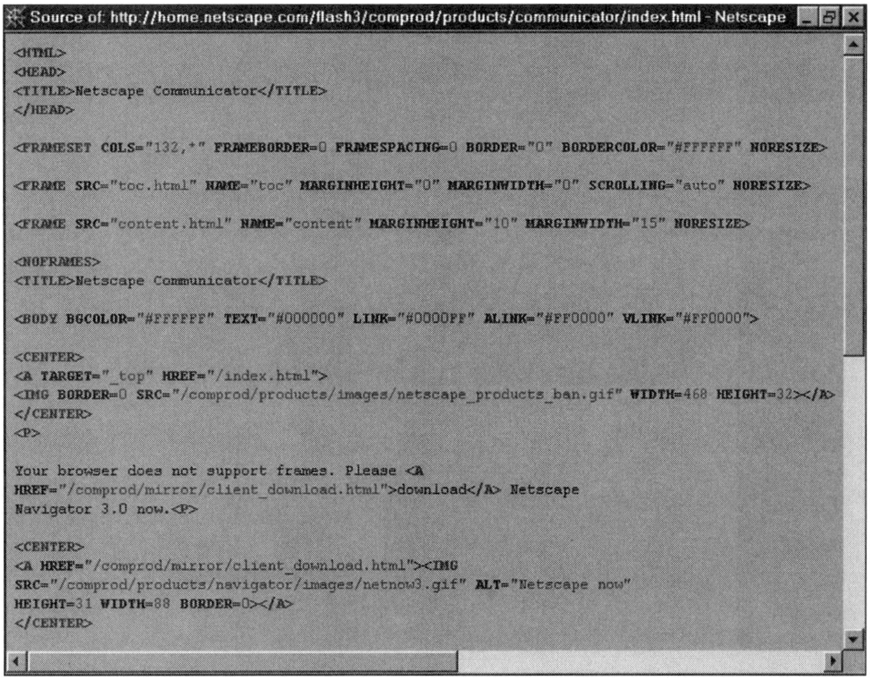

Source of: http://home.netscape.com/flash3/comprod/products/communicator/index.html - Netscape

```
<HTML>
<HEAD>
<TITLE>Netscape Communicator</TITLE>
</HEAD>

<FRAMESET COLS="132,*" FRAMEBORDER=0 FRAMESPACING=0 BORDER="0" BORDERCOLOR="#FFFFFF" NORESIZE>

<FRAME SRC="toc.html" NAME="toc" MARGINHEIGHT="0" MARGINWIDTH="0" SCROLLING="auto" NORESIZE>

<FRAME SRC="content.html" NAME="content" MARGINHEIGHT="10" MARGINWIDTH="15" NORESIZE>

<NOFRAMES>
<TITLE>Netscape Communicator</TITLE>

<BODY BGCOLOR="#FFFFFF" TEXT="#000000" LINK="#0000FF" ALINK="#FF0000" VLINK="#FF0000">

<CENTER>
<A TARGET="_top" HREF="/index.html">
<IMG BORDER=0 SRC="/comprod/products/images/netscape_products_ban.gif" WIDTH=468 HEIGHT=32></A>
</CENTER>
<P>

Your browser does not support frames. Please <A
HREF="/comprod/mirror/client_download.html">download</A> Netscape
Navigator 3.0 now.<P>

<CENTER>
<A HREF="/comprod/mirror/client_download.html"><IMG
SRC="/comprod/products/navigator/images/netnow3.gif" ALT="Netscape now"
HEIGHT=31 WIDTH=88 BORDER=0></A>
</CENTER>
```

Figure 16-1: A typical HTML document with many markup tags.

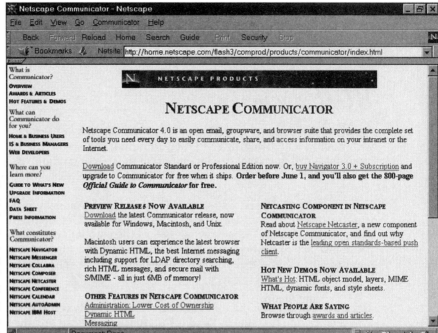

Figure 16-2:
If viewed by
a Web
browser,
the tags
disappear
and the
formatting
is added.

what the content looks like without all the HTML clutter. Other people choose to add formatting as they go along. Either method produces a text file with content and HTML tags, which is, after all, the goal.

Netscape Composer and other HTML creators

However, there is a third, and easier, way to create HTML documents: with a Web site creation tool like Composer. In Composer, you don't see the HTML unless you want to. Most of the time, you're using a WYSIWYG screen that looks a lot like a word processor, showing you how your text will be formatted. You can, of course, also see the HTML document that you're creating, but most of the time, you just use the WYSIWYG tools and trust Composer to do the HTML correctly.

With HTML editors, you don't need to type in each tag because the editor does it for you. This basic aspect of HTML editors makes them very useful to people who are creating several HTML documents. Most HTML editors immediately show you what your document looks like so that you can see if you made any HTML blunders.

The most common mistake in adding HTML tags to a document is to start adding formatting to some text but not finish it, as in the following example:

```
The <b>second word in this sentence is emphasized.
```

Notice that no closing </b> tag appears in the sentence, meaning that everything starting with the word second is now boldface. Almost all HTML editors, fortunately, can check for these kinds of mistakes; if it sees that you started boldface formatting and forgot to stop after a few sentences, it may point this out to you.

Many HTML editors are extensions to popular text editors and word processors. Microsoft, for example, distributes an extension to Microsoft Word for Windows called *Internet Assistant.* Internet Assistant enables you to use many of Word's normal word processing features as you create HTML documents. It even enables you to access parts of the Web as you work.

If you plan to set up dozens of HTML pages for your business or are converting a long, text-only document to HTML, you probably should look at using one of the currently available HTML editors or just use Composer. After you get the hang of a particular HTML editor, using that editor is often easier than typing in the HTML tags. The HTML editor — depending on the one you choose, of course — may even make some automatic conversion of old documents for you. Whether you choose to use an HTML editor or not, however, you should certainly know how to create your own HTML documents so that you can at least understand the output of an HTML editor.

Getting In and Out of Composer

As you saw earlier in the book, all of the components of Netscape are available from the Communicator menu. There, you'll find Composer listed as Page Composer. (What, did they think you wanted? A music composer?) Choosing that brings up the composer program, shown in Figure 16-3. Of course, you can switch back to Netscape Navigator using the Communicator menu or any of the other methods covered in Chapter 5.

Before you can use Composer to do HTML editing, you need to set it up with Preferences command from the Edit menu. There aren't many preferences, and only one is really important. The important preference is the name of the program you want to use as your editor for HTML source, meaning the name of the text editing program you want to use.

Figure 16-3:
The basic
Composer
window,
ready to
compose.

After you specify a text editor, Netscape will use this when you ask to see what the HTML you're creating looks like. To see your HTML, choose Edit⇨HTML Source, which will launch your text editor. You can then switch between the text editor and Composer as you edit your Web pages.

< *and* > Are Your Friends

HTML is one of those funny systems in which lots of rules exist for some things, while others have almost no rules. Certain tags, for example, must appear between certain other pairs of tags, yet they cannot appear between other, different tag pairs. On the other hand, you can place tags anywhere you want on the line of your text document — even on lines by themselves. The following two examples, therefore, result in identically formatted text:

```
<b>second</b>
```

and

```
<b>
second
</b>
```

Both versions give you the bold word **second** on your page.

As you learn HTML's rules, keep in mind that it was originally written for a much smaller audience than it has reached. Many contend that forcing people who want to set up simple Web pages to learn a language is inappropriate, particularly if that language has so many structural rules. In a more perfect world, people reading this book should not need to be concerned about editing text files by using arcane symbols and then checking their work by hand.

Because parts of HTML are quirky and overly technical, only the parts of the language that you commonly use are described here.

Starts and stops

As described earlier in this chapter, every tag starts with a < character and ends with a > character. So far, you've seen only two tags, the <b> and </b> tags, which turn the boldface formatting on and off. Most HTML tags work similarly to the <b> and </b> tags in that you put one tag at the beginning of what you want to format and the same tag with a / in it at the end. These pairs of tags are called *start tags* and *end tags*.

As noted earlier in this chapter, one of the most common errors you can make in adding HTML tags is to forget to add the matching end tag with the start tag. For this reason (among others), you really need to check your work carefully *before* putting it on the Web. All common Web browsers enable you to open HTML files on your hard disk and see how they will look as other browsers view them. Take advantage of this feature.

Capitals don't count

The case of the letters in tags is not significant, meaning that you can do whatever you want with it. Either <b> or <B> means exactly the same thing to every Web browser. This book uses lowercase characters for its tags simply because they're easier to read, but you can do as you please. The example we've been working with can just as easily appear as follows:

```
The <B>second</B> word in this sentence is emphasized.
```

For that matter, it can also appear as follows and still be treated the same:

```
The <b>second</B> word in this sentence is emphasized.
```

Where does the line end?

Another nice informality of HTML is that you can put HTML tags next to the text that they modify or on separate lines. Web browsers interpret line breaks as a space between words when they look through an HTML document. Although this may seem a bit odd to you, creating Web documents this way is much more flexible than having to keep tags on the same line with the text that precedes or follows it.

One side effect of this flexibility means that you can have very short lines in your HTML document and they will appear at the full width of the Web browser's window. This feature also means that you don't need to guess how long to make the lines in your paragraphs.

Check out the following example:

```
One side effect of this means that you can have very short
lines in your HTML document and they will appear at the
full width of the Web browser's window.
```

The preceding text looks the same in Web browsers as the following example:

```
One side effect of this means that you
can have very shortlines in your HTML
document and they will appear at the
full width of the Web browser's window.
```

Another nice advantage of this line-length freedom is that you can choose to put your HTML tags on the same line with the text they refer to or on separate lines. The following two examples, therefore, appear exactly the same if viewed in a Web browser:

```
One side effect of this means that you
can have <b>very short lines</b> in your HTML
document and they will appear at the
full width of the Web browser's window.
```

```
One side effect of this means that you can have
<b>very short lines</b>
in your HTML document and they will appear at the
full width of the Web browser's window.
```

Notice how the second example has the boldface characters on a single line in the HTML file, making the phrase stand out better. Many people prefer to add HTML tags to their documents in this fashion so that they can find the tags more easily if they revise documents.

Adding a Bit of Character

You've probably figured out that there is much more to HTML than <b> and </b>. The simplest tags in HTML are similar to these tags, however, so you should be able to build up your repertoire fairly quickly.

The pairs of tags in Table 16-1 are used to apply common character formatting to the text enclosed in them. You see them used most often for items such as book titles, quotations, and so on. Notice that you do not use these for emphasizing things such as headings — you'll see why in a moment.

Table 16-1	Common character formatting tags
Formatting	*Start and end tags*
Boldface	<b> and </b>
Italic	<i> and </i>
Underline	<u> and </u>
Fixed width	<tt> and </tt>

A second set of character formatting tags exists that is used less often. Instead of telling the Web browser how to format the text, these tags describe what kind of information is in the text. For example, the <cite> and </cite> tags tell the Web browser that the text is a citation. The browser then decides whether a citation should be in bold, underline, and so on. Table 16-2 lists these information-type character tags.

Table 16-2	Character formatting tags for typed information
Kind of information	*Start and end tags*
Citation	<cite> and </cite>
Program code	<code> and </code>
Emphasis	<em> and </em>
Keystrokes	<kbd> and </kbd>
Literal samples	<samp> and </samp>
Strong emphasis	<strong> and </strong>
Variable names	<var> and </var>

Again, you need to remember that different Web browsers display formatted text differently, particularly the tags shown in Table 16-2. The following example shows some HTML text with all of the character formatting tags, and Figure 16-4 shows how Netscape displays the text. (The `<br>` tag causes a line break, as described in the following section.)

```
All sorts of character formatting:<br>
<b>Boldface</b><br>
<i>Italic</i><br>
<u>Underline</u><br>
<tt>Fixed-width</tt><br>
<cite>Citation</cite><br>
<code>Program code</code><br>
<em>Emphasis</em><br>
<kbd>Keystrokes</kbd><br>
<samp>Literal samples</samp><br>
<strong>Strong emphasis</strong><br>
<var>Variable names</var><br>
```

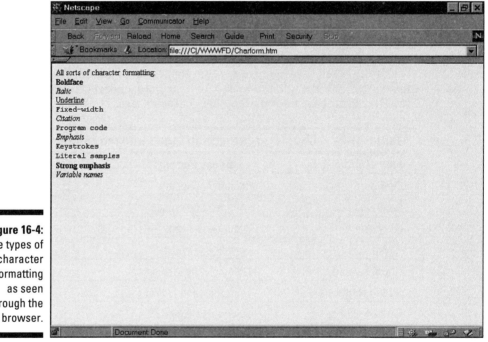

Figure 16-4:
The types of character formatting as seen through the browser.

Character Formatting in Composer

Okay, now that you have your first taste of how to do it that hard way, you'll be happy to know that creating the same HTML in Composer is easy. In fact, it's identical to the way you use any word processor. You simply select the characters you want and choose one or more of the character formatting styles.

There are two places that formatting styles appear in Composer: on the formatting toolbar and in the Format menu. The formatting toolbar is the second toolbar in the Composer window. Its elements are shown in Figure 16-5. For example, to make some text that you have typed bold, select it and click on the Bold icon in the formatting toolbar.

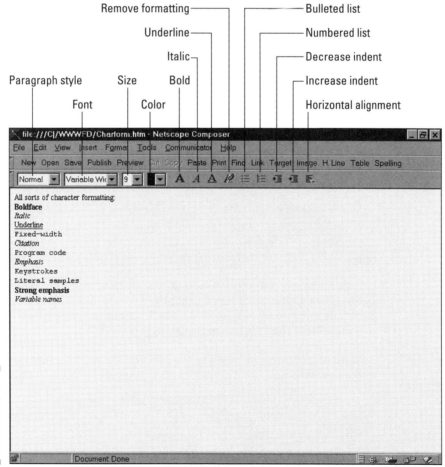

Figure 16-5:
The many tools on the formatting toolbar.

As you can see, there aren't icons for all the formatting that was listed in Tables 16-1 and 16-2. The Style command in the Format menu lets you apply some of the styles from Table 16-1 but none of those in Table 16-2. In fact, there is no way to use Composer to create many of these styles

That's right, you can't use Composer to create all of the kinds of HTML you can with a plain old text editor. In their infinite wisdom, the folks at Netscape have decided that some of the character styles aren't of interest to you, so they didn't make them available in Composer.

To insert tags you want, put the insertion point at the place you want the tag and then choose Insert⇨HTML Tag. This brings up a mini-editing window that you can type your tag in. When you close the window, Composer puts the tag into your HTML document.

Getting Things in Line

One does not live by character formatting alone. HTML also has a fairly complete set of line and paragraph formatting tags so that you can specify how your text lies vertically on the page. These tags are generally called *line formatting* tags or *paragraph formatting* tags.

The two most common tags used for paragraph formatting are the paragraph tag, <p>, and the line break tag, <br>. In most Web browsers, the <p> tag causes a blank line to appear, while the <br> tag simply starts a new line, as in the following example:

```
This would be the first sentence of the paragraph.
This would be the second. Guess what? There is
one more.
<p> This is the beginning of the next paragraph . . .
```

Do not make any assumptions about exactly how much space appears between the paragraphs when using the <p> tag. Some Web browsers add a full blank line and others add only a half line. In fact, a few Web browsers used to indent the first line of the paragraph!

As a point of style, you may want to put the <p> tag on a line by itself, as in this example:

```
<p>
This would be the first sentence of the paragraph.
This would be the second. Guess what? There is
one more.
<p>
This is the beginning of the next paragraph . . .
```

This organizational method makes reading your HTML files much easier.

In Composer, you add paragraph tags in a slightly odd manner. As you are typing, after the last word in the paragraph, press Enter *twice,* not once. If you press Enter once, you get a ⟨br⟩ tag; if you press Enter twice, you get a ⟨p⟩ tag.

Some HTML editors also insert a ⟨/p⟩ tag at the end of paragraphs. This isn't common, but you might see it if you look at the HTML for some pages you find on the Web. You can ignore the ⟨/p⟩ tags because most Web browsers ignore them.

Remember to use the ⟨br⟩ tag instead of the ⟨p⟩ tag if you just want things to appear on a new line, not as a new paragraph, as in the following example:

```
The answer, my friend,<br>
Is blowing in the wind.<br>
The answer is blowing in the wind.
```

If you have a great deal of text that has specific line endings, you may prefer to use the ⟨pre⟩ and ⟨/pre⟩ tags and not use the ⟨br⟩ tags at all. The ⟨pre⟩ tag is for *preformatted text,* which is text that already has all the line breaks you want. Generally, using these tags is easier if you have many lines that each end with ⟨br⟩ tags.

The preceding example, using the ⟨pre⟩ and ⟨/pre⟩ tags, would look like this:

```
<pre>
The answer, my friend,
Is blowing in the wind.
The answer is blowing in the wind.
</pre>
```

To mark a paragraph as preformatted text in Composer, choose Format⇨Paragraph⇨Formatted.

If you are using HTML to format a formal paper that has quotations indented from each margin, use the ⟨blockquote⟩ and ⟨/blockquote⟩ tags. Be aware that some browsers also put block quotes in italics, which may or may not be what you want. These tags are not used that often, although more and more academic papers are appearing on the Web, and everyone knows how much academics like to quote each other.

You may have noticed that many of the screens shown in this book display horizontal lines. To add a horizontal line to your HTML document, simply use the `<hr>` tag. (The *r* in *hr* stands for *rule,* the more correct term for a drawn line.) If they encounter an `<hr>` tag, Web browsers know to draw a line from one end of the window to the other. You should never draw horizontal lines across the screen by using hyphens (-) or underscore characters (_) because you don't know how wide the browser screen is or how wide those characters may appear on-screen.

To insert a horizontal line in Composer, use the Insert⇨Horizontal Line command. You can also just click the H. Line icon on the composition toolbar.

Learning to Love Lists

HTML's list features help you make nicely formatted lists with very little muss and fuss. Five kinds of lists are available, although only three are commonly used.

In other chapters of this book, you come across the two most common types of lists: *ordered lists* and *unordered lists.* Ordered lists are often called *numbered lists* because each item in the list starts with a sequential number. Unordered lists are often called *bulleted lists* because the items have a bullet before them.

Ordered lists are usually used for steps in a process, as in the following example:

1. **Turn on your television.**

2. **Find the remote control.**

3. **Sit down.**

Unordered lists are used to list items that have equal value but no particular order, as follows:

- Potato chips
- Soda
- Pretzels

The tags for ordered lists are `<ol>` and `</ol>`; for unordered lists, they are `<ul>` and `</ul>`. Each item in the list is marked with `<li>`, which stands for *list item.* The preceding lists, for example, would be tagged as follows:

```
What to do:
<ol>
<li>Turn on your television.
<li>Find the remote control.
<li>Sit down.
</ol>
What to have:
<ul>
<li>Potato chips
<li>Soda
<li>Pretzels
</ul>
```

The *definition list* is another type of available list. These are the two-column lists you sometimes see in glossaries or tables. Use the `<dl>` and `</dl>` tags to start and stop the list; use the `<dt>` tag in front of the items in the left column (the definition *terms*) and the `<dd>` tag in front of the items in the right column (the definition *definitions*). (Unfortunately, most Web browsers, Netscape included, don't format these lists as you would expect, with the two columns appearing on the same line. This fact can be confusing if you expect two-column lists to be in, well, two columns.)

The following example shows how you format a definition list:

```
What to watch:
<dl>
<dt>Dragnet
<dd>Cops and robbers in the '50s and late '60s
<dt>Mary Tyler Moore
<dd>Sitcom of the '70s
<dt>Dr. Who
<dd>Science fiction starting in 1963
</dl>
```

Figure 16-6 shows how these lists are displayed in Netscape. Notice that Netscape inserts a blank line before and after the list items; not all Web browsers add these lines.

You can also have lists within lists. This property is common in outlines but is also useful in many other areas. The following is an example of the formatting for a list that contains sublists:

```
What to have:
<ul>
<li>Potato chips
<ol>
```

(continued)

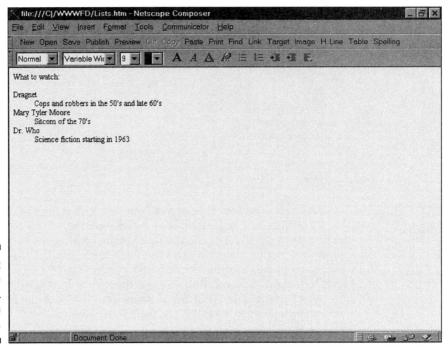

Figure 16-6:
An example
of an HTML
definition
list.

(continued)

```
<li>Find a bag that is not stale.
<li>Grab a second bag, just in case.
</ol>
<li>Soda
<ul>
<li>Caffeinated for the first hour
<li>No caffeine for the second hour
</ul>
<li>Pretzels
</ul>
```

Figure 16-7 shows how this combination of lists within lists appears.

Two additional kinds of lists, *directory lists* and *menu lists,* are rarely used. Their tags are `<dir>` and `<menu>`. Different Web clients also display these kinds of lists very differently. You'll be quite safe if you ignore them.

Turning a paragraph into a list in Composer is easy. Select any part of the paragraph, select the Format⇨List command, and choose the kind of list you want.

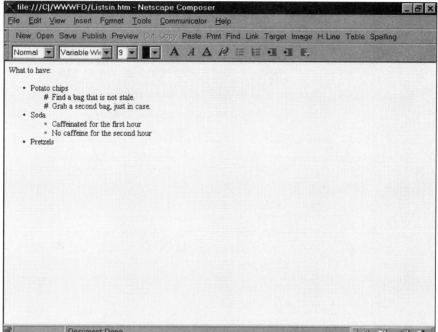

Figure 16-7:
Lists within
lists.

Headings

The last major set of HTML tags that you'll find yourself using all the time is
<h1>, <h2>, <h3>, and so on. These tags (and their ending partners </h1>,
</h2>, and </h3>) are used to mark headings in your text. They are also
some of the most misused tags in HTML.

The correct way to use the tags is around text that is a heading. The headings near the beginning of this chapter, for example, would be marked as
follows:

```
<h1>HTML: WYSLCDTWYG</h1>
<h2>What it looks like</h2>
<h2>HTML documents</h2>
```

Level 1 headings are the major headings in your document; level 2 comes
under level 1, and so on.

Most Web browsers put the headings in boldface characters and larger type
(usually) than the normal text in your HTML document. Of course, text with
<h1> tags should appear in larger type than text in <h2> tags, and so on.
Figure 16-8 shows how Netscape displays the first four levels of headings.

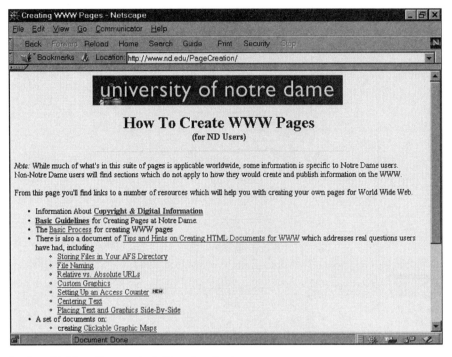

HotSpot 16-1: http://www.nd.edu/PageCreation/
This is an incredibly complete resource for how to create and maintain Web pages. Some of the material is specific to the computers at Notre Dame, but most of it is applicable to all Web page creators.

Unfortunately, some people use <h6> and </h6> to mean "Display this in really teeny, almost unreadable characters." Using headings this small isn't the smartest thing to do because some Web browsers show such headings in tiny type, but others don't.

Turning a paragraph into a heading in Composer is also easy. Select any part of the paragraph, choose the Format⇨Heading command, and choose the level of heading you want (such as 1, 2, and so on).

Top of the Doc

Every document should have a title. Connecting to a Web page and having no idea what's being discussed can be disconcerting to say the least. Fortunately, the <title> and </title> tags make creating titles easy. You can't, however, put these tags just anywhere in your HTML document.

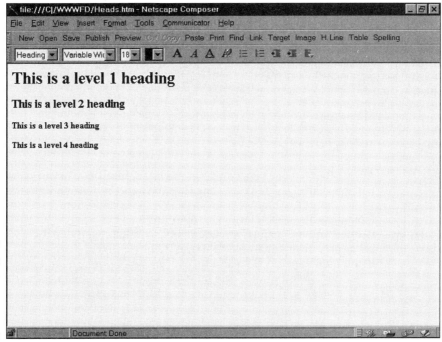

Figure 16-8:
Formatting
for heading
levels 1
through 4.

HTML documents have an overall structure that was intended to be manda-tory but has, due mostly to people's laziness, become optional. Knowing about the structure, however, is important because some Web clients still require it. Unfortunately, there is no way to know which clients require it and which don't without testing each one.

Every HTML document should begin with an `<html>` tag and end with an `</html>` tag. These tags mark the part of the document that is in HTML. For our purposes, the entire document is in HTML, so you would put these tags at the very beginning and the very end of the document.

Here's a place where using Composer makes life much easier. Every time you start a new document in Composer, it puts these tags in the document for you. You never had to worry about them. If you later want to change the title of the document, you can with the Format⇨Page Colors and Properties command.

Two parts exist between the beginning and end of the document. These parts are the head and the body, and they are marked by the `<head>`, `</head>`, `<body>`, and `</body>` HTML tags. This structure tells Web browsers what material applies to the entire document (the things in the head) and what applies to the body of what you want displayed. The `<title>` and `</title>` tags go in the head because the document's title applies to the entire document.

Thus the structure of an HTML document really looks like this:

```
<html>
<head>
<title>The title of this document</title>
</head>
<body>
The content of the document.
</body>
</html>
```

A few other sets of tags can go in the head, but they are rarely used and fairly obscure. For now, assume that the head is there to hold the title.

Most Web browsers allow you to put the `<title>` and `</title>` tags at the very beginning of an HTML document without specifying the rest of the structure. Others ignore a title that is shown in this manner and assume that if you didn't specify a structure, everything in your document is the body. Therefore, if you want a title on your document that can be read by everybody, you should include all the structure tags as shown here.

Other Bits and Pieces

As you can see, HTML is a bit quirky in how it is used. Some tags come in beginning and end pairs, others don't. You need to pay attention to the overall structure for some features but not for others. I hope, however, that you have clearly seen that not too many details get between you and writing Web content.

Chapter 17 covers the last two major parts of HTML that you are probably most interested in: hypertext links and pictures. A number of other little HTML features exist that that you should be aware of but that don't fit in any of the preceding categories. Consider this section the HTML's junk drawer.

Comments

You can put comments into your HTML documents that serve as notes to yourself. These comments are not displayed by Web browsers, but anyone looking at your HTML file can see them. Comment tags are a bit different than other HTML tags. Comments begin with the `<!--` tag and end with the `-->` tag. Thus part of your HTML document may look like this:

```
There are many things that I want to say to the world.
<!-- Boy, isn't that the truth... -->
However, the world never listens to me anyway, so
what's the point?
```

Giving your address

The `<address>` and `</address>` tags provide a special method of giving your address in an HTML document. Most Web browsers treat the text between these two tags as special, and most people put their address at the bottom of a document. You can include anything you want between these tags, but many people include a mail-to URL so that people can reach them easily. (URLs are covered in depth in Chapter 3.)

Special characters

You can't include just anything in your HTML documents. Specifically, you can't include certain characters either because they confuse the Web browser or because they may have different meanings on different systems. Fortunately, HTML anticipates these circumstances and makes them easy to take care of.

The three common characters that you *can't* include in an HTML document by themselves are <, >, and &. These characters are special in HTML; the preceding sections describe why the first two are so special (to hold formatting tags, remember?), and the use of the & is described in a moment. If you want to put the characters < or > or & in your HTML document, you must use the following text exactly as it appears here for each character: < or > or &.

To put it more simply:

```
&lt; = <
&gt; = >
&amp; = &
```

To represent the text x<y, for example, you would use the following text:

```
x&lt;y
```

As you can now see, the & sign (called the *ampersand*) is used at the beginning of special characters, which is why you can't just put it in your document on its own. You use a similar method for representing characters that differ between computers and operating systems.

Composer prevents you from having to know any of this arcane stuff. When you type a < character, it puts the < in your HTML document for you, and just displays the < on the screen.

The Web extends far beyond the United States, and HTML is an international language. Thus it must also account for characters that do not appear in normal English use. Many European languages, for example, have vowels with marks over them, such as ö. American computers have no standard way to represent ö, so HTML uses a special symbol for it: ö. The German city Köln, therefore, would be represented as follows:

```
K&ouml;ln
```

Inserting special characters in Composer is cumbersome, however. On Windows, you have to use the Character Map program that comes with Windows; on the Mac, you have to use the Key Caps program. Neither of these come with Netscape but instead are part of the operating system.

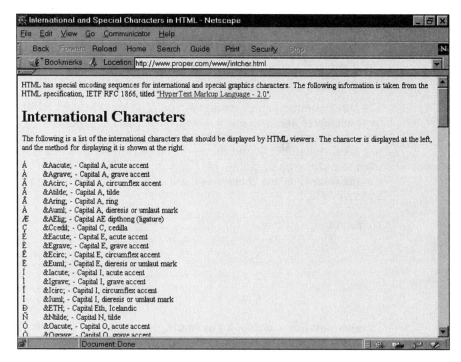

HotSpot 16-2: http://www.proper.com/www/intchar.html
Dozens of international characters and special symbols are defined in HTML. This Web site lists them all and shows how each character appears in your browser.

Chapter 17

The Best Parts: Hypertext and Graphics

● ●

In This Chapter

▶ Understanding links

▶ Creating links to other documents

▶ Linking within a document

▶ Including pictures in your HTML documents

● ●

Chapter 16 describes how to use HTML to add formatting to your documents. The HTML tags in that chapter are useful in making your documents more readable, but they ignore the two most popular parts of the Web: links and images. Both of these concepts are covered in this chapter.

Thinking about Linking

As discussed throughout the book, jumping from one document to another by using hypertext links is the basis for the Web. Many documents act as guides to other documents on the Web, enabling you to access those subsidiary documents with a single click. Other documents use links to point to parts of the same document.

Before you start merrily linking your Web documents to other documents hither and yon, a good idea is to first step back and think about what you really want to do with hypertext and the best way to do it. If you've been bopping around the Web as you read this book, you may have come across some Web sites that just didn't feel right. Maybe the links from the first page at the site weren't what you expected, or maybe some of the links were bad.

As you write, your best course is always to work from an outline or at least an overview of what you want to say. As you create Web documents, think about where you will link to and how those links may look to the casual Web user who has just breezed into your document but is unfamiliar with other related Web documents. Your outline or plan doesn't need to be anything formal — just a nudge to think about how your creation looks to the rest of the world.

The name of the link

In most fields, you need a consistent way to discuss the topics encompassed by the field; setting certain standards for the names of these topics, therefore, is important. Unfortunately, that's not true on the Web. If you create a link from one document to another, you can name the link whatever you want. The Web community has come to no consensus about the best way to name links, and this has caused all sorts of problems.

Web search utilities do not work nearly as well as the ones for Gopher because cataloging all the HTTP universe is impossible, while the Gopher universe is easily cataloged. Everything on a Gopher server is either the name of a menu or the name of a document. Because each Gopher menu is a list of names, people who publish at Gopher sites have adopted somewhat standardized strategies for naming menus: The names are all descriptive of what is in each menu. (Search utilities are described in more detail in Chapter 7.)

Not so on the Web. Some Web search systems index their text by the names of the links, while others index based on the content of the entire HTML document. Indexes based on the names of links rely on one style of naming, while indexes based on the content of the whole document rely on a different style of naming.

For example, imagine that you want to put a link in a document you are writing to another Web site that has a really fantastic collection of snail pictures. You may phrase the link as follows:

```
You can see lots of great photos of snails on the Web.
Click here to access Professor Kapha's
collection of snail photographs.
```

The underlined word *here* is the link to the other site. Another way to phrase the link is like this:

```
You can see lots of great photos of snails on the Web,
such as Professor Kapha's photo collection.
```

Notice that the link the user clicks is now the words *Professor Kapha's photo collection* (not including the period at the end of the sentence).

For search systems that index their content only by the names of the links (not by the content), neither of the names tells the index anything about what is really important. To make the Web searcher's index useful, you really want the word *snail* in the title of the link, such as in the following example:

```
You can see lots of great photos of snails on the Web,
such as Professor Kapha's photo collection of snails.
```

This approach, however, makes the sentence redundant.

Furthermore, you don't really want to base all your link name choices on what some search indexes may or may not do. Instead, you want the sentences you use to link to be easily readable and get the Web user your information in the clearest way possible. This usually means that you should avoid the "click here" kind of descriptions because any Web user knows that if they see a link, they "click here" to access it.

This may seem obvious, but you're best off avoiding link names that don't refer to the object of the link at all. As you traverse around the Web, however, don't be surprised if you find links such as this:

```
You can see lots of great photos of snails on the Web,
such as Professor Kapha's photo collection of snails.
```

Choosing good link targets

Another major problem with many of the links you may create in your Web documents is that your links could point to servers whose names have changed, servers who are no longer on the Internet, servers that don't allow access to the general public, or servers that are very slow. As you make links, think about whether the same information may be available at different sites, and choose the site with the best availability.

For example, you may have noticed that it takes a very long time to get documents from the site you intend to link to. If so, you probably don't want to send thousands of other people to that site without first asking the keeper of those documents for permission. Before linking to a slow site, send mail asking permission. You may get a reply telling about a better place with the same information or that the address of the site is about to change.

As a service to all users of the Web, you need to periodically check all the links in the Web pages you create. If you have many links that were valid when you wrote the document but later went bad (such as if the name of the host changes), you can be sending hundreds or thousands of people on a wild goose chase for naught. Make a habit of checking your resources and update your Web pages if the resources move or disappear.

In the future, Uniform Resource Names (URNs) will make these kinds of considerations much less necessary. URNs are not available now, but they should be soon. See Chapter 21 for more information on URNs and other future Web technologies.

Linking to the Outside World

The HTML tags that enable you to create hypertext links are `<a>` and `</a>`. (In case you just got here, HTML tags are described in excruciating detail in Chapter 16.) The *a* in these tags stands for *anchor,* which means that you are anchoring the text between the tags to the link. If linking to a document other than the document you are writing, you must specify that document by using a URL. The `<a>` tag includes `href=` followed by the URL in quotation marks.

For example, assume that you are linking to the home page for the Internet Society, the URL of which is `http://www.isoc.org`. You may include the following text in your document:

```
I'm also a dues-paying member of the
<a href="http://www.isoc.org">Internet Society</a>.
```

This text creates a link that looks like this:

```
I'm also a dues-paying member of the Internet Society.
```

This may be the first time you have seen an HTML tag with anything other than just a few characters between the `<` and `>` characters. The `href=` part of the tag is called an *attribute* of the `<a>` tag. Some tags have many possible attributes, but most have none.

You can use any kind of URL in an `<a>` tag. For example, you can refer to a specific file found on an FTP site as follows:

```
If you have a problem with the modem, be sure you have the
<a href="ftp://ftp.fastmodems.com/pub/text/settings.txt">
latest settings files</a>.
```

This last example shows a bit of HTML style. Don't put end punctuation, such as a period, inside the link: Always close the link with the `</a>` before adding the punctuation.

Another typical kind of link you see is the `mailto:` URL, which causes e-mail to be sent to someone (as described in Chapter 3), as in the following example:

```
This Web page was written by
<a href="mailto:aji@salary.com">Aji Tsutomo</a>.
```

If a Web user chooses that link, the Web browser starts a letter with the specified mail address in the "to" section.

The text between the `<a>` and the `</a>` is no different than the text in the rest of your HTML document. You can use the formatting tags described in Chapter 16 on some or all the text if you want, as in the following example:

```
If you liked that one, you may enjoy the even-sappier love poem,
<a href="ftp://ftp.std.com/obi/Tennyson/Fatima"><i>Fatima</i>
</a>, by Alfred Lord Tennyson.
```

Creating links in Composer is a snap. Simply select the text that you want to be the link, and then click the Link icon on the composition toolbar (or give the Insert⇨Link command). In the dialog box, enter the URL for the place that you want to link to and click OK.

Linking within Your Document

So far, all the links you have seen have been to other documents on the Internet. You can, however, also make links to specific spots in your document by using the `<a>` tag. These spots are called *targets* because they are the target location for other links. Instead of using the `href=` attribute and a URL, use the `name=` attribute and a name you'd like to use as a marker for the target area. You can then link to the point by using the target's name.

For example, assume that you want to link to each first-level heading in a long document. You may have a heading that looks like this:

```
<h1>Chapter 4. Bertha and Althea</h1>
```

You can make this heading a target named *"ch4"* by adding the following tags:

```
<h1><a name="ch4">Chapter 4. Bertha and Althea</a></h1>
```

The `<a>` tags that point to targets use the `href=` attribute, but instead of a URL, you use the # character and the target's name. If, for example, you were creating a table of contents with links to targets such as the one in the preceding example, it would look something like this:

```
<a href="#ch4">Chapter 4</a>. Bertha and Althea
```

Remember that the # character appears in the ⟨a⟩ that *links to* the target, not in the ⟨a⟩ that names the target.

Using target names in the URLs of HTML documents to which you are linking is also legal. This is a bad practice, however, because the author of the document could change the names of the targets without warning, thus breaking the URL you use. If you really want to do this, however (if, for example, you are the author of both the target document and the one pointing to it), you can create links such as those in the following example:

```
See <a href="http://www.bigstate.edu/students/willy/thesis#ch4">
Chapter 4</a> of my thesis for a deeper discussion on
the theme of commitment, and lack thereof.
```

Linking within a file is just as easy in Composer. In fact, it's even easier, because Composer lists all of the targets in the current file or the file you specify and you just pick out of the list. I have a tendency to give my targets similar names, and misspelling is always an issue for me, so this feature is pretty handy.

Mixtures with Pictures

Okay, it's time for pretty pictures! Well, pretty is in the eye of the beholder, but pictures seem to be one of the most compelling parts of the Web, and you may be itching to include them in your Web pages. HTML makes adding the images easy; the hard part is getting images that enhance your pages without looking tacky or taking too long for users to download.

On the other hand, not everything is so automatic outside of HTML. Dozens of different formats exist for graphics files, and most Web browsers understand how to display only one or two of these formats. By far, the most popular format is GIF, a format popularized by CompuServe almost a decade ago. The next most popular format is JPEG, which is a newer open industry standard that has not caught on as well as GIF. Other formats exist, but most Web browsers understand only one or both of these two; Netscape handles both just fine.

Two types of images can be found on the Web: those that are part of HTML documents and those that you download just like other files. The ones that are part of HTML documents are called *inline images* because they appear in the same line as text. Downloadable images are no different than any other downloadable file.

To include an inline image in your HTML document, use the ⟨img⟩ tag and the src= attribute. The value of the src= attribute is a URL — namely the location of the image you want to display.

You may, for example, display some images as in the following example:

```
<img src="http://geog.bigstate.edu/minelli/tindell-bef.gif">
The Tindell river before the flood<br>
<img src="http://geog.bigstate.edu/minelli/tindell-day2.gif">
The Tindell river on the second day of the flood<br>
<img src="http://geog.bigstate.edu/minelli/tindell-day7.gif">
The Tindell river two days after the flood<br>
```

You probably already guessed how Composer lets you insert images. In case you didn't, you use the Insert⇨Image command or the Image icon on the composition toolbar. Doing so brings up the image properties dialog box where you can specify the location of the graphic and various formatting. To later edit this information, simply select the graphic and give the Insert⇨Image command again.

Where images go on the line

Inline images you specify in the <img> tag appear on the same line with your text. Most images are much taller than a single line of text, and you may want to vertically align the text after the image with the top, the middle, or the bottom of the image. For this procedure, you use the align= attribute with the words top, middle, or bottom. For example, if you wanted the text after the flood pictures to be centered vertically with the pictures, you would instead use the tags as shown in this example:

```
<img src="http://geog.bigstate.edu/minelli/tindell-bef.gif"
align=middle>The Tindell river before the flood<br>
<img src="http://geog.bigstate.edu/minelli/tindell-day2.gif"
align=middle>The Tindell river on the second day of the flood<br>
<img src="http://geog.bigstate.edu/minelli/tindell-day7.gif"
align=middle>The Tindell river two days after the flood<br>
```

Images as links

Inline images can act just like text in that they get wrapped by Web browsers, can act like links, and so on. Of course, you can't add formatting such as bold or italics to an image (although it would be kind of fun if you could), but you can treat inline images just like anchors. In fact, many Web pages use small inline images as links to other documents. Although these images act similarly to buttons in dialog boxes, they are just simple inline images.

To make an inline image a link, simply have it as the only content between the `<a>` and `</a>` tags, as in the following example:

```
Would you like to take the tour?<br>
<a href="http://www.lilac.com/users/wally/tour.html">
<img src="http://www.lilac.com/users/wally/yesbutton.gif"></a>
<a href="http://www.lilac.com/users/wally/home.html">
<img src="http://www.lilac.com/users/wally/nobutton.gif"></a>
```

In Composer, insert the image first, select it, and then turn it into a link with the Link icon on the composition toolbar or by giving the Insert⇨Link command.

In this case, the two buttons would appear next to each other on-screen and would be shown as links. Choosing the first one (the one that displays `yesbutton.gif`) takes you to the link `tour.html`; the other takes you to `home.html`. Figure 17-1 shows a typical page that uses fancy-looking graphics as buttons.

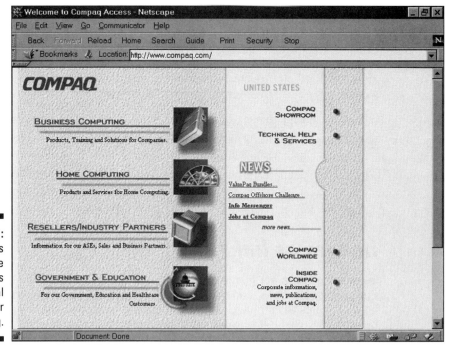

Figure 17-1: Compaq's Web site uses graphical buttons for linking.

What about character-based browsers?

Instead of joining the rush toward the all-graphical Web, you should remember that millions of Web users can't view the images in your Web pages. These people are already quite familiar with being frustrated by thoughtless Web page designers who blithely assume that everyone can see graphics. You can, for example, all too easily find Web pages written up as in the following example:

```
Click the picture of the house to go home, or click the
picture of the stadium to see the statistics for the home
team.
<img src="http://www.baseball.com/images/house.gif">
<img src="http://www.baseball.com/images/stadium.gif">
<img src="http://www.baseball.com/images/question.gif">
```

For someone who is using a character-based browser, however, the preceding example appears on-screen as follows:

```
Click the picture of the house to go home, or click the picture
of the stadium to see the statistics for the home team.
[IMAGE][IMAGE][IMAGE]
```

Not too helpful, eh?

Fortunately, HTML enables you to put text where an image would have appeared, providing that the Web browser allows this feature. Most character-based browsers show this text, enabling their users to at least get a hint of what the image may have looked like. To specify alternative text for the image, you use the alt= attribute, as in the following example:

```
Click the picture of the house to go home, or click the picture
of the stadium to see the statistics for the home team.
<img src="http://www.baseball.com/images/house.gif" alt="House">
<img src="http://www.baseball.com/images/stadium.gif" alt="Stadium">
<img src="http://www.baseball.com/images question.gif"alt="Help">
```

Remember, too, that many people turn off automatic image downloading as they browse around the Web so that they can get information faster. This is particularly true of people using Web browsers other than Netscape. Not all graphical browsers, however, show the alt= text if image downloading is turned off.

Adding alternate text in Composer is a bit more cumbersome, but not too bad. When you insert the graphic (or when you later edit the formatting), in the image properties dialog box, choose the Alt. Text/LowRes button. Doing so brings up yet another dialog box where you can enter the alternate text.

Where do images come from?

Like most things in life, you can take images from someone else, or you can create your own. If you aren't artistically inclined or don't want to take the time to design your own graphics, you can use GIF or JPEG files that already exist. You can find many places on the Web from which you can download small icons and buttons for your Web pages, and you can, of course, include larger pictures that you get from the many FTP sites that have graphics collections.

On the other hand, if you like to create your own graphics, many paint programs save their output in GIF or JPEG format. If your paint program doesn't save files in these formats, you can easily find graphics conversion programs that take the output of your paint program and convert it to GIF or JPEG format. Windows users can find freeware and shareware graphics programs at `ftp://ftp.cica.indiana.edu/pub/pc/win3/desktop`; Mac users can find some good conversion programs at `http://mirror.aol.com/pub/info-mac/`.

Again, remember that not all browsers support both graphics formats. You are generally safer with GIF than with JPEG, but that could change in the future because of legal problems with the GIF format that have cropped up recently. You are pretty much forced to guess which format is the most supported by the client software on the Web and then go with that one if you can. For today, GIF is more popular, but that could change in a year or two.

The Trouble with Tables

HTML tables are a mixed blessing: You can create very nice-looking information with them, but the HTML tags needed are quite complicated. In fact, I'd say that creating tables without an HTML editor is folly. Having said that, I want to assure you that the table features in Composer are just fine, and you can create tables easily with them.

To start a table, choose the table icon in the composition toolbar, or give the Insert⇨Table⇨Table command. Doing so brings up the large dialog box shown in Figure 17-2. Don't be daunted by its size: Choosing what you want is actually quite easy.

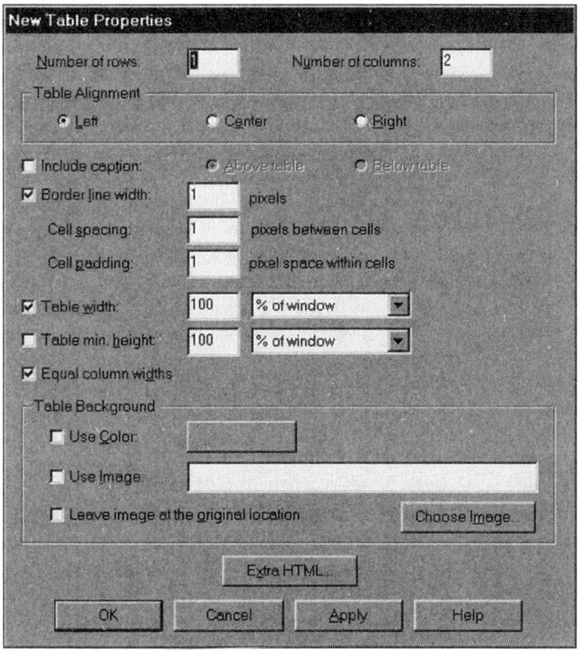

Figure 17-2:
Choices for
creating a
new HTML
table.

The main choices you have to make are how many rows and columns you want. Don't worry about this choice too much, for that matter, because you can always add or delete rows and columns later. The other choices you can make include the following:

- ✔ The alignment of the table relative to the Web page.
- ✔ Whether or not the table has a caption, and if the caption is above or below the table.
- ✔ If the table has a border around the cells, and if so, how thick the line is.
- ✔ The spacing around the text in the cell.
- ✔ How wide the table is, either relative to the page or as an absolute width.
- ✔ The minimum height of the table.
- ✔ Whether or not the columns will maintain equal widths.
- ✔ The background for the table (a color or a picture).

After you create a table, you can fill in the cells just by typing into them. You can enter and format the text in table cells just like you can in the rest of your HTML document.

For example, Figure 17-3 shows a typical table after it is created. It has five rows, two columns, is centered in the page, and has the default borders. The text was entered as normal, and the text in the first row is formatted with both bold and italics.

Incidentally, if you want to know why I said that the tags for tables were much more complicated than other HTML tags, create a table like this one and take a look at the HTML source. Pretty ugly, eh?

Composer also lets you manipulate tables in many ways in order to get exactly the look you want. The most convenient method for making these changes is in the table properties dialog box. Select any part of the table and give the Format⇨Table Properties command. The first part of this dialog box looks just like the Insert Table dialog box, but the properties dialog box also has tabs for the current row and current cell.

A few of the interesting things to experiment with are cells that span a few columns and cells that have different widths than the other cells in the table. Both of these are easy to change with the table properties dialog box.

You can even have tables inside tables. This is particularly visually attractive if the tables have no borders. Create a table, put the insertion mark in one of the cells, and insert another table. The possibilities are endless.

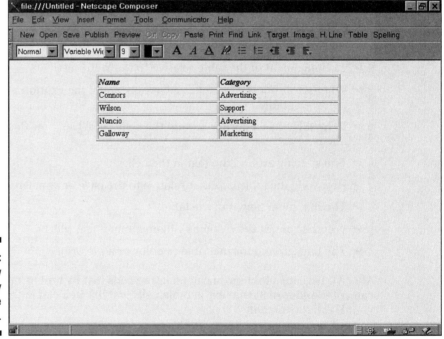

Figure 17-3:
A new table, ready to be filled in.

Using HTML in the Real World

Now that you have an overview of the major parts of HTML, you may be wondering what to do next. The best way to start is to take some existing text and add HTML tags to it. Open that newly edited file in Netscape or whatever browser you are using, see how you did on the first try, and keep refining your work.

You may find that the HTML tends to take over your document, letting the formatting take precedence over the content. When WYSIWYG word processors became common in the mid-1980s, the same thing happened with business memos and reports. Try to resist the urge to overformat; let the words speak for themselves. Chapter 18 gives you many more ideas about things to remember as you create Web documents.

Chapter 18

Think Twice; Then Think Again

● ●

In This Chapter

▶ Recognizing good and bad Web page design

▶ Learning to keep Web pages small

▶ Thinking about legal issues with Web pages

▶ Checking out forms and image maps

● ●

*A*s preceding chapters describe, Web content consists of more than just the text and pictures you see as you visit a site. Some Web sites have good style, nice design, and an enjoyable layout; others are ho-hum, and their design makes them a bit hard to read; still others are just plain awful.

Beyond the issues of design, however, are questions about what is good or not good to put on a Web page. In the excitement of publishing on the Web, you can easily forget that some of your readers may have cultural, political, religious, or geographical points of view that may cause them to be offended by some of what you decide to publish. This is not to say that you should not publish your views; if your intention is to make your site attractive to as many people as possible, however, you certainly need to think about more than just the appearance of your content.

This chapter covers many topics that you may want to consider when putting your Web pages together. Still, the best way to see what works and doesn't work is to explore the Web with an eye toward how others have made their sites attractive. If you find yourself drawn to a particular kind of site, consider emulating it. Of course, you don't need to simply copy what others have written on the Web: You can be creative and generate inviting Web pages at the same time.

Looking Good (or Bad) in Print

No hard-and-fast rules exist about designing Web pages to make them attractive. On the other hand, plenty of rules about how *not* to design pages can be derived from looking at sites on the Internet.

You don't need to have an artsy, mod look to your pages for them to be appreciated. In fact, a bit of a dull (but very functional) look often wins out over snappy but difficult-to-read text. This section covers many design ideas that you can incorporate (or avoid) in your Web pages.

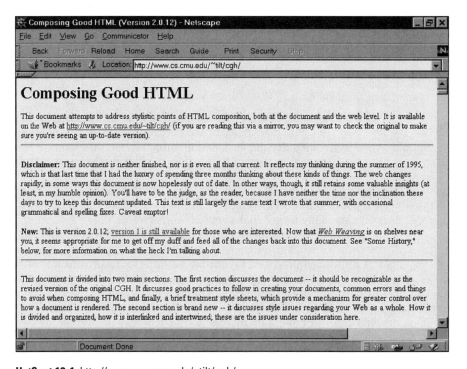

HotSpot 18-1: http://www.cs.cmu.edu/~tilt/cgh/
You can find many guides to using HTML but not so many guides to Web page design. This HTML guide is one of the most rigorous available. It is full of good suggestions, and it avoids the fluffy recommendations that many HTML guides give.

Avoid excessive vertical space

Most people on the Web have small screens on their computers. Web pages that have lots of extra white space between lines give users less text to look at on a single screen. As you add HTML to your content, remember that many tags cause white space to be added following the text they enclose, so avoid using those tags together.

For example, don't use <br> tags after lines that already have a blank line inserted after them as shown in the following example. Such an action results in excess vertical space after the list.

```
<li>I finally found out the correct way to get the car
started!
</ol>
<br>
```

On most Web browsers, all the heading tags such as <h1>, <h2>, and so on place a blank line after the heading; most also insert blank lines after paragraphs. As you use your Web browser to review how your HTML looks, think in terms of reducing the amount of excess vertical white space so that your readers don't need to scroll so much.

Lists are your friends

Information seems to be the emphasis on this superhighway that we are supposedly on, and information often comes in lists. Much of the informational content on the Web is somewhat organized as lists and menus. Many commercial sites that provide sales and customer service information, for example, display a menu of choices as their initial Web page; many of the links from that page also lead to menus.

In HTML, menus are most appropriately shown as lists by using the <ul> and </ul> tags. Notice that menus are better shown as *unordered lists* (lists prefaced with bullets) rather than as *ordered lists* (lists prefaced with numbers) because users normally choose only one item from the list rather than each item from the list in succession.

Many people have made lists of links that are not terribly interesting. You can use a bit of creativity in creating your lists by including helpful text as part of the list (but not as part of the link). For example, assume that you are making a list of physics departments at universities that have Web sites. A simple list may look something like the following example:

```
<ul>
<li><a href="http://www.physics.brown.edu/">Brown</a>
<li><a href="http://www.physics.unlv.edu/">University of
Nevada, Las Vegas</a>
<li><a href="http://string.harvard.edu/">Harvard</a>
</ul>
```

A more descriptive list would look like this:

```
<ul>
<li><a href="http://www.physics.brown.edu/">Brown</a>'s
server has descriptions of its research groups and various
seminars
<li><a href="http://www.physics.unlv.edu/">University of
Nevada,Las Vegas</a> is fairly mundane, but there are phone
lists and a bit of overview of the department
<li><a href="http://string.harvard.edu/">Harvard</a> has an
extensive Web page with many topics such as current re-
search, home pages for some of its undergraduate courses,
and links to other Boston-area physics sites
</ul>
```

Don't feel constrained to put your links at a particular place in a list. If you are giving longer explanations of the items in your list, you don't need to put the links at the beginning of the list. You could, for example, set up your list as follows:

```
<ul>
<li>The Web site for the physics department at
<a href="http://www.physics.brown.edu/">Brown</a>
has descriptions of its research groups and various
seminars
<li>The Web page for the
<a href="http://www.physics.unlv.edu/">University of
Nevada, Las Vegas</a> physics department is fairly mundane,
but there are phone lists and a bit of overview of the
department
<li>As you might expect,
<a href="http://string.harvard.edu/">Harvard</a> has an
extensive Web page with many topics such as current
research, home pages for some of its undergraduate courses,
and links to other Boston-area physics sites
</ul>
```

Use headings as headings

One of the current popular misuses of HTML is to use high-numbered headings such as ⟨h5⟩ and ⟨h6⟩ as methods for putting "fine print" on-screen. This is a bad practice for many reasons:

- ✔ On most Web browsers, fine print is unreadable. Many browsers, such as Netscape, put a gray background behind the text on-screen. Trying to read fine print on a gray background is almost impossible.

- ✔ Even without a gray background, most computers don't display text smaller than eight points very well.

- ✔ Some automated systems use the heading levels not as formatting commands, but as indicators of structure of a document. Those automated systems create virtual tables of contents from the headings; in doing so, those systems assume that this fine print is, in fact, a long heading.

Before trying to make fine print, you should ask yourself why you even want to put something in your page that is hard to read. Most people are perfectly adept at ignoring unimportant information on a page; just put your unimportant information at the bottom of the page in normal-sized letters, and trust people to either read it or skip right over it.

Although less common, some Web sites have been known to use ⟨h3⟩ and ⟨h4⟩ tags to get boldface characters instead of just using ⟨b⟩ tags. Obviously, this is not a good idea because you have no idea what kind of formatting each browser uses for headings.

When the Web Is Slow, Small Is Fast

One of the biggest temptations of creating your own Web pages is the desire to publish lots of content as quickly as possible. You've got a hard disk full of pictures and written material you've found interesting, and you're just dying to let the world at it. After all, Web access is almost free, and your Web provider isn't charging much for you to publish this content, right?

Maybe. The fact that the Web has flourished is partially based on the custom of people publishing loads of information and entertainment that wasn't available on the Internet before. You should feel free to continue that trend, but you should also consider how you can do so without wasting the overall bandwidth of the Internet.

If you have a graphical browser such as Netscape, you have probably already discovered Web sites that have huge inline graphics that take more than a minute to download. Face it: Huge inline graphics are usually a pain in the butt. Yes, they're sometimes nice to look at; and yes, they may even be useful. If you own a 14.4 Kbps modem, however, or if the Internet (or your Internet provider) is slower than usual at the moment you are accessing a Web page, viewing a huge graphic can be frustrating and time-consuming.

If you don't like huge graphics other people create, why create them yourself? You have many ways to make smaller graphics: You can use fewer colors in your pictures, show smaller pictures, or use pictures that are created at lower resolutions. Various paint and graphics conversion programs include options that enable you to create smaller files; use those features whenever possible.

Of course, graphics files are not the only ones that can be extremely large. Even a very useful 50K text file can seem huge to someone using only a 2400 bps modem or who lives in an area where Internet connections are always slow. If you post a long text file at your Web site, consider breaking the file down into smaller chunks. Often, a long file can be broken into chapters or sections.

For now, most people do not pay much to access the Web, and the Internet is running fairly rapidly in most parts of the world. To assume that this will be the case even two years from now, however, is dangerous. If the Internet, and thus the Web, becomes expensive or slow (or both!), large files will be shunned. We may as well all start looking at conservation so that the resources of the Internet are not squandered.

Just Because It's Cool Doesn't Mean It's Good

Then there's the delicate subject of taste. Similar to what you may find in many forms of media, much of what is on the Web is junk. Just because you *can* put some content on a Web page doesn't mean that you *should* put it there.

The wild freedom of Web publishing is a double-edged sword. Easy access to publishing on the Web means that some people who want to publish for a small audience can now do so at low cost, and the small target audience can access the material easily and cheaply. On the other hand, the same material is being presented to a much larger audience that is uninterested in it; and many in that audience may be very offended, outraged, or hurt by what is said or how it is said.

Even if you can publish for free, remember that publishing is a privilege. If you are writing something that is likely to provoke strong reactions in people outside your intended audience, try to think of ways to dissuade outsiders from visiting your Web site (or at least from reading the parts that will provoke strong reactions). This is plain courtesy and provides a bit of self-protection. If you publish an article that attacks the beliefs of a particular religion, for example, you may want to precede the article with a page that describes the tone of the article and suggests that people who may be offended by such an attack not follow the link to the article.

At one time or another, every one of us has said things that have angered other people. Sometimes that was our intended result; other times, it was an unanticipated side effect. Particularly when we were children, most of us were punished for some of the things we said. As adults, some of the ways we speak and the things we speak about in public can cause reactions in others so strong as to make them want to silence us. Every country in the world has dealt legally with how much expression to allow and to disallow.

The Web is basically no different than most other publishing media. Like everything from magazines to television, parts of the Web are of general interest, and other parts are of very narrow interest. All publishers deal with the same issues of rights, responsibilities, freedom, and costs.

Pay Attention to the Law

As you can tell, nothing in this book tries to discourage thoughtful publishing on the Web. Keep in mind, however, that not everyone is so generous. Legal restrictions are placed on a wide variety of publishing applications in many countries, and Web publishers can run afoul of the law in many ways.

For one extreme example, consider the statement "I would like to kill the President of the United States." Publishing that statement on a Web site in the United States could easily be considered illegal, and you could end up in jail within hours of putting it on your Web page. In other countries, such a statement may be discouraged and even condemned, but would be perfectly legal. In still other countries, such a statement would be applauded. (A statement such as "I would like to kill the President of *fill in the country*" can have different legal repercussions depending on where the statement is made and where it is read.)

Now, consider the fact that all three of these types of countries are on the Internet. A Web page published in the United States is readable in more than 100 countries. A Web page published in any of those countries is readable in the United States.

The law adapts very slowly to new technology. In the United States, it is not clear how the law deals with the fact that someone can read content published in other parts of the country (and other parts of the world) without physically "importing" the content. Already, cases are in the courts that raise this question relative to pornography, and it is likely that other forms of currently restricted speech (such as death threats, slander, and fraud) will soon follow. There are also moves in many countries to ban some types of speech from the Internet that are acceptable in other media, and many countries are actively moving to ban types of speech that are currently legal.

Sadly, no legal guidelines currently exist for what you can and can't publish safely on the Web. Of course, you should assume that anything that is illegal to print on paper is probably illegal to distribute on the Web, although even that isn't always a foregone conclusion. The kinds of content that are often prohibited in various states and countries include, but are not limited to, the following:

- Disparaging various religions and beliefs.
- Encouraging insurrection.
- Sexually explicit material.
- Threats against leaders.
- Descriptions of how to make weapons.
- Trade secrets of companies.

Of course, every one of these areas has shades of gray; that's one reason we have judges and lawyers to sort these matters out. Given the newness of the Web, it's likely that something that may have been considered legal on paper could be considered illegal on the Web — or vice versa. In other words, be careful.

If Only I Were a Programmer: Forms and Image Maps

One last bit of unfinished business that the more observant of you may have noticed: I've so far included no description of how to create HTML forms. Everything else in HTML is reasonably easy to grasp, but creating forms is not quite so easy. To create forms, you must be a programmer, and most Web sites that let you create your own documents don't let you create forms for just that reason.

Think for a moment about the forms you've seen as you moved around on the Web. Most forms have a few sets of buttons, and forms often have some fill-in fields as well. Every form has a button — usually labeled *Submit,* or *Send,* or *OK* — that causes the contents of the form to be sent to the host site for processing. Notice that word *processing*. To process the results, you need a program of some sort, and each program is tailored to a particular form.

Even if you know a bit about programming, you shouldn't think, "Hey, I can create the form and the program myself." On many systems, unless the program associated with a form is very carefully written, that program can become a huge security hole for the system. Hackers have already broken into various Web sites via badly written form programs, and it is likely that they will continue to do so.

Image maps are pretty much the same as forms. (By the way, the techies like to refer to them as one word, *imagemaps;* feel free to use either form.) After you click a certain part of an image map, the location of where you clicked is sent back to the host site for processing. The program at the host site then says "Ah, he clicked at this spot; therefore, he wants to get this information" and sends it to you. Again, you need a program to determine what to do with that information, and those programs also are susceptible to hackers and crackers (although image map programs aren't likely to be as vulnerable as forms programs).

Part V
The Web in the Future

The 5th Wave — By Rich Tennant

"It's a letter from the company that installed our in-ground sprinkler system. They're offering Internet access now."

In this part . . .

*E*veryone likes to pretend to be able to predict the future. The Web today, in fact, has been seriously affected by people making such future guesses about multimedia and HTML. Yet, here we are today without much multimedia and the same HTML we've had for years. The two chapters in this part give you an indication about what may — and may not — change on the Web in the coming years.

Chapter 19

Multimedia Mirage

● ●

In This Chapter

▶ Dealing with speed problems

▶ Getting a handle on multimedia

▶ Finding helper applications

● ●

*O*kay. You're reading Chapter 19 and this book is just getting to the subject of multimedia. You had heard all this great stuff about the Web and multimedia, but you haven't seen much about it in this book until now. So what gives?

Multimedia refers to content that incorporates more than one kind of medium. Because text is considered to be one kind of medium, text plus anything else is multimedia. Because most of what you can download from the Web consists of single kinds of media, however, each file isn't really multimedia.

Mmmm, Fast Is Good

Basically, the problem with multimedia and the Web is one of size. All multimedia files are too big to enable you to view or hear them interactively over the Web even if you have the fastest modem available today (28.8 Kbps). And even if you have a fast Internet connection such as a dedicated ISDN line, multimedia video is jerky and small, although you can get reasonable sound on an ISDN connection.

ISDN is a type of telephone service that enables you to get high-speed data connections through your phone line. ISDN lines carry data about five times faster than a 28.8-Kbps modem. Essentially, few people have ISDN lines today. In a few years, *many* people may have them, but that *many* will probably be fewer than 5 percent of the people on the Web. Thus multimedia on the Web isn't destined to be anything popular or even desirable for many years.

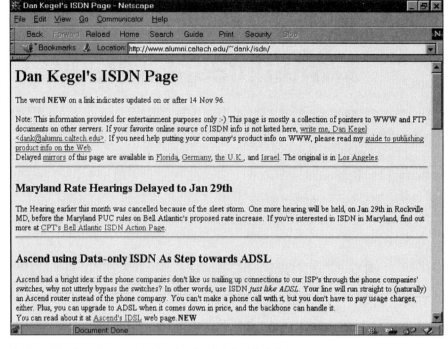

HotSpot 19-1: http://www.alumni.caltech.edu/~dank/isdn/
This Web page is one of the best resources for finding out about ISDN, sources for ISDN, rates for ISDN, and so on. This resource also has a complete list of ISDN hardware and software manufacturers.

Some people predict that many homes will soon have ISDN, but the telephone companies have priced ISDN service so high that few people are interested in signing up for it. The not-so-funny part of this is that these same phone companies say that they are pricing ISDN low now to get people interested!

If you're thinking, "Hey, I'll just get something faster than ISDN," I have some sad news for you: It's probably still not good enough. I know from personal experience: You can have a line that runs many times faster coming into your house, and multimedia still is jerky and not terribly interesting. Problems exist throughout the Internet, and having a big "data pipe" at your end won't fix them.

CD-ROMs still rule

The preceding discussion doesn't mean that all multimedia is unavailable. In fact, millions of people currently use CD-ROM multimedia on their PCs and Macintoshes. For many people who don't mind the limitations of current

CD-ROM-based multimedia, the combination of a CD-ROM drive and a computer works well. For other users, even CD-ROMs and standard PCs are too slow to deliver compelling video graphics.

You can't, however, compare CD-ROM-based multimedia and Web-based multimedia. CD-ROMs can deliver data to your computer more than 100 times faster than the fastest modem, which gives CD-ROMs a great advantage in delivering video and sound. CD-ROMs are much faster than ISDN lines for delivering multimedia, and they probably always will be.

You can still use the Web to receive multimedia; you just can't view that multimedia interactively as you receive it. If you've got an hour or two to download a large file, you can still do so and then watch or listen to it after it's all downloaded. This kind of delayed gratification is certainly not like the instant gratification of the rest of the Web, but if you want to take the time to slowly download large multimedia files, you're welcome to do so.

The basic problems

Even if you have an incredibly fast connection from your home to the Internet, many Web sites do not. You can't get the data any faster than it can be sent. Many sites aren't capable of sending out multimedia streams for a variety of reasons, such as the following ones:

- ✔ Getting high-speed connections to the Internet can cost thousands of dollars per month. Low-speed connections cost much less.

- ✔ Many Web sites are at universities. Universities may have high-speed Internet connections, but those connections are supporting tens of thousands of users inside the universities in addition to those users coming in from the outside.

- ✔ Just because you and the Web site have high-speed connections doesn't mean that all the connections *between* you and the Web site are fast. You can only get information from a remote site as fast as it can go through the slowest link along the way.

What's Multi?

You may still be hot on multimedia, even if you can't get it interactively off the Web. Many kinds of multimedia are available, but most of them really consist of "unimedia." Confusing? Yes.

As described at the beginning of this chapter, multimedia is content that incorporates more than one kind of media, such as text, pictures, and sound. Many people call Web pages that have inline graphics *multimedia* because they contain both text and pictures. Well, that kind of multimedia has been around for more than ten years. Embedding video and sound in documents has also been around for years, but it usually appears only on CD-ROM systems because of the large size of the files.

The different kinds of *media* that people usually associate with *multimedia* include the following:

✔ Plain text

✔ Formatted text

✔ Still pictures

✔ Audio

✔ Video

✔ Animation (nonvideo)

Plain text and formatted text have already been fully covered throughout this book. In fact, so have still pictures. As described in Chapter 5, the most common formats for pictures are JPEG and GIF. Netscape and other popular Web clients handle JPEG and GIF formats just fine.

Audio

Sound files come in many formats. These formats differ significantly, so one particular program usually can't play all the different kinds of sound files. For instance, Netscape version 2 couldn't play any sound files at all, but Netscape versions 3 and 4 can play the most common sound file formats: AIFF, AU, and WAV. Each of these files has different features that makes them attractive to different multimedia providers.

Unfortunately, sound files have the same problems as most multimedia: The files are quite big. Even the AU format, whose files are 8K per second of sound, require modems faster than the standard 28.8 Kbps to play in real time. A few companies have gotten around this problem, however, by using better compression. The RealAudio plug-in for Netscape lets you hear special sound files as they come over the Internet, so you don't have to bring the whole file in before playing it.

Video

If you think audio is a space hog on your hard disk, wait until you see video. The most common video formats are AVI and QuickTime movies, both of which can be played directly in Netscape. If you are using an earlier version of Netscape or a Web browser that can't play video, plenty of free applications are available that can do the job just fine. Videos are huge, usually taking up many megabytes per minute. Thus downloading anything other than a few seconds of a video clip is unlikely; and even then, downloading takes much longer than you would hope just for a few seconds of tiny-screen viewing.

Animation

So far, no well-accepted standards for nonvideo animation exist. Many programs that create animation are available, but few free or cheap programs exist for viewing the results. This situation may change in the future, but even then, not many animated images are available that people want to see.

Java

Version 2 of Netscape introduced another interesting extension to the browser. Web sites can create small programs, download them to your computer through Web pages, and execute them in Netscape. These programs, written in a relatively new language called Java, are used to create animation, perform live updating of information, and do other tasks that are well beyond what normal HTML can do.

Java has caused quite a stir in the Internet community (not to mention spurring a zillion bad coffee-related jokes). Java allows programmers to create a single program that can run on PCs, Macintoshes, and any other computer platform to which Java has been ported. It is supposedly very secure, so a program cannot come onto your system and read your files or destroy your hard disk.

On the other hand, it is (surprisingly) still mostly unproven. This isn't to say that you can't find Java programs around: hundreds exist. However, very few of them do much that is useful. Maybe by the time you read this, the situation will have changed, but even years into the "Java revolution" finding many useful Java programs on Web sites is a difficult task.

Further, Java's security was supposed to be sound, but university researchers have found numerous, very serious security bugs that Sun and Netscape have to keep fixing. So far, no one has exploited the security holes that have been found, but I really do worry that some lurking holes may exist that can turn into nightmares for novice (and not-so-novice) users.

VRML World: Virtual reality for virtual fun

Netscape has jumped on the virtual reality bandwagon with both feet. VRML World is Netscape's foray into providing a browser for VRML (Virtual Reality Modeling Language), the most popular way of showing three dimensional worlds. VRML worlds are pretty difficult to navigate in, however, and like other multimedia, are slow to download.

Like Java, how much interest VRML will generate is unclear. People had hyped VRML for many years, but recently, the main companies making VRML creation tools have started shutting down. Finding almost any useful VRML sites around the Web is still a difficult task.

Plugging into plug-ins

The folks at Netscape went well beyond Java when they extended version 2. They included two other major extension features that will probably get more and more use as programmers discover them. Although neither does much by itself, both open up Netscape so that it can work with a vast range of other kinds of programs. Generally, plug-ins fall into the nebulous category of multimedia, meaning that they let Navigator show you content in formats not normally supported by the program.

Many companies — such as Adobe, Macromedia, and Apple — are using *inline plug-ins* to make it easier to view materials you get from the Web outside of Netscape. For example, if you get a document that is prepared with Macromedia's Director program, that document can start a Director plug-in, which causes the content to be shown in Netscape's window using the program from outside of Navigator. The viewing program can even have links back to Netscape, so documents being viewed can have links back to the Web.

Helpers for Browsers

Every major browser enables you to specify what programs it should use if you select a link to a sound or video file. In Netscape, you specify the helper files in the Applications page of the Preferences dialog box, which is described more fully in Chapter 6. Essentially, a helper application is one that gets launched if your browser gets data it doesn't know how to handle. Every Web response from a server comes with a two-part description of the kind of data that is in the response. MPEG videos, for example, have a standard description of *video/mpeg*. In the helper application preferences, you choose a separate program for each kind of data. If you don't have a program that can display the data, you can always choose to simply save the data on disk.

Chapter 20
HTML: The Next Generation

In This Chapter

▶ Looking at how HTML will change

▶ Making rough guesses about when it will change

Chapters 16 through 18 describe the most important features of HTML version 2.0. The HTML features described in those chapters are available in every major Web client program.

As you may guess, HTML will not end with version 2.0. In fact, future versions of HTML are already being planned, debated, and formalized. Given how important HTML is to the Web, HTML is likely to keep changing and getting better (and more complicated).

Many suggestions have been made about what features should appear in future versions of HTML. Some make a great deal of sense right off; others seem a tad obscure. Some are of interest only to a small number of people, but those people have a strong desire for these features. (Such is the way computer standards are established.)

This chapter was last updated in the summer of 1997. The information presented here is correct and current for that time. If you are reading this around, say, the beginning of 1998, the material here may be out of date. The standards process will certainly have moved forward, and things described here as proposed standards or experimental may be real standards by the time you're reading this.

On the other hand, the features being considered also may have significantly changed or even been discarded from the HTML standards process altogether. Further, it may turn out that the large Web client companies such as Netscape and Microsoft pay less and less attention to the HTML standards and create their own extensions. The best way to find out where the HTML world is today as you read this is to go to the Web sites discussed in this chapter and see what they have to say.

Where the Future Is Being Shaped

Until 1996, the future of HTML was in the hands of the HTML Working Group of the Internet Engineering Task Force, better known as the IETF. The Working Group valiantly tried to make some sense of what the standard should look like and where it should go, but they ended up failing at getting the agreement needed.

In 1995, the World Wide Web Consortium (also called the W3C) took a much more active role in trying to coordinate the various extensions to HTML that were being proposed by companies such as Netscape, Microsoft, Spyglass, and others. Because all these companies are members of the W3C, that group is a good place to try to get some consensus about what should and shouldn't be in HTML. The W3C is now where most of the HTML work is taking place. In 1996, they finally standardized the next generation of HTML, called version 3.2. Version 3.2 is the result of the members of the W3C getting tired of all the wrangling and fussing by the IETF HTML WG. The W3C went their own way, picked their own number (there was never anything between 2.0 and 3.2), and chose the feature set they could all agree on. It's too soon to know if there will be a 3.3 or 4.0 or something like that, but if there is, it will almost certainly come from the W3C and not the IETF.

If you're interested in the state of HTML, you should probably keep track of the W3C work. Figure 20-1 shows their main HTML page, which is at

```
http://www.w3.org/pub/WWW/MarkUp/
```

The W3C is not stopping at HTML version 3.2. They are working on ways to add more features to HTML to make Web pages more useful in more environments. As I write this, they are considering adding features like:

- Making HTML pages more useful for people with disabilities
- Standardizing frames and subwindows
- Creating more powerful forms
- Allowing for dynamic page updates through programming
- Mathematical formatting

All of these projects are described on pages off of the main W3C HTML page.

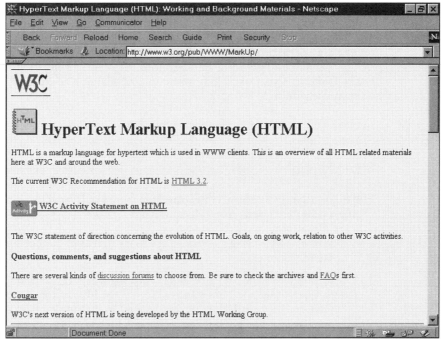

Figure 20-1:
Learning
about
HTML from
the W3C.

Why Netscape Is Different

Most Web browsers keep up with the HTML development effort. By the time HTML version 2.0 was made final, they all worked with that version almost perfectly. Before 1995, few Web browsers implemented HTML features that weren't part of the standard.

Then along came Netscape. The rough-and-tumble programmers at Netscape decided that the HTML standards process wasn't moving ahead fast enough for them, so they started adding their own HTML features. Immediately, this action raised a storm of criticism, with many people on the Internet accusing Netscape Communications of subverting the standards process.

In fact, nothing could be farther from the truth. The standards don't say: "Thou shalt not do anything except what is in this standard." Rather, the standards tell you what you must do to conform to that standard. People who write software are, of course, allowed to do more than that. If a Web browser sees some HTML that it does not recognize (such as tags that are not part of the standard), it is supposed to gracefully ignore them. Thus, non-Netscape browsers reading HTML tags invented by Netscape have the option to simply ignore them.

Still, many Internet users (including people who work for companies that make competing Web browsers) fumed that Netscape's additions made moving the HTML standard ahead in an orderly fashion impossible for others. Netscape programmers disagreed, saying that they just added a few things that seemed obvious. Furthermore, Netscape promised to follow any future standards that used different tags to do what Netscape's standards were already doing.

Netscape documents its changes to the HTML version 2.0 specs in the following file:

```
http://home.netscape.com/assist/net_sites/html_extensions.html
```

The top of this file is shown in Figure 20-2. Some of the major additions and changes Netscape made are as follows:

- ✔ The new `<nobr>` and `</nobr>` tags mark text that cannot have a line break in it.

- ✔ You can specify the font size to use with the new `<font>` and `<basefont>` tags. These tags are handy for enlarging the first letter of a paragraph, adding another kind of emphasis in the documents, and so on.

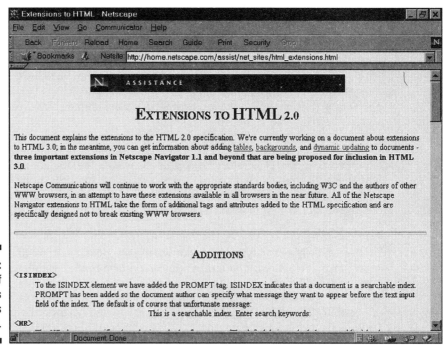

Figure 20-2: Some of Netscape's improvements to HTML 2.0.

✔ The new `<center>` and `</center>` tags (you guessed it) center text horizontally on the page.

✔ By using the `<hr>` tag, you can also say how wide the line should be, how thick, whether you want it against the left, center, or right side of the page, and whether you want it shaded.

✔ The `<img>` tag now has lots of options to enable you to align an image with different parts of the page. You can also specify the height and width of the image, which makes it easier for Web browsers to lay out the page before the image has been downloaded. And, for a bit of flair, you can add a border to the image.

✔ The `<ul>` tag enables you to specify the kind of bullets you get. You can choose between disks, circles, and squares.

✔ You get a bit more control in numbered lists. You can say what kind of numbering you want: plain digits, letters (upper- or lowercase), or roman numerals (upper- or lowercase). You can also specify with what number the list starts.

✔ You can specify lists in general by using the new `<list>` tag. For example, instead of using `<ul>` to start a bulleted list, you can use `<list type=ul>`. This gives you a bit more flexibility if you decide to change the type of list later.

✔ For pages with searchable indexes using the `<isindex>` tag (which is used to indicate that the document is searchable by a program on the server), you can also specify a prompt for the search.

✔ Two new special characters are available: `&reg;` for a registered trade-mark (®) symbol and `&copy;` for a copyright (©) symbol.

Whew! That list is just what Netscape added in version 1.1. Version 2 went even further, extending HTML in many ways that became part of HTML 3.2 (before that version was made official, however).

Nonetheless, you'll find it useful to know what additions to HTML appeared in Netscape version 2. You can find out more at

```
http://home.netscape.com/assist/net_sites/
html_extensions_3.html
```

Briefly, the extensions are as follows:

✔ The new `<big>` and `<small>` tags make text larger and smaller. For example, you can make one word larger with something like the following:

```
Hey, this is <big> important</big>, so please listen up!
```

✔ You can create subscripts and superscripts with the `<sub>` and `<sup>` tags. This feature made it into HTML version 3.2.

✔ You can change the alignment of a paragraph with the attributes. Instead of using the normal `<p>` tag, you use `<p align=center>` to center the paragraph after the tag. Instead of `center`, you can also use `left` and `right`.

✔ There is a new concept of *frames,* which allows you to create separately scrollable areas of the window. To create a frame, you use the `<frameset>` and `<frame>` tags. You can even create alternate text, for people who don't have frame-enhanced browsers, with the `<noframes>` tag. These tags are described in much more detail at

```
http://home.netscape.com/assist/net_sites/frames.html
```

✔ Netscape version 2 allows *client-side imagemaps,* which are like the clickable images in version 1 except that they allow you to use them when you are not connected to the Internet. This has many advantages, the main one being that the processing of "what does clicking here mean" is done on your local computer, which is fast, instead of causing a request to go to the host computer, which may be slow.

✔ Although it's not really an extension, you can specify in an HTML page that particular inline plug-ins and Java programs should appear at a particular part of a page. You specify these with the `<embed>` and `<applet>` tags.

✔ Forms in Netscape version 2 support the type of file upload described earlier in this chapter.

Some Features You May See Soon

Many of these Netscape-specific features may appear in the future versions of HTML, but debate continues about whether they will appear as Netscape designed them. This is one of the hazards of designing new features without waiting for the standards body to approve them; on the other hand, you can die waiting for the W3C to put out new standards.

A slew of other features are likely to show up within the next few rounds of crafting the HTML standard at the W3C. Some already appear in some of the more advanced Web browsers. As discussed earlier in this chapter, it's impossible to predict how and when any of these suggested features may appear. Knowing what's being suggested is a good idea, however, so that you aren't too surprised if a new version of your browser has these features built in.

Tables

Virtually everyone working on the HTML standard agreed that a tables feature had to be included in HTML. When the W3C released HTML 3.2 with a robust tables feature, most of the browser makers made sure that their tables worked like that in the specification. Since the spec was almost exactly based on Netscape's tables, Netscape didn't have much to do in order to conform.

Because of its popularity, the tags Netscape chose to use for tables have already started to be used on the Web. Figure 20-3, for example, shows a typical table as displayed by the Netscape browser.

Additional character sets

Right now, HTML is limited to the characters defined in the HTML specs. However, many other character sets certainly should be available to people creating HTML documents. Character sets are discussed widely (and heatedly) in many IETF working groups, as well as in many other computer forums, such as the International Standards Organization (ISO).

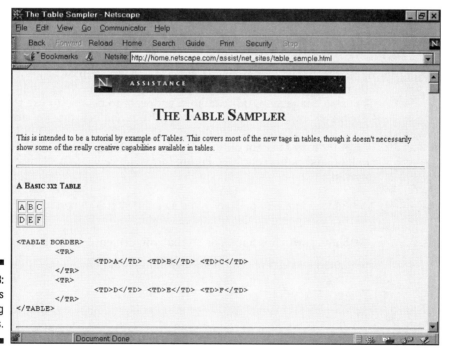

Figure 20-3:
Netscape's rendering of tables.

Future versions of HTML may enable you to specify that a document use a different character set. Discussions also are underway on whether you can specify that the overall document uses one character set but that parts of a document can use different sets. This would give users outside the United States much greater flexibility and would enable those who use specialized character sets (such as the Greek character set used by scientists) to publish more of their information on the Web.

Better horizontal control of text

One of the most common mistakes beginners make in using word processors is in the method they use to place text where they want it on a line. Every word processor has a way of setting tabs, for example, yet most word processing novices use the space bar to move to the place they want. Getting text to line up this way is usually quite difficult — and centering lines this way is even more difficult.

It really shouldn't be hard to add tags to HTML for tab stops and other tools for aligning text on a line. Netscape has already added its own tags, <center> and </center>, for centering text on a line and <p align=center> to center the paragraph after the tag. Such features seem likely to appear sooner rather than later in future versions of HTML.

Much more advanced forms

HTML's form features are nice (and certainly better than any equivalent on other Internet services), but much more can be done with them. You may like using image maps, for example, and want to be able to use them in forms. That capability should certainly be added in future versions of HTML.

Currently, forms accept only a few kinds of information — namely text, list choices, and button choices. Future forms, however, may also accept the following:

- Picture images (perhaps offering a little scratch pad into which you can draw or paste an image).
- Sliding switches and dials so that you can enter a number from a range.
- Audio and video input (two-way multimedia).

Math equations and formulae

Academic computer users have long been able to lay out equations and formulae by using various word processing and publishing software. Because this is an absolute requirement for many academic papers, the Web hasn't been used much for academic publishing. If HTML had reasonably simple ways for expressing these kinds of data, you could expect to see an explosion of academic publishing on the Web.

Footnotes

What is an academic paper without footnotes? Although footnotes are not common in normal book and magazine publishing, academics live by them. Actually, many other fields also rely on footnotes; both the legal and accounting professions, for example, must have them as well. These should be fairly easy to put in a future version of HTML.

So When Will I See All This?

Who knows? Some of these "future" features are already appearing in Web browsers such as Netscape. If the standards bodies such as the IETF and the W3C don't move as fast as the market demands, Netscape and others will probably keep adding their own implementations of these features. On the other hand, this practice will probably lead to fragmentation of the HTML market, which would be a bad thing all around.

Remember, too, that many other features not listed in this chapter may appear in future versions of HTML. Someone may think of a small new feature that most people agree is pretty great, and it gets fast-tracked into the next version. As the Web grows and more people ask, "Why doesn't this do such-and-such?" you're more likely to see such features added to newer versions of HTML.

Part VI
The Part of Tens

The 5th Wave   By Rich Tennant

"I don't care what your E-Mail friends in Europe say, you're not having a glass of Chianti with your bologna sandwich."

In this part . . .

This part gives you a few quick chapters containing lists of ten various things having to do with the World Wide Web: ten things the Web doesn't do yet, ten bothersome things about the Web, and ten charming Web sites to visit. Well, that's thirty, total, but you get the idea.

Chapter 21

Ten Things the Web Won't Do for You ... Yet

In This Chapter

▶ Looking into many possible futures

▶ Imagining the Web that you want

*E*ven though you may never have the fancy multimedia computer that you want and HTML may never be easy enough for mere mortals to use without help, the future of the Web looks bright. Many people today may look at the Web and say, "So what?" But many things could change within the next few years to make the Web an even more exciting place to be.

This chapter lays out ten ways in which the Web may improve. The future Web features described here are not based on miracles or any huge technical improvements. In fact, they could have already existed today if people a year or two ago thought they were important enough.

Depending on when you read this book, some of these "future" items may, in fact, be part of the present. One of the hard parts in writing about the future is that the future can come to pass before the book has a new edition. Remember, however, that all these features can keep improving, just as many parts of the Web have improved over time.

Publish Software That Never Gets Out of Date

The Web is up-to-date. A company with a Web site can put information on it at any time. This process is very different from the traditional way of publishing software, in which the software is distributed on floppy disks and CD-ROMs. If that software is revised or the content on the CD-ROM is updated, the disks already sold are out of date. (In fact, the disks still on the store shelves are also out of date.)

Combining software publishing with the Web can change the nature of publishing software. Conceivably, a user could at any time run an update program that goes out to the publisher's Web site and grabs the latest changes and updates to the software. Imagine a CD-ROM encyclopedia that is automatically updated to include this week's news or a medical reference that has new studies added every month.

Put the Content Close to You

Looking at a Web site that is far away almost always takes longer than looking at one closer to you. If you are in the U.S., browsing sites in Asia or Europe can be tediously slow. It doesn't have to be this way, however, because these sites can set up *mirrors* in the U.S. (and U.S. sites can set up mirrors in other parts of the world).

Mirror sites and smarter Web clients can make getting information much faster and reduce the load on the Internet at the same time. For example, your client could see that you were linking to a site in Taiwan, remember that a mirror is located much closer, and get the information from there (possibly asking you first). This action by your client reduces both your frustration and the amount of information traveling on the trans-Pacific Internet cables.

Use Names Instead of Locations

Most URLs point to a location where information is stored (the notable exception is the `news:` URL). What if the same information is stored in many different places? Shouldn't a way exist to choose the "best" of many possible locations?

One of the next big advances on the Internet (that will particularly help the Web) will be *URNs,* or *Uniform Resource Names.* If you link to a URN, you get back one or more URLs for the thing named in the URN. You can then choose the URL you want for the URN. Getting the list of URLs from a URN is called *resolving* the URN.

Asking for information by name (or URN) has many advantages over asking for it by its location (or URL):

  ✔ If the owner of a document moves the document, the owner must update only the pointer in the published URN, and everybody who later accesses that URN will find the information at its new location. (People who try to access the document using an out-of-date URL won't reach it after the move.)

✔ URN client software can be smart. For example, when you request resolution of a particular URN, you can also tell the URN client where on the Internet you are, and the software can give you the closest URL that has a copy of the information. You may also specify a preferred language; if the information is available in many languages, the URN program could give you just the URL of the document in the desired language.

✔ URNs are incredibly flexible. A good URN publisher can give you many URLs for a single URN request. For example, if a URN is "*Hamlet* in many languages," it may resolve to a set of many URLs, one for each language. That way, you don't need to specify a preferred language, and you can choose from the set of URLs returned to you using your URN client.

Let People Write Content Reviews

As the Web gets more and more content that costs money to access, you will probably want to start getting other people's opinions of the content before you access it. Services that support opinion polls and reviews of content will become as popular on the Web as they are in current paper media such as magazines.

Reviews of Web content will also be important even if the content is free, just because so much is out there that you don't want to waste your time jumping around from site to site. These reviews may be free or cheap, but the most useful ones will cost more. Of course, given how easy it is to link things on the Web, the reviews will probably have links directly to what is being reviewed, making them more useful than paper reviews.

Send You the Daily News

The "personalized newspaper" is a recurring theme in computers and communication. The idea is that each night a computer goes through all its available resources and creates a summary based on your preferences. Many companies have claimed to have created such publications, but none have come close to succeeding. So far, they have all been based on too limited content from which to choose and unnatural methods for users to express their preferences.

The Web, however, may help push this concept more toward reality. Given the much larger content base of the Web, more interesting newspapers can be created. The Web is also fertile ground for people studying the best way to get content preferences from many people. As the Web expands, the likelihood of interesting and inexpensive personalized newspapers increases.

Enable Whole-Web Searching

The best catalogs on the Web right now are the ones created by individuals on particular subjects. Searching the entire Web, or even a significant portion of it, is still impossible. The Web spider sites described in Chapter 7 are still primitive, incomplete, and of limited research value.

The technology to make the Web search sites better and more useful, however, is already available. Dedicated sites with advanced spiders, aided by the Web site administrators themselves, could lead to much better, searchable indexes.

Tell You Where the Problems Are on the Internet

In many areas of the world, you can listen to news stations on the radio to find out the traffic conditions on the highways. This service helps drivers avoid areas congested by accidents, or at least lets them know that they need to plan on taking more time in their travels. Some areas even have toll-free telephone numbers with this kind of useful information.

Not so on the Web. There is no way to find out, for example, "the Web server at BigComputers is down," or "trying to get information from Web servers in Australia right now is twice as slow as it was an hour ago." Mind you, it would not be hard for someone to set up such an information service. However, because no central authority on the Web exists, no one is really in the business of servicing Web users this way. Also, no standards exist for how a site might report its status.

Bring You Real BBSs, Real Fast

Two-way communication is an important part of everyone's personal life and business life. Yet, if you take out Usenet news, the Web is still 99 percent a one-way medium. On the other hand, non-Web computer BBSs throughout the world thrive because they give people a place to chat about things that concern them most.

Nothing is stopping anyone on the Web from setting up BBS systems. In fact, some already exist. These two-way parts of the Web, however, are hampered by poor design and the inherent speed problems of the Web, even for text. In the near future, many sites will develop and test better BBS interfaces for the Web, and parts of the Web will become more conducive to two-way conversation.

Build Real Communities

The talk about "virtual communities" on the Internet usually is well off the mark. Connection does not equal community. Just because you can chat with a group of people on the Web doesn't mean that you have the kind of long-term commitment to understand, support, and enjoy those people. Yet these things are requirements for real communities. Although very useful for many people, Usenet newsgroups are not communities in the sense that anyone can join them, no one must support anyone else, and understanding is often last on the list of importance.

This is not to say that communities cannot be built on the Web. In fact, just the opposite is true. Real communities, however, take much more personal work than has been put into many Web sites to date. People must be committed; they must work within the limitations of the Web's communications capabilities; and they must keep at it even when it doesn't work the way they imagined it might.

It is likely in the coming years that the Web will help get some communities together that might otherwise never have been able to do so. Better BBS software will be part of this process, but a bigger part will be a shift in what people expect from the Web. An even bigger part will be a shift in what people expect from each other when they communicate without seeing or hearing each other. The outcome could be wonderful.

Bring Everyone into the Tent

Today, the Web is used mainly by people in the major industrialized countries in North America, Europe, and Asia. The number of countries with almost no Web presence, either in terms of Web sites or Web users, however, is staggering. Smaller countries and poorer people are grossly underrepresented on the Web, more than on any other popular communication medium.

It doesn't need to be this way, and the tide is changing. The Internet Society is one of the prime movers in bringing the Internet to all countries of the world; it offers many programs that help countries share Internet technologies. Furthermore, many communities in the countries already on the Web are moving to bring Web access to more people by putting Web-enabled terminals in libraries and other public places.

The spirit of inclusion was one of the founding premises of the Web. Its open structure was designed to let as many Internet hosts as possible participate. The next step is to help as many users as possible participate. This step, if taken, will in turn certainly fuel the growth of the number of Web sites, as well as the depth and thought put into the current Web sites.

Chapter 22

Ten Reasons Why the Web Bothers Some People

● ●

In This Chapter

▶ Looking at the bits that folks don't like

▶ Enjoying diversity

● ●

*O*kay, so the Web isn't all happiness and joy. What is? We humans manage to find fault with almost everything, and something as big and expansive as the Web is certainly a target for such criticism.

Understand that the ten reasons described in this chapter do not bother the same people. In fact, some people view some Web features as positive, while others view the same features as very negative. A few people don't like anything about the Web, but we can't do much for them, can we?

Using the Web Is Too Unpredictable

Because of how the Internet is set up, you have no idea how long it takes to follow a link before you try. You cannot tell if a link points to a small or a huge file without accessing the link. Even after you do that, you may not be able to determine how big the file is until it's completely downloaded.

Even trying the same link twice during different times of the day can lead to wildly different access times. Parts of the Internet may get busy at different times of the day, and the reliability of the paths between you and a host site can vary, depending on which company is servicing those paths.

URLs Are Cryptic

URLs are hard to read and are often hard to type. You commonly find URLs that are more than 40 characters long. URLs are fine if you find them in links that are already on the Web, but many of them appear in other parts of the Internet or from the print media, such as this book.

Links Break

Because URLs point to a specific location, they all too often break when the location of the information changes. Links frequently break when a filename changes, the name of the host server changes, or simply when the person who created the document decides to change the name on a whim. In any case, if you try to link to a broken URL, you receive an error message.

Pornography Is Too Easy to Find

Probably the most common complaint about the Web and the Internet is that too much pornography is too easy to find. By coincidence, one of the shortest URLs on the Web, news:alt.sex, is a discussion about sex. You can find plenty of sex on the Web if you want to. However, I believe that the people who say that you can easily come across pornographic sites "by accident" are exaggerating. Pornography is such a charged topic, people on all sides of the debate tend to not be completely honest.

Pornography of many kinds is easily available on the Web; it's also easily available in print. As most men know, just about any boy old enough to want to read print pornography can get access to it; accessing it on the Web is obviously easier for kids who have unrestricted Internet access.

It's Too Much Head, Not Enough Heart

Cruising the Web for a few hours can be an agitating experience. Most of the sites on the Web are very information based and not at all emotion based. Some people live in their minds much more than in their spirits, but many people are just the opposite. Today's Web has very little to offer to people who try to lead from their feelings.

It's Too Masculine

Similar to the head/heart split, the Web as it stands now is predominantly masculine. This fact isn't surprising, given that more than 90 percent of Web users and Web providers are men. Still, it is quite disturbing to many people (yes, including many men) that so little feminine sensibility exists on the Web. Bigger, faster, more powerful, unconcerned with appearance, irregular, and so on seem to be the driving forces of the Web.

Few Sites Give You Two-Way Communication

If people come to the Web after having experienced electronic mail, mailing lists, and Usenet news, they usually notice that most of the Web is one-way communication. For some things, that's fine; after all, books such as this one are one-way communication. But two-way communication could obviously be used to a great effect in many places on the Web.

No Maps of the Web Exist

No one likes to get lost, but getting lost on the Web is easy. Links can take you in unexpected directions and down blind alleys. Stumbling around the Web may be fun for some folks, but it is disturbing for many others. Because users can get to any site without having come "from" somewhere, most Web users don't know the meaning of "go back" unless they use that feature in their Web browsers.

Services Such as FTP Have Archaic Interfaces

The fact that the Web encompasses older Internet technologies is great in that it makes a huge amount of older information available. However, those older technologies are burdened with older user interfaces that are difficult for most people to use. FTP is a great example. Many of the files in the directories are not meant to be read by humans, but they appear in directory listings anyway. The names of FTP files are also often cryptic and assume that the user understands a great deal about UNIX.

It's Not as Interesting as TV or Books

Probably the most damning criticism of the Web is that it just isn't as fun as other things that people are already used to. In some ways, the Web is more interactive than television, but the content is just not as compelling to the vast majority of people. It is more immediate than books, but it still feels very computerish and not as comfortable as many print books and magazines. These facts won't kill the Web, of course, but they will probably turn many people away from it for the foreseeable future.

Chapter 23

Ten Charming Places on the Web

• •

In This Chapter

▶ A reminder that the Web is more than just "information"

▶ Places you'll want to visit

• •

*T*he Web can be a restful, enjoyable place if you let it. Many of the sites described in this book are useful, informative, and so on, but there's more to life than that. Sometimes the Web is useful for finding out about what else is available off the Web, and sometimes it's nice just to sit and be while you are roaming the Web.

Bill's Lighthouse Getaway

`http://zuma.lib.utk.edu/lights/`

People travel, people have hobbies, and people take pictures. Some of the "personal" sites on the Web have wonderful pictures of what people do when they are on vacation, when they're doing their hobbies, and so on. This Web site shows many pages of pictures and descriptions of lighthouses.

Zen Page

`http://sunsite.unc.edu/zen/`

Many people view Zen Buddhism as one of the most contemplative religions in the world. Whether or not that is the case, you can find many Web sites with Buddhist themes, particularly those of quietude and tranquillity. This site features many such Zen pages.

ExploraNet

http://www.exploratorium.edu/

If you've ever been to the Exploratorium in San Francisco, you know that it is one of the least peaceful museums anywhere. Kids run around, trying all sorts of science experiments and teaching exhibits, generally having a wild, science-filled experience. Parents and teachers can often be found sitting exhausted on the benches.

ExploraNet, the Exploratorium's Web site, however, is much more calm. It still provides much of the sense of wonder of the full Exploratorium; much of the magic of the museum has been translated to the many Web pages.

Plugged In

http://www.pluggedin.org/

What do you get when you combine creative but financially poor kids with multimedia technology and training? Pretty amazing results. Artwork is just a fraction of what is created at Plugged In, a center in East Palo Alto, California, that is geared toward helping underprivileged kids learn to use multimedia equipment and facilities that are clearly beyond their financial reach.

The Peace Page

http://www.ccnet.com/~elsajoy/index2.html

Okay, call me an old hippie. A page about spiritual awareness and being centered touches my heart. This personal page is one of my favorites, a testimony to someone who cares enough to tell the world that she likes things of the soul. What's so funny about peace, love, and understanding?

Positive Vibrations

http://newciv.org/worldtrans/positive.html

On a similar note, this page has lots of links to other places around the Web that are "positive." Yes, sure, it's all relative, but I guess I like knowing that a few Web pages are out there that help to balance out all the pages extolling violent games, hatred, and just plain "negative" stuff.

Crossword Puzzles

```
news:rec.puzzles.crosswords
```

If you like to relax with a word puzzle or two, you probably do crossword puzzles. The `rec.puzzles.crosswords` newsgroup is a wonderful place to hang out when you're not putting pencil to paper. Some people post humorous clues; others point to other puzzle locations; and still others just like reading and writing about words.

GardenNet

```
http://trine.com/GardenNet/
```

Sitting in a garden can be the most relaxing thing many of us get to do during a busy week. Whether you like to tend gardens or just sit in them, the resources in GardenNet can be enjoyable in and of themselves.

Bird Watching

```
http://www-stat.wharton.upenn.edu/~siler/birding.html
```

Another activity that is quite calming for millions of people is watching birds. You can find birding organizations all over the world whose interests vary from simply counting different varieties of birds to preservation and collecting.

Pete's Pond Page

```
http://reality.sgi.com/employees/peteo/
```

Some folks are lucky enough to have a pond in their garden. This Web site is another one of those personal pages that serve as a resource spot for others with similar interests. No Web page can replace the tranquillity of going out and watching the goldfish, but this one certainly helps the experience.

Glossary

The Internet is full of jargon, and much of it applies as much to the Web as it does to any other service. This glossary covers general Internet- and Web-specific terms that you may need to know. Many abbreviations are used on the Web, and you may also see these terms spelled out in places. Such terms are listed here with the more common usage appearing first — be it abbreviation or the full name — and the less common appearing in parentheses after it.

America Online

A large online service with more than five million users. America Online, also called AOL, was the first of the "big three" online services (Prodigy, America Online, CompuServe) to have more than just a mail connection to the Internet. It introduced both a Gopher client and a Usenet news client in the spring of 1994 and a Web browser in 1995.

anonymous FTP

The most common way to search for and download files. Hundreds of host computers on the Internet enable anyone to connect to their systems and look through directories for files they want.

Archie

The preferred method for searching for files in anonymous FTP archives. Archie servers throughout the world enable you to log in or use Archie client software to search for files and directories by their titles.

ARPAnet

The network run by the U.S. Defense Department's Advanced Research Projects Agency that was the original "backbone" of the Internet. The ARPAnet was originally intended as a research network that would also link Defense Department affiliates. ARPA handed the ARPAnet to the U.S. National Science Foundation, which turned it into the NSFnet.

ASCII

Plain text characters. ASCII is a standard that says which computer-readable number is associated with each letter, digit, and punctuation mark. An *ASCII file* is a text file that can be read by almost any program.

BBSs (bulletin board systems)

Computer systems that enable people to dial through modems and use their services. A BBS may be a single computer with a modem or a local network of many computers that can accept dozens of connections at a time. Some BBSs are on the Internet, although most are not. BBSs often feature downloadable files, discussion areas, and other features that make them popular. You can use some BBSs for free, although others charge a monthly or hourly fee.

BITNET

A network of university computers that is separate from (but connected to) the Internet. BITNET is slowly fading away as the mainframe computers on which most of it runs are decommissioned, but it is still a major force in academic computing. BITNET computers are not on an active network but instead have intermittent connections.

bookmarks

Method of remembering specific Web sites. Many Web browsers (and a few other Internet clients) enable you to store the name and locations of interesting sites in bookmark collections. You can use these collections as quick ways to get to where you want to go.

browser

Software used for roaming the Web. Web browsers are client software that enable users to view the many kinds of information on the Web, such as HTML documents, Gopher pages, and FTP directories. Netscape is the most popular Web browser, followed in popularity by Internet Explorer. See also *client program*.

c shell

The most common user interface for people whose Internet providers run on character-based UNIX systems. The c shell is also one of the oldest user interfaces still widely used, and it shows. Unless you are a computer weenie, it is unlikely that you will like using the c shell very much.

cache

An intermediate storage location that keeps a copy of information you have already seen. In Web browsers such as Netscape, if you access a location that you have already been to and the information from that location is still in the cache, you don't need to get the information again from the Internet. Caches help reduce network traffic and make using the Web faster.

CERT *(Computer Emergency Response Team)*

A security force for the Internet. CERT is a clearinghouse of information about network security, known security problems on the Internet, and attempted (or successful) break-ins. It has an FTP site that has definitive versions of common Internet server software.

CGI *(Common Gateway Interface)*

A programming standard used by most Web servers for handling forms. CGI helps one type of software (in this case, Web server software) present information to other types of software (the programs that handle Web forms) in a standard fashion so that the two don't need to know anything about each other.

chat

An old multiuser discussion system for the Internet. It has almost completely been replaced by Internet Relay Chat (IRC).

CIX *(Commercial Internet Exchange)*

The first major industry group for companies that provide Internet access. Because it is made up of competitors in a constantly changing market, CIX is a somewhat volatile group. CIX also lobbies the U.S. government on Internet-related issues.

client program

A program that a user runs to interface with server software. Client software often looks different on each computer it runs on, taking on the best features of that computer. Many different client programs can interact with one server program. See also *browser*.

client-server software

Software that is split between two programs: clients and servers. The term *client-server* has become widely used in the computer industry to describe database and information retrieval systems in which users run programs on their personal computers that interact with database programs on host computers. Most of the major Internet services (such as mail, Usenet news, and the World Wide Web) use the client-server model.

CNIDR *(Clearinghouse for Networked Information Discovery and Retrieval)*

A government-funded group that supports Internet search software. CNIDR (pronounced "snyder") collects these tools and, in a few cases, maintains them.

CompuServe

A major online service with more than two million users. CompuServe was one of the earliest of the large systems not directly connected to the Internet to offer Internet mail access to its users. Recently, CompuServe has embraced the Internet by giving its users access to features such as Usenet news and a Web browser.

CoSN (Consortium for School Networking)

A nonprofit organization for K-12 teachers, hardware and software vendors, and Internet providers. It has taken an active role in helping educate teachers and parents about the Internet and how it can be used in education.

DNS (domain name system)

The method by which Internet addresses (such as mit.edu) are converted into computer-readable IP addresses (such as 182.156.12.24). The DNS is one of the most flexible and powerful technical features of the Internet, enabling computers to appear and disappear from the Internet without causing problems. It also makes sending messages much easier because it does not require a central repository of all names.

download

To copy a file from a remote system to your computer. Downloading files from anonymous FTP servers is a popular way to get freeware and shareware files.

dweeb

See *geek*.

EFF (Electronic Frontier Foundation)

One of the first large groups concerned with Internet-related privacy and access issues. The EFF does extensive education and lobbying in Washington and often educates local law enforcement agencies about computer technology. The EFF is one of the strongest supporters of personal freedom on the Internet.

e-mail

Electronic mail. Internet users often use the term *e-mail* to differentiate those messages from postal mail.

encryption

Scrambling a message so that it is virtually impossible for other people to read unless they have a key. You use encryption to maintain privacy when sending messages and also to verify the identity of the sender of a message. Many different types of encryption are used on the Internet, none of them compatible with each other.

ERIC (Educational Resources Information Center)

Funded by the U.S. Department of Education, ERIC is a clearinghouse of general information for teachers. It sponsors AskERIC, an Internet site with lots of online teaching resources for K-12 teachers.

FAQ (Frequently Asked Questions)

A file that contains a list of questions that appear regularly on a Usenet newsgroup and the answers to those questions. FAQs are useful for preventing the same questions from being asked repeatedly by newcomers. The term FAQ has now moved beyond Usenet and is used for anything that answers the most common questions on a topic.

file

A group of characters stored electronically. Files can contain anything from text to pictures to programs to movies, and so on. Most programs refer to files by their names.

finger

An Internet service that enables you to find out information about a user on a computer. Computers that run finger servers tell you when a user was logged on last and give some information about the user.

flame

To attack someone in a discussion, usually with language much harsher than necessary. It is also used as a noun to describe the message(s) sent. Flames are usually personal even if the flamer is attacking ideas. The term comes from the concept of a "heated" debate.

Freenets

Bulletin board systems connected to the Internet that are free or charge only a nominal amount for use. The idea is to give all the people in a community free access to computing and to information on the Internet. Freenets are usually supported by volunteer staff and local donations.

freeware

Software that you can use and copy with no obligation. People write freeware because it feels good or as a way to hone up their programming and design skills. Although you can give it away, most freeware restricts you from selling or altering the program.

FTP (File Transfer Protocol)

The Internet's file transfer program. FTP is one of the older standards on the Internet; most FTP client software is fairly unfriendly and difficult to use. On the other hand, FTP is still an efficient way to transfer files between systems and to distribute information on request to Internet users.

FYIs (For Your Information files)

A subset of the Internet RFC files that give information to Internet beginners. FYIs are often much simpler to read and cover less technical information than other RFCs.

gateway

A translator between two different interfaces. Many kinds of gateways exist, but on the Internet, the term is most commonly used to indicate a protocol gateway that converts between two Internet services. For example, a mail-to-Web gateway enables users who have only mail access to get files from the Web.

geek

A somewhat affectionate term for someone who is overly interested in computers. Similar terms of partial endearment/partial criticism include *nerd, dweeb, weenie,* and *wonk.*

GIF files

Graphics files stored using the GIF format. The GIF format was designed by CompuServe as a way of compacting images and making them easily viewable on many kinds of computers. The GIF standard has been widely adopted on the Internet.

Gopher

Service that enables you to navigate through Internet information easily. More than 1,000 Gopher servers are on the Internet, and you can find Gopher client programs for almost every computer. Gopher presents all information as either a directory or a file; most Gopher servers enable you to search for information as well.

home page

The initial page you see when you enter a Web site. The term is somewhat ambiguous because it is also commonly used as the page you see when you first start your Web browser.

host computer

Any computer on the Internet to which you can connect. Generally, a host computer is any computer to which you can send mail or that has a Web server, an FTP server, or something similar.

HTML (HyperText Markup Language)

The formatting language used by World Wide Web servers. HTML documents are text files with extra commands embedded into them.

HTTP (HyperText Transfer Protocol)

The protocol used for passing hypertext documents on the Web. HTTP has become popular as a result of its somewhat simple nature and the fact that you can easily write both client and server programs that can communicate with HTTP.

hypertext

A type of document that contains links to other documents. When reading a hypertext document, you can quickly jump to linked documents and then jump back whenever you feel like it. Hypertext enables you to organize the information you read into different formats.

Hytelnet

A program that works with telnet that enables you to easily browse through library catalogs. Hytelnet has a database of all known public library catalogs, and it contains information about how to operate them after you are connected.

IAB (Internet Architecture Board)

The group that oversees Internet technical issues. It oversees the IETF and the IRTF and acts as a liaison with other nontechnical Internet bodies.

IETF (Internet Engineering Task Force)

The group that oversees the technical standards on which the Internet is based. The IETF is an all-volunteer organization and is heaven for computer geeks. The technical decisions made by the IETF affect how the Internet functions, how fast it operates, and how it will look in the future.

inline images

Pictures that appear in a Web page. An inline image is different from a regular picture that you may find on the Internet in that it appears as part of a Web document, not as a stand-alone image. Many Web browsers enable you to download and save these images by themselves.

Internet Society (ISOC)

A voluntary group that acts as a focal point for Internet building. The ISOC has been particularly active in bringing non-U.S. users onto the Internet and in coordinating other Internet-related groups.

Internet Talk Radio

A broadcast station that uses the Internet as its medium. It is an experiment that looks at how the Internet may be used in the future for real-time data transfer and what kind of entertainment and information people on the Internet want.

InterNIC

A government-funded group that tells users how to get on the Internet and what to do after they are there. The InterNIC has a wealth of online information and can answer phone calls, FAXes, and postal mail. It is also a good resource for other people who support Internet users.

IP

The standard used by computers to transmit information over the Internet. IP, which stands for Internet Protocol, defines how the information looks as it travels between computers, not what the computers do with it. IP also defines how Internet addresses work.

IRC (Internet Relay Chat)

A program for coordinating many people talking at the same time. Using IRC, you can talk with groups of people by typing. Using IRC is similar to being in many conversations at the same time at a party.

IRTF (Internet Research Task Force)

The research arm of the IAB. The IRTF looks at issues that affect the Internet's future, such as what happens after the explosive growth that the Internet has been experiencing and how certain technologies will affect Internet traffic.

ISDN

A digital form of data transfer over regular telephone lines. ISDN stands for Integrated Services Digital Network, which doesn't really mean anything to the typical person. Using ISDN phone service enables you to have both voice and data on the same phone line. ISDN modems run about ten times faster than popular 14.4 Kbps modems, although they cost much more than regular modems. ISDN service from the telephone company is also usually more expensive than regular telephone service.

JPEG files

Graphics files stored in JPEG format. The JPEG format is an open industry standard that is used widely for storing photographs in a compact form. A few variations on the JPEG format exist, but most programs like Netscape can read them all.

LISTSERV

A program used on some computers for handling mailing lists. LISTSERV has an arcane interface but has been around for more than a decade. Many important mailing lists are still run from LISTSERV computers. Many LISTSERV mailing lists also enable you to retrieve files related to the mailing list.

local area network (LAN)

A network of computers that are all in the same location, such as at an office or building. LANs have become much more common in the past few years as more companies have realized the importance of communication. Some LANs are attached to the Internet, giving each person on the LAN access to Internet resources.

Lynx

A character-based client program for accessing the World Wide Web. Although Lynx is not as flashy as other Web clients such as Mosaic, it works well for the millions of Internet users who have only character-based access.

mail

Messages that are sent over the Internet by using the Simple Mail Transport Protocol. Internet mail is by far the most popular and most used feature of the Internet. Most of the supposed 20 million people on the Internet (if even that many are out there) have only mail access.

mailing list

A system of duplicating one message and sending it to many people. A single letter is sent to the mailing list host and a copy is sent to every person on the mailing list. Some mailing lists have thousands of people.

markup language

A method for specifying types of content and formatting in a text file. Markup languages enable you to enter text strings in your file to denote various features of the file, such as which words should be boldface and which words are part of the title.

MIME

The standard for enclosing binary files in Internet mail. MIME stands for Multipurpose Internet Mail Extensions, and it enables you to specify the type of attachment you are making to your Internet mail. Many nonmail programs, such as the World Wide Web, also use the MIME standard to make reading files easier for client programs.

mirror

A duplicate of an FTP site. Mirrors help reduce long-haul Internet traffic by enabling people to choose to download files from hosts that are closer to them. Usually, mirror sites are updated each night so that they have the same contents as the main site.

modem

A piece of hardware for connecting computers over telephone lines. Most personal computer users connect to the Internet over modems, although some have direct connections through company networks. The most-common modems cost less than $100, although faster modems can cost much more.

Mosaic

A graphical browser for the World Wide Web. Mosaic has contributed a great deal to the Internet's recent surge in popularity by being the first easy-to-use Web browser. Netscape, however, has supplanted Mosaic in popularity.

MUD (Multi-User Dungeons)

A program that simulates a place where you can move around, talk to other users, and interact with your surroundings. Most are centered around fantasy themes such as dragons, science fiction, and so on. Many MUDs on the Internet enable you not only to interact but also to create parts of the environment for others to interact with.

netiquette

A play on the word etiquette, this term refers to the proper way to behave on the Internet. This includes respecting the rights and desires of others, setting an example of how you want strangers to treat you, and acknowledging that the Internet is very different from face-to-face communication.

Netscape

A graphical browser for the World Wide Web and the main subject of this book (along with the Web itself, of course). Netscape is produced by Netscape Communications, which also produces other Web-related software such as server software. Netscape offers more features than any other popular Web browser and is inexpensive or even free.

netstorm

The nastiness that happens when packets get lost or undelivered on the Internet. Netstorms have many causes and sometimes last only a minute or two. Sometimes, however, netstorms can last for days on small parts of the Internet.

newsgroups

Topical divisions of Usenet. A newsgroup generally has a single topic (such as the communications software for Microsoft Windows), but within that topic anyone can ask or answer questions. The term "news" is outdated; the majority of the discussion in newsgroups has to do with old items, not news. See also *Usenet*.

NII (National Information Infrastructure)

A broad proposal for the U.S. government to set up standards and governing bodies for the transmission of digital data. The NII is still under debate, and the final content may be affected more by corporate lobbyists than by citizens because of the significant effect it will have on how private networks operate.

NSFnet (National Science Foundation network)

The network run by the National Science Foundation that was previously the backbone of the Internet. The NSFnet is now in transition, most of its usefulness supplanted by commercial networks.

packet

A group of bytes that are going from one Internet host to another. Packets have variable lengths and can contain any kind of information.

PEM (Privacy Enhanced Mail)

The standard for encrypting Internet mail. PEM enables you to make your mail messages unreadable by anyone other than the desired recipient. It also enables you to authenticate your mail, meaning that the person who receives it can be assured that you were the person who sent it.

plug-ins

Programs external to Netscape that can display different types of documents inside Netscape's window. Plug-ins are generally used to display formats that would be hard for Netscape to incorporate, such as page layout or animation formats. Some plug-ins are free; others are commercial.

POP (Point Of Presence)

A place you dial into to get Internet access. Many Internet service companies have POPs in many cities. Usually, all the POPs for one service provider are connected to a single set of computers.

POP (Post Office Protocol)

The most popular way to get Internet mail by using a mail client such as Netscape. When you have mail stored on a remote mail server, you use POP to see what the mail is and to download it to your personal computer.

port

A number that helps TCP identify what kind of service you are asking for from another computer. Most common Internet features such as Gopher have standard port numbers (for example, 70 for Gopher) that client software uses if you do not specify a different port number. The only time you need to know about ports is if a server requires that you use a nonstandard port number to communicate.

PPP (Point-to-Point Protocol)

A fast, reliable method for connecting computers on the Internet over serial lines, such as telephone wire. PPP has become more popular than SLIP in the past few years, and many Internet service providers offer PPP connections. Using PPP or SLIP, your personal computer can be directly connected to the Internet. See also *IP*.

protocol

A set of rules. On the Internet, protocols are generally considered to be the rules used for communicating between computers. Some common protocols are FTP, HTTP, and SMTP.

RFCs (Requests for Comments)

Documents that define the technical aspects of the Internet. Originally, these documents were used to get input from other technical users of the Internet before standards were set down, and many RFCs today still serve that purpose. Other RFCs are simply statements of reality.

root domains

The main domain names assigned by the root domain of the Internet. The main root domains in the U.S. are `.com`, `.edu`, `.gov`, `.mil`, `.net`, `.org`, and `.us`. The other root domains are the two-letter country codes, such as `.ca` (for Canada) and `.jp` (for Japan).

router

A device that connects two networks, enabling only certain traffic to pass through. Routers are used at almost every intersection on the Internet to both limit traffic going to smaller networks and to help choose the most efficient way to get packets to their desired destination. Some routers cost less than $2,000; others cost more than $25,000.

S-HTTP

A secure form of HTTP, mostly used for financial transactions on the Web. S-HTTP is slowly gaining acceptance among merchants selling products on the Web as a way to pass credit card numbers and other sensitive information without the chance that someone snooping on the Internet can see the information as it goes by.

server program

The program that a host computer runs that communicates with users running client programs. Server software establishes a standard for communication, and all client programs must act in that standard fashion to work correctly. Many different client programs can interact with one server program.

service

The generic term for a communication protocol and the content that goes with it. Electronic mail, FTP, and HTTP, for example, are all services.

SGML (Standard General Markup Language)

The language from which HTML was spawned. SGML is much more flexible than HTML and is used by many large companies for creating structured text that can be searched and indexed. Many text purists feel that HTML has too many faults for real formatting and that SGML is the only way to go.

shareware

Software that you can freely copy and try before buying it. Shareware enables you to test software and pass it along to others without paying for it. If you continue to use the software for a specified amount of time, however, you must send the author money to license the software.

shell

A program that enables a user to interact with an operating system. Programs such as the MS-DOS command line and Microsoft Windows are shells to the MS-DOS operating system. Many popular shells run under UNIX, such as the c shell, Bourne shell, and so on.

SLIP (Serial Line IP)

A fast, simple method for connecting computers on the Internet over serial lines, such as telephone wire. PPP has become more popular than SLIP in the past few years, although many Internet service providers offer SLIP connections as well as PPP connections. Using PPP or SLIP, your personal computer is directly connected to the Internet. See also *IP*.

SMTP (Simple Mail Transfer Protocol)

The rules that govern how Internet mail moves from the sender's computer to the recipient's. Mail on the Internet is quite flexible, mostly thanks to the fact that SMTP has been around so long and is well understood by mail administrators. Netscape users need to know which SMTP host they can use to send mail from their accounts to other places on the Internet.

spiders

Programs that roam the Web collecting information for indexes. Spiders are automated programs that can wander aimlessly or can try to follow particular kinds of links.

SSL (Secure Sockets Layer)

A protocol developed by Netscape to let all types of client software (not just Web clients) securely communicate with servers. Using SSL prevents someone who is watching a conversation going across the Internet from determining what is being said. It is thus useful for transmitting things like credit card numbers and other sensitive information.

STD (Standards file)

A type of RFC file that has been anointed by the IETF as an official Internet standard. STDs are, in fact, the same as the RFC files; they simply have an additional designation.

tags

Text you add to an HTML document so that Web clients can format the document. In HTML, tags always begin with the ⟨ character and end with the ⟩ character. Tags often come in pairs, called *start tags* and *end tags;* for example, the tags ⟨title⟩ and ⟨/title⟩ are a pair of start and end tags.

TCP (Transmission Control Protocol)

The standard used on the Internet to identify the kind of information in packets. TCP is almost always used with the IP standard, and you normally hear of them together as TCP/IP. TCP also makes sure that data is passed without any errors.

telnet

An Internet service that enables one computer to act as a terminal on another computer. Using telnet, you can type on another computer as if you were directly connected. In this way, telnet is somewhat like common communications programs (sometimes called *terminal programs*) for personal computers.

terminal program

Software that makes your computer act like an old-style computer terminal. Terminal programs are still useful because so many Internet hosts enable users to attach to them through terminals. Literally hundreds of terminal programs are available.

UNIX

The most common operating system for servers and hosts on the Internet. Almost any computer can be an Internet host, but since the early days, such computers more commonly run UNIX.

upload

To send a file to a remote computer. A few UNIX hosts enable anyone to leave files on the computer for others to read. About 99 percent of the people on the Internet, however, only download files and never upload them.

URL (Uniform Resource Locator)

The current method for specifying the addresses of things on the Web. URLs are also starting to be used by non-Web client software as a way of identifying the location of files, mail addresses, and so on.

URN (Uniform Resource Name)

Perhaps (if we are lucky) the future method used to specify how to find things on the Web. URNs differ from URLs in that they don't specify where something is. Instead, they simply give many things a name; you must then fetch the information about that name to find where the object resides.

Usenet

A widely used Internet service that organizes people's comments by topic. These topics, called newsgroups, have their own structure, with people commenting on previous comments, starting new threads of discussion, and so on. Usenet is probably the most popular Internet feature other than mail. It is sometimes incorrectly listed in all caps as *USENET*.

UUCP

A common method used to communicate among computers that are connected to the Internet only part of the time. UUCP, which stands for UNIX-to-UNIX-Copy is a very old standard that enables mail messages, Usenet news, and files to be transferred from computer to computer. It has become less popular in recent years, although many bulletin board systems use it to pass mail.

Veronica

A type of server used for searching for files on Gopher servers. You access a Veronica server by using a Gopher client and then sending a search request. Veronica servers can give you answers in a variety of fashions; they may, for example, list only those directories that match your request.

VRML (Virtual Reality Modeling Language)

A language used to display three-dimensional information on the computer screen in a way that looks somewhat realistic. VRML programs often make it look like you're walking or flying around a scene and allow you to interact with objects in the scene.

WAIS (Wide Area Information Server)

A method for searching databases over the Internet. WAIS was once trumpeted as the next big thing on the Internet, but the free versions of WAIS server software and client software are not very easy to use, and few sites are running commercial versions. WAIS is also used by many Gopher and Web sites as a method for searching just within those sites.

wide area network (WAN)

A network of computers spread out across a great distance. Some of the connections in a WAN are typically through telephone lines or over satellites. WANs are often networks of networks, linking local area networks (LANs) into a single network.

Winsock

A standard that Microsoft Windows programs use to interact with the Internet and other TCP/IP networks. Winsock is short for "Windows sockets." Today, all Windows TCP/IP programs use standard Winsock interfaces.

workstation

A very high-powered personal computer. The line between the most powerful PCs and the least powerful workstations is blurry, but workstations usually have much more RAM and hard disk space and are much faster. Workstations are also often used as servers on the Internet.

World Wide Web (WWW)

An Internet service that enables users to retrieve hypertext and graphics from various sites (often just called "the Web"). The Web has become one of the most popular Internet services in the past few years. In fact, many Internet information providers are now publishing only on the Web.

Index

• *X* •

• *Y* •

• *Z* •

IDG BOOKS WORLDWIDE REGISTRATION CARD

RETURN THIS REGISTRATION CARD FOR FREE CATALOG

Title of this book: **Netscape Communicator™ 4 For Dummies®**

My overall rating of this book: ❑ Very good [1] ❑ Good [2] ❑ Satisfactory [3] ❑ Fair [4] ❑ Poor [5]

How I first heard about this book:

❑ Found in bookstore; name: [6] _____   ❑ Book review: [7] _____

❑ Advertisement: [8] _____   ❑ Catalog: [9] _____

❑ Word of mouth; heard about book from friend, co-worker, etc.: [10] _____   ❑ Other: [11] _____

What I liked most about this book:

_____

_____

What I would change, add, delete, etc., in future editions of this book:

_____

_____

Other comments:

_____

_____

Number of computer books I purchase in a year: ❑ 1 [12] ❑ 2-5 [13] ❑ 6-10 [14] ❑ More than 10 [15]

I would characterize my computer skills as: ❑ Beginner [16] ❑ Intermediate [17] ❑ Advanced [18] ❑ Professional [19]

I use ❑ DOS [20] ❑ Windows [21] ❑ OS/2 [22] ❑ Unix [23] ❑ Macintosh [24] ❑ Other: [25]_____
(please specify)

I would be interested in new books on the following subjects:
(please check all that apply, and use the spaces provided to identify specific software)

❑ Word processing: [26] _____   ❑ Spreadsheets: [27] _____

❑ Data bases: [28] _____   ❑ Desktop publishing: [29] _____

❑ File Utilities: [30] _____   ❑ Money management: [31] _____

❑ Networking: [32] _____   ❑ Programming languages: [33] _____

❑ Other: [34] _____

I use a PC at (please check all that apply): ❑ home [35] ❑ work [36] ❑ school [37] ❑ other: [38] _____

The disks I prefer to use are ❑ 5.25 [39] ❑ 3.5 [40] ❑ other: [41]_____

I have a CD ROM: ❑ yes [42] ❑ no [43]

I plan to buy or upgrade computer hardware this year: ❑ yes [44] ❑ no [45]

I plan to buy or upgrade computer software this year: ❑ yes [46] ❑ no [47]

Name: _____   Business title: [48] _____   Type of Business: [49] _____

Address (❑ home [50] ❑ work [51]/Company name: _____)

Street/Suite# _____

City [52]/State [53]/Zipcode [54]: _____   Country [55] _____

❑ **I liked this book!** You may quote me by name in future
IDG Books Worldwide promotional materials.

My daytime phone number is _____

IDG BOOKS

THE WORLD OF
COMPUTER
KNOWLEDGE

❏ **YES!**

Please keep me informed about IDG's World of Computer Knowledge.
Send me the latest IDG Books catalog.

NO POSTAGE
NECESSARY
IF MAILED
IN THE
UNITED STATES

BUSINESS REPLY MAIL
FIRST CLASS MAIL   PERMIT NO. 2605   FOSTER CITY, CALIFORNIA

IDG Books Worldwide
919 E Hillsdale Blvd, STE 400
Foster City, CA 94404-9691